MW00577917

When Your Mind Sabotages Your Dreams

"This book contains an innovative approach to negotiating inner conflicts in ways that result in integrated action. Lasater, Kinyon, and Stiles take the principles of NVC that work so well for external conflict and apply them to the parts of us that are at war in important aspects of our lives. The result not only fills a hole in the NVC framework but also empowers people to get all their parts to work together to achieve their dreams."

—RICHARD C. SCHWARTZ, PHD,
developer of the Internal Family Systems Model of psychotherapy

"The authentic path to peace is an inner journey. And yet, there is very little practical guidance available. John, Ike and Julie fill that need with eloquence, and take a lifetime of experience and reflection to provide a map that is both accessible and inspiring. A must read for those motivated to have more peace in their lives."

—JOHN FORD,
author of *Peace at Work: The HR Manager's Guide to Workplace Mediation*, founder of The HR Mediation Academy
hrmediationacademy.com

"*When Your Mind Sabotages Your Dreams* is an exceptionally valuable addition to the growing literature on subpersonalities, and the theories contained in this marvelous book have much in common with the Internal Family Systems model developed by Dr. Richard Schwartz. Each chapter provides helpful tools for managing the negotiation within, and then demonstrates the use of these tools by various individuals whose internal struggles we follow from the beginning of the book to the end. I highly recommend this book for anyone seeking a psychologically sophisticated manual for managing emotions and implementing dreams."

—DAVID A. HOFFMAN,
John H. Watson Jr. lecturer on Law, Harvard Law School;
founder, Boston Law Collaborative, LLC

"When Your Mind Sabotages Your Dreams is an insightful addition to John Kinyon and Ike Lasater's Mediate Your Life series that brings the focus back to *ourselves*, where we have the greatest power and opportunity for change. This book will empower you to create a life brimming over with joy and meaning!"

—MARY MACKENZIE,
author, *Peaceful Living: Daily Meditations for Living with Love, Healing and Compassion*; co-founder, NVC Academy; executive director, Peace Workshop, International

"When Your Mind Sabotages Your Dreams is the book I've both wanted and needed for years. It is like an old friend that I've just met, a discussion companion who senses and responds to my needs by offering practical resources for getting unstuck. Its message is powerful, and yet the strategies accessible: We can explore and navigate both our dreams and the challenges that accompany them even when we don't believe we can. I often smiled at how familiar and authentic the example scenarios were, and then I found myself drawn into experimenting with the well-constructed activities, surprising myself at what I learned. I absolutely recommend this to anyone who wants compassionate and wise strategies for listening and remaining true to your inner voice."

—PJ NELSEN, PhD,
associate professor, Appalachian State University

"We all want to change the world—and our own lives in the process. But how do we turn dreams into reality? Once again, with their newest work, the Mediate Your Life team weaves insight with the practical and doable. Their advice: listen carefully to the wisdom of our competing internal voices, for once we hear them, really hear them, we find that the voices can sing in harmony. In other words, by learning to hear, we move reliably toward our dreams. Like all great teachings, theirs seem obvious once understood, and yet completely illusory beforehand. I marvel at their continued contribution to my own internal life. Read this book!"

—LARRY C. ROSEN,
founder of the mediation law firm Through Understanding
ThroughUnderstanding.com

"Getting stuck when pursuing your dreams? When many of us are despairing, hopeless and concerned about ever reaching our dreams—this book elevates the monologue and dialogue both within and with others by offering a toolbox of possibilities to 'dream, plan, and implement' our greatest longings for contribution and fulfillment."

—SYLVIA HASKVITZ, MA, RD,
CNVC certified trainer and assessor, author of *Eat by Choice, Not by Habit: Practical Skills for Creating a Healthy Relationship with Your Body and Food*

"Connecting with feelings and needs in the workplace isn't something most of us talk about, yet I've seen what happens when the principles in this book are taught and practiced in the workplace: teams feel safe, ideas flourish, and companies transform. *When Your Mind Sabotages Your Dreams* is actually a perfect change management how-to manual, because it's practical, actionable, and it works!"

—PAUL JOHNSON,
marketing excellence manager, Microsoft USA

"This book has a lot of very useful tools if you are looking for joyful ways of doing inner work. Becoming your own best friend can be an adventure instead of one more thing to achieve."

—LIV LARSSON,
mediator, CT NVC trainer, author of *A Helping Hand: Mediation with Nonviolent Communication* and *Anger, Guilt and Shame: Reclaiming Power and Choice*
friareliv.se/eng

"Another gift from the dynamic team of Lasater, Kinyon, and Stiles! Their new book, *When Your Mind Sabotages Your Dreams*, explores how to 'mediate' our own worst critics—the naysayer and often conflicted internal voices that get in the way of our living our dreams and living big. A comprehensive and insightful approach to applying NVC-based mediation as an 'inside job.'"

—DIAN KILLIAN, PHD, trainer, coach, and consultant,
Work Collaboratively, LLC; certified NVC trainer;
author, *Connecting Across Differences* & *Urban Empathy*
workcollaboratively.com

"If you want to get out of your own way and create internal and external conditions that will result in a life you truly want to inhabit, this book offers you a path. With *When Your Mind Sabotages Your Dreams,* readers receive guidance for responding skillfully to the internal barriers that get in the way of health, healing, peace of mind, and well-being. Readers are supported in developing a relationship with that self that is orchestrated by the Mediator Mind (MM) state. The MM is marked by friendliness and autonomy rather than the misguided hostile and neglectful efforts to control the self in ways that only cause harm. Those who cultivate MM can better meet their universal needs for love, connection, meaning, and more. Universally relevant examples illustrate how readers can apply these effective tools for cultivating a compassionate relationship with the self. Highly accessible, and easy-to-relate-with stories show readers how to address the barriers within that interfere with changing a range of habits, from establishing an exercise routine and eating food that nourishes to discovering more meaningful and fulfilling work. The wisdom in this book for overcoming struggles to living a desired life will be relevant to a broad range of people, and those who practice these tools can enhance health of mind, body, and behavior."

—CHRIS MOLNAR, PHD
president, Mindful Exposure Therapy for Anxiety and Psychological
Wellness Center (META Center), Inc. and Mindful Therapists
editor, The Evidence-Based Practitioner (EBP)

"This wonderful book provides a detailed and concrete pathway to identifying blocks to your dreams and finding a new way forward. For anyone who feels that their life is not what they want it to be, you need to read *When Your Mind Sabotages Your Dreams.* Based on sound psychological principles, it will help you turn your life around."

—KRISTIN NEFF, PHD, author of *Self-Compassion:*
The Proven Power of Being Kind to Yourself
self-compassion.org

"The Japanese say, 'Vision without action is a daydream. Action without vision is a nightmare.' This book contains transformative maps to viscerally crystalize and deeply live your vision—beyond daydreams and nightmares. As such, it is an excellent travel guide for pilgrims of wholehearted living. Mediate Your Life makes accessible the magic Marshall Rosenberg created in his workshops. I learned this model from John and Ike years ago, and it is enriching for my personal path and very useful in my daily work with people in deep emotional dilemmas and life-threatening crises. One of the precious qualities of this approach, as opposed to many mainstream psychotherapy and inner-work models, is that it emphasizes the deep integration of seemingly obstructive inner experiences instead of fighting, changing, or ignoring them. Through this, it naturally enables our access to countless inner resources instead of "cutting" something out of us. May this book and work be a deep contribution to peace and the rich, full, and meaningful life of living beings."

—GÜNTHER MILD,
psychotherapist and psychiatrist

Praise for

FROM CONFLICT TO CONNECTION

"In this profound yet practical guide, John Kinyon and Ike Lasater show us that within every conflict lies the seed of transformation. *From Conflict to Connection* doesn't just offer a better way to resolve conflict, it provides a means of using conflict to deepen our connection to others and to ourselves."

—CHRIS KRESSER MS, L.Ac,
author of *NY Times* bestseller *The Paleo Cure*
chriskresser.com

"*From Conflict to Connection* gives you the ability to develop valuable and effective skills for dealing with conflict in personal and work relationships. When you apply what John and Ike teach in these pages, you'll move closer to the life and relationships you most want."

—MIKE ROBBINS, author of *Nothing Changes Until You Do*
Mike-Robbins.com

"Written with tender precision, this book is a complete guide to navigating interpersonal engagement. A happy by-product is how these external practices inexorably move us to a greater capacity for inner peace."

—LEE GLICKSTEIN,
founder of Speaking Circles International and author of
Be Heard Now! Tap Into Your Inner Speaker and Communicate with Ease
speakingcirclesinternational.com

"This amazing book is like having a GPS for navigating conflict. It offers step-by-step, concrete tools to get you to where you want to be—in a place of harmonious, peaceful, and meaningful relationship with yourself and others. A true roadmap to happiness."

—KRISTIN NEFF, PHD,
author of *Self-Compassion: The Proven Power of Being Kind to Yourself*
self-compassion.org

"Kinyon, Lasater, and Stiles describe a concise and thorough path for anyone seeking to transform the habitual cycles of conflict that plague our culture, families, organizations, and selves. Walking this path gradually frees us up from habits that otherwise undermine our lives and our work; instead, we develop our capacities and abilities for greater freedom, clarity, creativity, and service to others. Thus, these practices are crucial to building a better future for us all."

—JEFF BARNUM, Magenta
magenta.fm

"From Conflict to Connection is a beautifully and thoroughly written offering that can provide clear and powerful support to everyone in a relationship. The clear, everyday examples that illustrate the concepts make this an eminently practical book. I am happy to know that John and Ike are in the world sharing NVC in such an accessible way. I feel a partnership in their work and believe this book will go a long way to giving people a way through conflict to real communication. A wonderful and important enhancement to the legacy of Marshall Rosenberg."

—ROBERT GONZALES,
author of *Reflections on Living Compassion*; CNVC certified trainer
living-compassion.org

"John and Ike offer a unique approach to responding effectively in difficult and crucial conversations, in personal life and at work. Their work is a valuable contribution to how human beings are learning to create peace and resolve conflicts compassionately and collaboratively."

—CORT WORTHINGTON,
faculty, UC Berkeley Haas School of Business
cortworthington.com

"They've done it again! Written a book that is engaging, stimulating, thought-provoking, and potentially life-changing for those who are willing to do the exercises and apply the principles to their lives. *From Conflict to Connection* is a winner!"

—SYLVIA HASKVITZ, MA, RD,
CNVC certified trainer; author of *Eat by Choice, Not by Habit*

"Gandhi said, 'In a gentle way you can shake the world.' *Choosing Peace* offers radical, yet practical instruction to do just that. Don't merely read this book. Practice the wisdom you discover in it to harness the transformative power of choice that resides within every conflict. You will be astonished."

—CHRISTINE FLAHERTY,
healthcare executive and CNVC certified trainer

VOLUME 3

WHEN YOUR
MIND
SABOTAGES
YOUR
DREAMS

WHEN YOUR
MIND
SABOTAGES
YOUR
DREAMS

Turning Your Critical
Internal Voices *into*
Collaborative Allies

———

IKE LASATER, JOHN KINYON &
JULIE STILES

GLOBAL REACH BOOKS

Published by
Global Reach Books

Ike Lasater
97 Linden Street
New Haven, CT 06511
www.mediateyourlife.com
Ike@mediateyourlife.com

To inquire about bulk orders or special programs:
connect@globalreachbooks.com

ISBN: 978-0-9899720-7-9
Library of Congress Control Number: 2017912921

Editing and book design by Stacey Aaronson

Printed in the United States of America

WHEN YOUR
MIND
SABOTAGES
YOUR
DREAMS

TABLE OF CONTENTS

INTRODUCTION

IN EACH MOMENT, YOU ARE CREATING YOUR EXPERIENCE OF YOUR LIFE.

This may seem like a bold statement. Most people go through their lives as if they are entirely at the mercy of what happens around them. If they don't have what they desire in their lives, they may blame outside circumstances, their past, or other people, saying things like, "Well, I just haven't met the right person yet, that's why I'm not married" or "I didn't grow up in an entrepreneurial family, so I don't have it in my genes to get a business going." They may also internalize the blame and find themselves at fault: "I'd love to make more money, but I'm not smart enough." Frequently, people feel hopeless and helpless, as if they play no part in getting what they want.

All of this is understandable, since most people were never taught how to "create" their lives. When you grow up in a family and culture where people tend to look outward for responsibility, and blame and shame are the predominant responses to what happens, being willing to look at your part in creating your life takes courage and openness to a whole new way of seeing the world.

Why?

Because taking responsibility for the part you play in *creating* your life starts *within*. Of course, there are many circumstances out of your control that influence your life, but you *do* have significant control over how you relate to your circumstances. Thus, it's what you do *within* you, how you relate to yourself, others, and the world—that is where creating your life begins.

Ask yourself:

+ Am I satisfied with my life?

+ Is there anything I can do to make it better?

People often find some areas of life that work in their favor, but others that simply don't, whether they understand why or not. For example, perhaps business is the arena where you are effective at reaching your goals, and yet you can't seem to create a relationship that works, or vice versa. Maybe you feel comfortable taking responsibility for your health, but your financial situation is out of control.

It's probable that you would like to change some aspect of your life, or create something entirely new and different, but what? Perhaps you:

+ long to start a business

+ already have a business and aspire to greater success

+ wish for a lifestyle that has greater balance between taking care of yourself and your responsibilities to family and career

+ yearn for financial stability

+ desire a healthier body and mind

+ would like to be a better parent, partner, or friend

Shelves of books already exist that give strategies for the nuts and bolts of creating these and myriad other dreams. While those resources are all helpful, many do not touch on how to get through the internal barriers that can often arise. In other words, before these nuts and bolts can be put into place, you have to learn how to get out of your own way.

In contrast to other books on this topic, *When Your Mind Sabotages Your Dreams* addresses the internal responses to whatever you choose to do. We give you the maps—specific steps to take— to navigate this territory, showing you where to focus your mind and what actions to take, so that you can remove those barriers that might be stopping you, and in doing so, move toward the life you wish to create.

In the pages that follow, you will not be creating vision boards for your life or crafting visions and missions for your business. While useful, these subjects are covered in other great resources. We are also not focusing on task management; plenty of people have written excellent resources to help you with time management and productivity, such as David Allen in his book *Getting Things Done*. It's also not a book that's going to tell you to simply try harder, be more focused, beat or force yourself, or power through.

Instead, this is a book about collaborating with *yourself*. As such, we will guide you to identify the conversations you would like to have with yourself to create what you desire in life. While this may sound strange at first, this practice will enable you to be clear about what you would like to do, plan the conversations to have, know what outcome you desire from those conversations, and develop the tools to prepare for and act mindfully in each moment. Further, this book is about how to have compassion for yourself wherever you are in the creation of your dream, along with resilience to face what comes up at each stage of the journey. Ultimately, we teach you how to meet yourself with awareness, presence, and choice—and when you can meet yourself this way, you can meet the world in the same way.

In the first volume of the Mediate Your Life series, *Choosing Peace*, we set the foundation by exploring the basic components of Nonviolent Communication—Observations, Feelings, Needs, and

Requests—that the rest of our work builds upon. In the second volume, *From Conflict to Connection*, we explored the maps and skills that are necessary when you are in a difficult conversation with someone else.

While this book is about the conversations you have with *yourself*, in particular those that tend to get in the way of living the life you desire, it is a close companion to *From Conflict to Connection* in that as you go about creating your dream, you'll likely be talking with other people. We refer you to that book for the maps and skills that will help you be more effective in those conversations.

HOW THIS BOOK IS ORGANIZED

While creating your dream is not a linear process, there is generally a flow or order to it. Before you can plan, you have to dream, and before you can take concerted action, you need a plan. Thus, reaching any dream follows the basic structure of dream, plan, implement. The chapters follow this flow of what takes place so that you can work through the process while reading the book. Chapter 1 will teach you to embrace your thinking mind, Chapter 2 will help you clarify your dream, Chapter 3 will aid in creating a plan, and Chapters 4–10 will cover various aspects of implementing your plan to achieve your dream.

CHAPTER 1 begins by exploring awareness of thinking and how you create your life one conversation at a time, which are the foundation for everything to follow. We'll see how parts of you can sometimes be in conflict, how your own thoughts become barriers to achieving your dream, and how to embrace the concept of mediator mind to learn to change your internal conversations from contentious to harmonious.

CHAPTER 2 starts where creating your life starts—with a dream. Sometimes it's difficult to be clear about your dream, and creating clarity requires becoming aware of the internal barriers that may be blocking your dream from emerging. When you can empathize with all the internal parts of you that come up in thinking about your dream, you can become clear about who you are, and your dreams and goals suddenly emerge from the confusion.

CHAPTER 3 moves to the next stage, which is planning. Creating your dream will involve planning conversations (and the outcome from each) with yourself and others. Because you may feel overwhelmed, want to know every step along the way, or even resist the process of creating a plan, you may find your progress is halted. The key to moving ahead is knowing where to focus your attention, so that in the next moment you can have awareness, presence, and choice. We teach you a simple activity to do just that.

CHAPTER 4 begins the process of implementing your plan, with a discussion of taking action. One of the primary barriers to moving forward is when you have two internal voices, each advocating something different. Since all voices are speaking to meet some need, learning to mediate between them helps you make better choices, as you take into account each aspect of yourself that is showing up.

CHAPTER 5 focuses on making agreements with yourself. Since many people find it difficult to be accountable to themselves, we teach you three types of agreements to make it easier. We will also touch on what to do if you don't keep the agreement.

CHAPTER 6 recognizes that as you implement your plan and take action, you are likely to judge yourself afterwards for what you did or didn't do. In this type of internal conflict, a part of you speaks up that is upset about what you did (the Educator), and another part of you responds with the good reasons for choosing that option (the Chooser). Mediating between these two parts of you transforms your judgments, helping you to find the needs behind your judgments as well as your actions.

CHAPTER 7 introduces the important role habits play in achieving your dream. Habits, whether they are behavioral or mental, can either be a significant barrier or profoundly supportive. We'll show you a process by which you'll learn to identify what habits you'd like to create to help you achieve your dream, along with what habits you already have that are a form of self-sabotage you'd like to change.

CHAPTER 8 acknowledges that as you implement your plan, you will encounter obstacles and experience setbacks. How you deal with them can lead you further along the road or stop you in your tracks. Bringing compassion to yourself in difficult times, escaping from self-judgments about what you might have done differently, making new decisions about how to move forward next, and re-motivating yourself are essential elements of dealing with setbacks.

CHAPTER 9 suggests that when conflict arises with other people as you work toward your dream, there is an internal component to that external conflict. When you resolve the internal driver, the outer conflict is more likely to shift. As such, you may find a smoother path toward achieving your dream.

CHAPTER 10 expands the view to encompass how all the maps and tools in this book can apply across different aspects of reaching for your dreams, anytime you find voices sabotaging your efforts or feel blocked in moving forward. We teach you to recognize what is coming up for you so that you know which tool to use.

Early chapters each introduce a map or tool to support you on the journey to living your dream, and you will see in later chapters how these maps interrelate and how to choose which process to use as you go through different stages. For many processes we include a link to a video demonstration so that you can see in action a concrete example of how that process unfolds.

As in the previous books in our Mediate Your Life series, we will be following our fictional family as they face the internal conflicts that keep them from creating the lives they desire. We'll see how Sally works through the internal conversations about starting her own business while still being a mom and taking care of her family, how James faces his own uncertainty about what his dream is, and how teenaged Corey takes steps toward what he'd like to create.

In addition to the family, we will also follow three people in short snippets throughout each chapter to highlight the different ways people can get into internal conflicts that sabotage their efforts, and how they work through their internal conversations. Let's meet these three companions.

CHRIS

In his recent physical exam and lab tests, Chris's doctor told him he was pre-diabetic and that his blood pressure was too high, and the doctor wanted to put him on medication. Chris knew that he'd been under a little stress lately; he was working long hours and was unable to spend as much time with his family and do the things he enjoyed. He also knew he was a little overweight; in fact, he has struggled with weight since graduating from college ten years ago. During those ten years, he sometimes went on a diet and did quite well, but then he always slowly gained the weight back, usually adding on a few pounds more. Because he hadn't been paying much attention to it lately, he was a little shocked when he stepped on the scale at the office and was heavier than ever. The doctor told him losing fifty pounds was likely to help him lower his blood pressure and avoid developing diabetes.

DAWN

Dawn is in her fifties, happily married to her husband of thirty years. She mostly stayed at home to raise their two children, the youngest of whom is now away at college. She did some part-time work and volunteering now and then while the kids were growing up, as well as being involved in all of their activities. Now that the kids are gone, she is feeling a little out of sorts, spending a lot of time puttering around the house and yard, unsure of what to do with herself.

KEVIN

Kevin and his wife got married and started a family in their early twenties. Kevin threw himself into work, striving to get ahead and live the American dream, and has been climbing the corporate ladder. He's read lots of self-help books about self-actualization and has attended multiple events with one of the leading personal development "gurus."

Though initially he got a rush from putting in long hours to get everything done and move ahead, he's finding it exhausting and draining now that he's in his forties. Aware of feeling a bit empty inside, Kevin has been reflecting more on how it seems harder to keep going, and how there's not much time or energy for him to be able to enjoy the things he's working so hard for: his family and his nice lifestyle.

HOW TO USE THIS BOOK

If you see ways you are not progressing in creating your life and you'd like to change that, then take this book on as an experiment in living. We recommend reading each chapter, both so that you have all of the maps available to you and understand the entire process, and also so that you can address the internal barriers that may arise at each step. You will then more readily recognize your own sabotaging thoughts, and when they emerge you can return to specific chapters in the book as a resource to shift the internal conversation.

The Practice Pauses in each chapter are designed to give you a chance to apply what you're reading to your situation right now. Besides the full version of each map, which we recommend you practice often until it becomes embodied, we also outline ways to use each map more quickly once you are familiar with it. In this way you can more easily integrate the maps into your daily life.

Here are some possible ways you can make this book benefit you:

+ Do you already know your big hairy dream? Would you like to create world peace, start a social movement, or increase compassion and consciousness on the planet? If you're clear about your dream but feel stuck in some aspect of moving forward, use this book as your barriers and challenges arise.

+ Don't have a clue what we mean by a dream? That's okay, we'll help you get there with Chapter 2, and then you can use the rest of the book to start taking action.

+ Prefer to test some of these tools? Pick a smaller project, such as having a dinner party, going on vacation, or completing a project for work. Barriers come up with small dreams too, and they provide an excellent training ground for using the skills and tools.

+ Feel stuck but aren't sure where to begin? Read through the book and learn to identify the different voices in you that are vying for attention. As you become more adept at hearing them, you'll gain clarity about what will help unstick you.

However you decide to use the book, try out the exercises and maps we lay out in these pages. Identify the thoughts that come up, capture them, and use the processes in this book to work with them. If you find that you get better outcomes, enjoy the process more, or simply discover that your life flows more easily than with your habitual way of being in conversation with yourself, keep going! Do small test experiments, integrating one map into an internal dialogue to see if it improves your outcomes, both in the way you feel and in your ability to take action in the world. Embrace the ongoing process of being more skillful at recognizing self-sabotaging thoughts when they flit through your mind, and of using strategies to make them work to your advantage.

What we're talking about can seem overwhelming, as in some ways it is about changing the way you habitually interact with yourself and the world. Yet, it doesn't have to be overwhelming if you approach it through small changes. Yes, it does take some focus. But as you remind yourself to notice your feelings and thoughts and to use processes to have better internal conversations, you will indeed reap the benefits.

Aren't you and your life worth the effort?

1 | MEET (AND EMBRACE) YOUR THINKING MIND

We are what we think.
All that we are arises with our thoughts.
With our thoughts we make our world.
—BUDDHA

———∿∿∿———

SALLY GLANCES AT HER PHONE AND NOTICES THE TIME. *Oh no, three o'clock? I'm already late!* She throws her bag in the car and sits behind the wheel. *I didn't think the meeting would run that long. Maggie's going to be so upset with me for being late.*

Sally calculates how long it will take to drive to Maggie's school. Clearly marked in her calendar is the three p.m. meeting with Maggie and her teacher. Sally remembers how excited Mags had been when she gave Sally the request from her teacher for the conference. Bouncing up and down, she had tried to explain what it was about, but all Sally understood was that it had something to do with a special science program the teacher wanted Maggie to participate in. Sally had felt unsure about adding another activity to Maggie's schedule, but seeing her excitement, Sally knew she at least needed to consider it.

Thinking about Maggie's schedule prompts Sally to reflect on her own busy day: getting the kids up and to school, meeting with her website developer, finishing a proposal, and the meeting that had just run over, in which she presented the proposal to a potential client. *Then again, every day is a busy day,* Sally thinks, impatiently tapping her foot as she waits for the light to turn green. Between running the kids around to school and various activities, managing her fledgling consulting business, and taking care of the household, Sally feels like she is on the go from the moment she wakes up to when she finally goes to bed at night. It's even worse when her husband James is gone, like he is now, even if it's only an overnight work trip. Wondering how long she can keep it up, she pulls into the school parking lot as a wave of exhaustion flows through her body and settles in her stomach.

—⁓—

Whatever you would like to create, this book can help you achieve it. But in order to understand how you can change anything in your life from within, we must first explore how human beings think.

How aware are you of the thoughts that run through your mind each day? Imagine waking up in the morning and the string of thoughts that may follow:

Oh, warm covers . . . it feels cold out . . . maybe I can hit the snooze button for another few minutes. No no, I need to get up because I've got that early call at work . . . I can't be late today. I wonder what Bill will say when he hears I've landed that sale! Oh wait, I haven't landed it yet, but I know I will . . . we had a great conversation last week . . .

And it continues on through breakfast and into your commute to work:

Oh god, I really hate this traffic. It should only take fifteen minutes to get to work but no, add another hour to that . . . if they'd just change the way these lanes merge, it would be so much easier for traffic to flow. Maybe I should start going in earlier, but I don't want to miss time with my family in the morning. At least I can listen to some good podcasts while I'm sitting here, so it's not a complete waste of time . . .

A popular online meme suggests that we have thousands of thoughts a day, though no one seems to be able to cite actual research on which to base specific numbers. Still, there's no denying that thoughts—however you define them—accompany you as more or less a continuous background stream of commentary throughout the day. These thoughts run your life, unless you become aware of them.

While this may seem overwhelming, it's important to note that you are not the sum total of your internal commentary. When you can become aware of your thoughts, you realize that just because you think them, they are not necessarily true. Many meditation and spiritual traditions include practices that allow you, over time, to notice your thoughts, realize their impact on you, and be able to witness them instead of being run by them. But paying attention to and noticing thoughts, rather than allowing the constant stream to buffet you one way or the other, requires practice.

So how can you become more aware of your thoughts?

While thoughts may be ubiquitous, they often take place underneath conscious awareness, hence it may only be when you notice you're ruminating on distressful thoughts about something that happened that you become aware of the stream and its impact on you. Alternatively, you may notice feelings, and since thinking and feeling are connected, thoughts will produce feelings that affect you. If you notice you are feeling upset, for example, you can backtrack to uncover the thoughts associated with it. Here it's helpful to ask yourself, *When did I start feeling this way?*

Of course, for many people, being aware of either thoughts or feelings may be difficult. If you are focused outward all the time, being in touch with your internal state—whether feeling or thinking—may take some practice. This is when creating a system to regularly check in and pay attention to what is going on internally is extremely beneficial. For example, you can set a timer on your phone or computer that prompts you regularly to "check in" with yourself. Each time it goes off, ask yourself, *What am I thinking?* You could also choose a behavioral trigger, such as walking through a door, using the bathroom, or eating or drinking to cue you to focus on what you are feeling and thinking in the moment.

PRACTICE PAUSE

How aware are you of your thoughts and feelings? What structure would you like to try for a few days to become more aware of them?

PARTS IN CONFLICT

As you become more aware of this constant stream of thoughts, you might notice you are having an internal conversation, as if there are different parts of you speaking to each other. To take a simple, and somewhat silly, example, let's say you're in the middle of writing an email and your stomach growls. You have an internal conversation about getting up for a snack or waiting a few minutes until you finish. When you go to the refrigerator, you see there's not much in there, and another internal conversation ensues about when to go to the store.

In the earlier example of the commute, at least two voices are speaking to each other—one frustrated about the traffic and wondering about going in earlier to avoid it, and the other desiring to spend more time with family in the morning. Once you start to pay attention, you'll begin to notice how often your internal conversation is actually a conflict. Part of you wants one thing (avoid frustration of commute) and part wants something else (family time). In a sense, you have an internal split where these two parts of yourself are in conflict with each other, pulling you in different directions.

Being in conflict internally implies that there are (at least) two parts of you that have different strategies or ideas about what you *have* done or what you *ought* to do. For many people, the idea that they have different parts of themselves vying for attention may seem disturbing; however, take comfort in knowing that this is a well-established concept in psychology and quite normal. For example, Hal and Sidra Stone's well-known Voice Dialogue work is based on the concept that you have many internal voices that determine your worldview and behavior; Jonathan Haidt's analogy of the Elephant and the Rider introduced in *The Happiness Hypothesis* describes how the mind has different parts that can be in conflict; and Chip and Dan Heath further developed this idea in their book *Switch* to elucidate how people change (or don't). In addition, the idea of there being many parts within the psyche is the basis of a model of psychotherapy called Internal Family Systems developed by Richard Schwartz.

Thus, a growing consensus recognizes that there is not one

unified voice within the mind; instead, there are competing modules in the brain vying for control of consciousness, with the prefrontal cortex acting as a kind of traffic cop, deciding which module will have control of conscious thought from moment to moment. This all goes on behind the scenes, without your being consciously aware that it is happening. Yet, despite how overwhelming it may seem, with practice you can learn to become consciously aware when these shifts between various components take place. This is the beginning of true self-awareness.

CREATING YOUR LIFE

When you think about creating your life, what do you think of first? If you're like most people, you might focus on what you *are* or *are not* doing. What you do is, of course, a crucial aspect of creating your life. Yet in our view, there's actually a step before the doing.

You create your life one conversation at a time.

Think about this for a moment. If you and your colleagues are working on a project together, you get on the same page by having conversations—who will do which tasks, what outcomes you're looking for, etc. To create anything in the world with other people, you have conversations with them.

Often overlooked is the fact that the same process happens within. Unlike with other people, however, you may not even realize you are having a conversation, and maybe even a conflict, with yourself, or how you can change the relationship between your internal voices so that it serves what you'd like to create. Because you live one moment after the next, as each moment arises and you are living in that moment, you are in an internal conversation about what is happening now and what to do next. You create your life moment by moment in a whole series of conversations.

Now, people are not typically aware of every single internal conversation occurring from one moment to the next, and that's fine. In fact, it might hinder your day-to-day activities to a degree if you did. After all, many of these conversations flow easily and effortlessly, and life proceeds smoothly from one action to another.

Except when the conversation isn't so easy.

—◆—

"Well that sounds like an exciting program, doesn't it?" Sally puts her arm around Maggie's shoulders as they walk through the school doors and out into the sunshine.

Maggie pulls away. "You're not gonna let me do it, are you?" she says, throwing an accusatory glance toward her mom.

Sally sighs. Maggie had made it clear through the meeting that she was angry. As her teacher explained to Sally that the local university was starting an after-school program for elementary school girls who showed promise in the sciences, Maggie sat with her arms folded, practically glaring at Sally or at the floor.

"I think it's a wonderful opportunity for you. I know how much you love science," Sally says, "but I'm concerned about how many activities you're already doing and how to fit this in too. You're already in soccer, chess club, science club, plus volunteering at the animal shelter. That's why I said we'd talk it over with your dad tonight."

Maggie shrugs. "But I can do this too. Just because you can't handle everything doesn't mean I can't."

Sally feels the sting of Maggie's words and barely remembers to take a few deep breaths instead of letting what she wants to say fly out of her mouth. As they get into the car, she finally manages to say, "We'll talk about it later. Right now we need to get you to soccer practice." Sally feels like she's struggling to breathe in the thick silence on the short ride to the soccer field.

Maggie jumps out and runs to the field as Sally grips the steering wheel. Without her daughter there, Sally lets the emotions and thoughts she's been holding at bay come to the surface. *Mags is so angry. Maybe she's right, though. What am I thinking anyway? Maybe I shouldn't be trying to start my own business. It's too much to take on, especially while the kids still need me. Maggie especially. Am I a bad mom to be doing this? I'm only human. I can't do it all.* Sally peels her hands off the steering wheel to rub her shoulders.

But I should be able to do it all! I mean, it shouldn't be this hard. Other women seem to manage a career and family just fine. What's wrong with me that I feel like I'm barely hanging on? And I'm letting everyone down. The heaviness and sadness settle deeper in Sally's body, and she notices how run-down she feels. *And I guess I'm letting myself down too. I don't have time to take care of myself, so I'm exhausted and feel like I may be getting that cold Mags just got over.* Sally leans the seat back slightly and closes her eyes. *Maybe I should just stop trying to do it all,* she thinks before dozing off.

—⁓—

THOUGHTS AS BARRIERS

In order to create what you desire, you must first have a dream, create a plan, and then begin to implement the plan. In taking action, you must then deal with what arises, including changing your habits, working with other people, and managing the unexpected. Obstacles will arise—some external and others internal—but one of the most common obstacles people experience is their own thinking. We call these obstructive thoughts *barriers*.

> barriers *n.pl.*
>
> thoughts or judgments about yourself or external reality that result in blocking creation of or forward movement on a dream

You have likely heard vivid metaphors that describe how you stop yourself, such as "shooting yourself in the foot," "getting in your own way," or "being your own worst enemy." Have any of the following barriers stopped you in your tracks before?

+ Worry
+ Fear of what might happen
+ Self-sabotaging thoughts
+ Unworthiness
+ Overwhelm
+ Despair
+ Concern about other's judgments
+ Hopelessness, helplessness, or powerlessness

When these barriers arise, the internal conversation turns into an internal conflict, whereby part of you would like to act on your dream, and yet one or more voices speak up to express a different opinion. For many people, the conversation stops there.

They simply believe the self-sabotaging thoughts and come to a standstill. Hence, they don't take any further action on their idea.

Let's experiment with an exercise.

Think of some dream you have, something that you'd like to create in your life. Feel free to choose something big—it could be anything from "I'd like to be able to negotiate a raise with my boss" to "I'd like peace in the Middle East." Perhaps you'd like to be in a relationship. Or you have a business idea you'd love to get off the ground. Maybe you'd like to buy a house, or sell your house and travel around the world. Maybe you'd like to find a job that would bring you more joy.

Name it clearly to yourself.

Once you have it named in your mind, notice what happens.

+ Do you sense any shift in the way you feel?

+ What's the first thought that comes to mind?

+ As you think about what it would take to fulfill your dream, what comes up for you?

+ Do you notice any voices speaking up?

+ What do you feel, and what are those voices saying?

Take a moment now to jot down on a piece of paper what you are feeling and thinking.

If you feel excited and your thoughts jump to what you can do to create your dream, great! Put this book down and go create it! If you're like many folks, however, numerous possibilities might come up, such as:

+ "You could never do that."

+ "That's too big—you're powerless to make an impact on world peace."

+ "It's doubtful she'd ever say yes to a date with you."

+ "Even if he gives you a raise, he'll just pile more work on you, and you're already overwhelmed."

+ "What do you mean you're going to sell your house and travel? Are you crazy? People will think you've gone off your rocker!"

What comes up for you when you explore the idea of your dream? Did any typical self-defeating thoughts and feelings pop into your mind? If so, how do you normally respond to that self-sabotage? Here are the common strategies people use.

IGNORE IT

You pretend that if you don't pay any attention to them, the problematic thoughts will go away. This approach strives to push away the disturbing voices by shifting your thoughts to something else or simply trying to not think about them.

Difficulty: Try to not think about a pink elephant. What's now on your mind? A pink elephant.

REASON WITH IT

This might sound like, *Well, let's just do a little bit and see what happens.* Or *Why don't we go ahead . . . I'm sure we'll learn from it.*

Difficulty: Reasoning with a voice generally comes from the perspective that you know the "right" thing to do, and this voice is wrong and you have to reason with it (like you would a recalcitrant child) to get it to come on board and do the right thing. If someone talked to you that way, how would you feel?

TALK BACK TO IT

We need to do this. I know you don't want to, but once we do it, you'll feel better.

Difficulty: This tactic often comes from a place of frustration or irritation about not moving forward. Instead of listening, your internal conversation is about making a demand of the wayward parts of yourself that they get in line.

OFFER REWARDS

Promise yourself a reward if you can accomplish the task.

+ *If I go work out, I'll be able to eat a piece of chocolate.*

+ *Once I complete this proposal, I'll take a break and call my friend.*

+ *When I reach my sales goal, I'll take a day off from work.*

Difficulty: Persuading some part of you to go along with what you want by promising a reward later is not the same as listening to what that part of you has to contribute.

While there's nothing inherently wrong with any of the above approaches—they can all seem to "work" for some period of time, and if they do, then by all means keep using them!—the question is, do they *truly* work? In other words, they may get you over the hump of the self-defeating behavior in the moment, but at what cost?

For example, have you ever reasoned with a child to get him to do something he doesn't want to do, perhaps get into the car to go to the store? When he resists, you reason, cajole, or offer rewards; eventually he acquiesces. Yet all the way to the store, he's sullen. Once you arrive, he's uncooperative and difficult, reaching for items on shelves, complaining, and throwing out what you've added to the cart.

This example isn't to imply that our internal voices are all a bunch of unruly children. The point is that being heard is a fundamental need that everyone shares, including you and all the different parts of you that speak up. Anyone who isn't heard—whether a child, your partner, a friend or coworker, or an internal voice in your mind—will be angry and attempt to find another way to be heard, sometimes through more subtle means, and sometimes through outright sabotage.

What this means is that if you conquer self-defeating thoughts by discounting some part of yourself, that part is more likely to rebel, cause problems down the road, or sabotage your efforts. As a result, you may find that riding roughshod over the voice carries a cost either immediately or later.

Of course there are times when you will choose the above strategies simply for ease or time, and that's okay. We never suggest that you take on any practice out of a "should" or "have to." But if you find that any of your usual ways of responding to your internal conversations have consequences you don't enjoy, then try what we suggest—or try it just for fun to see what happens.

PRACTICE PAUSE

What are your typical ways of responding to internal barriers? What consequences have you noticed from responding that way?

MEDIATOR MIND:
CHANGING THE INTERNAL CONVERSATION

In our view, all internal voices have something important to contribute toward actualizing your dream. What we are offering is a
way to *mediate between* the conflicting voices that arise in the
course of pursuing it. When two people are in conflict, a mediator
listens to both parties and assists them in coming to an agreement
about how to proceed. When the two parties are both in your own
mind, you can act as your own mediator by accessing what we
call *mediator mind*.

> **mediator mind** *n.*
>
> the state in which you can hold all the parts of
> yourself without being pulled into the limited point
> of view of any one voice

From this state, you can listen to your internal voices and
hear what they have to contribute, and in doing so help them begin to collaborate to create new possibilities.

When you listen to your internal voices from mediator mind,
you don't merely listen to what each is saying, you listen for the
components of Nonviolent Communication (NVC): Observations, Feelings, Needs, and Requests.

Here is a quick recap of these components (See *Choosing Peace*
for more details and techniques to practice these components):

Observation is the stimulus—what happened, what was said or
done or not said or done—that is being responded to. It may be
something in the external world, or it can be a thought in your
mind.

Feelings are body sensations that arise due to *needs* (the fundamental qualities every human being shares to survive and thrive in life) being met or unmet. Examples of needs are sustenance, contribution, love, connection, respect, autonomy, trust, and beauty. When needs are met, feelings of exhilaration, aliveness, hope, joy, satisfaction, and appreciation may arise. When they are not met, feelings may be more along the lines of anger, hurt, disappointment, heaviness, sorrow, impatience, or boredom. (See Appendices A and B for lists of Feelings and Needs.) Everything you do moment to moment is to meet needs, and all internal voices are also speaking up in an attempt to get needs met. Once needs are identified, then you make *requests* of yourself or others to try to get the associated needs fulfilled.

Empathy is the process of listening for the components of observations, feelings, needs, and requests. But when you're listening within to what your internal voices say, the needs may not be immediately evident. In other words, the thoughts may be clear, you can tap into your feelings, and the strategy that part of you is advocating for is often obvious, yet finding the need underlying all of that requires some questioning, and it is your mediator mind that engages in the inquiry. The ability to empathize—to identify the needs of each part of you and then hold the needs of all parts of yourself—is the capacity to be in mediator mind.

When you're in internal conflict, every voice represents some part of you that has a need not being addressed. Thus, you can treat the conflicting internal voices the same way you would if you were mediating between two people: uncover the needs of both parties, and then help them collaborate to find a solution that will meet those needs. The maps in this book will guide you in learning how to do all of this, starting with the foundational skills to empathize from mediator mind with a part of you. When you change the internal conversation by listening in a new way, you can begin creating your life from a space of collaboration instead of conflict.

Let's take a closer look at how this works.

FOCUS AND ACTION

You have control in two distinct places: where you focus your mind, and the action you take. By mental focus, we are talking about where you put your attention internally. You can focus on your thoughts or feelings, or on the meaning you place on what's going on around you. In short, you have choice about what thoughts you have and the meaning you make. Action, on the other hand, is everything you say and do in the outer world. These two "controlled aspects" of your life tend to be intimately connected, as where you focus your mind leads to the actions you are likely to take. Between these two is how you create your life. Unfortunately, people often tend to create what they *don't* want through a tragic expression of unmet needs.

Let's break these two components of attention and action down a bit more with a simple example so they're clear.

> Your partner leaves dirty dishes in the sink, and you've asked before that he put them straight into the dishwasher.

Here are two possibilities for the focus of your mind and the action you take:

Mental Focus: Upset, anger, irritation. You make it mean that he doesn't care about you, and your thoughts might sound like: *Again? What the hell? I've asked him before to put these away. I mean seriously, how difficult can it be?*

Action: Could be anything from lashing out at your partner, angrily putting them in the dishwasher, leaving a nasty note, or (insert your go-to angry reaction).

OR

Mental Focus: Connecting to yourself and finding your observations, feelings, needs, and requests. Your thoughts might sound like: *Okay, I'm feeling frustrated. I've asked him before to put dishes away, and I'd really like support and to know that I matter. I feel such pleasure when I come into the kitchen and it's clean.*

Action: Connected to your need for cleanliness, you go ahead and meet that need by putting the dishes in the dishwasher. When you see your partner later, you ask about the dishes, making a guess about what was going on for him, looking for the need he was meeting in leaving the dishes in the sink. After hearing him and expressing your own needs, you end with a request.

We're not suggesting that the first one is wrong or bad. The question is, which one is more likely to create a life you'll enjoy? In either case, the needs you are acting from are the same; what's different is whether you are *aware of* and *connected to* those needs. When you're not aware and connected to unmet needs, you are more likely to act in ways that create further upset and conflict, both within you and with other people. In addition, when the mental focus and action is along the lines of the first example, you will tend to carry the anger and frustration forward, perhaps complaining to someone at work and feeling irritable the entire morning (or longer). These small resentments feed into larger conflicts in the relationship down the road.

PRACTICE PAUSE

Think about a recent situation in which you felt upset or irritated. Where was your mental focus, and how did that focus manifest in your actions?

All of our work at Mediate Your Life is about how to change your mental focus and actions so that instead of the tragic expression of your needs, you can act in ways that are fulfilling. We give you the maps and tools to focus your mind on finding the feelings and needs that are driving your reactions, and then choosing what to say or do that will better help you meet those needs. If you'd like to create something different, start with the question of what to focus on and how to act in the way you desire.

Learning and practicing these maps and tools is necessary, because where you focus your mind is a matter of habit. Have you noticed that you respond in typical ways in similar situations? Perhaps with your mother you find yourself easily frustrated and short in your responses. When a coworker challenges a decision you made, you feel devastated and question your own abilities, or you defend yourself and the rightness of the decision. In short, based on your specific history, you've built up patterns of responding that tend to recur in similar situations.

These patterns develop because as a child, you lacked the resources to deal with situations and therefore did the best you could with what was available. You made decisions and handled the situation, often developing beliefs about yourself and other people that you then built on, choice after choice, into present time. These patterns are rooted in the amygdala, a key part of the brain involved in emotional learning and motivation. Because people tend to perceive the world out of these lifetime patterns—even though they may be largely unaware of the patterns them-selves—every time a situation arises that feels at all similar to the pattern, people pick from a short "menu" of choices present in the amygdala. They then act from that feeling instead of from what is actually happening. Hence, these patterns are easily trig-gered when striving to achieve a new goal that requires you to do what you haven't done before.

So how do you break out of this "menu" of embedded patterns?

An effective mode of disconnecting the pattern-response way of perceiving and interacting with the world is through em-pathy. When you empathize, you first make more of the pattern conscious, then you begin to see what actually happened (the observation) and what was triggered in you, then you identify the feelings and needs that prompted you to act as you did. Practicing over time, you disconnect the automatic response of the amygdala, giving you the opportunity to experience different feelings and thoughts, and act in a new way.

—◦◦◦—

"Why don't you take some time for yourself, hon?" James asks, rubbing Sally's arms. "I'll clean up from dinner and get the kids to bed." Sally's shoulders drop and she lets out a sigh of relief. "Thanks. I know you're tired since you just got back from your trip, so I really appreciate it."

Earlier, Sally had filled James in on how the afternoon had unfolded, including how stuck she had felt in the car. During dinner they talked with Maggie about how she might partici-pate in the science program and arrived at some agreements with her.

Plopping down on the couch, Sally's mind goes back to the familiar internal conversation of the afternoon. Now that she is not so caught up in it, she feels able to more easily recognize her need for empathy and give it to herself. And, since she's empathized with similar thoughts in the past, she drops in quickly, starting with her judgments about being late to meet with Maggie's teacher. *I'm upset about that because the kids are a priority and I'd like Mags to trust that I'll be there for her, even if I'm working. I got so caught up that I didn't pay attention, so maybe in the future I'll set an alarm to alert me, and let others know too when I have to finish.*

Even though Sally feels good about this strategy, the voice telling her she shouldn't be starting her own business jumps in. *It's way too much, you're letting your family down while saying they're your priority! You're just being stupid and arrogant thinking you can have it all.* Sally feels the harshness of this voice and places her hand on her heart to give some comfort, then talks to it. *So you're feeling angry . . . you'd like to protect me from taking on too much and for me to act with integrity about my family being my priority, like to live up to that value, is that it?* She feels a slight softening in her belly.

Then she hears, *You can't do it all, you'll just crash and burn and take everyone else with you.* On hearing this, Sally understands what this part of her wants to express and responds to it internally. *I get it . . . you care that I don't overdo it and create some mess that would be difficult for all of us?*

The deeper release Sally feels tells her that she's guessed correctly, and she connects more to how she wants to care for her family, to be a good mom, and to care for herself too. *No wonder this part of me says I should stop the business. That does seem like the only option from its point of view.* But then another voice speaks up. *This is ridiculous, what's the problem here? The kids are older now and this is something I want to do . . . it's been time to get back to professional work. Other women have their own business and raise kids too. What's wrong with you? Buck up and get to work.*

Sally takes a deep breath, aware of the tension that arises when she thinks that way. She asks that part of herself, *Are you frustrated because you'd like to contribute to the world in a bigger way?*

The answer comes to her easily.

Yes! I was bored silly staying at home with the kids all the time. And sure, I got involved in different activities and that was fine, but I've wanted to get back to my profession in a big way for a long time. Now what, I'm going to give that all up just because it's a little challenging?

She continues responding to herself.

So you're saying that it's important that I get back to what I'm interested in professionally and be engaged in that, and that I persevere even when things get tough.

Her inner voice answers back.

Of course. There's a way through this . . . find it!

Once again, a knot loosens in Sally's chest at the trust she hears from that part of herself, that there is a solution even if she isn't seeing it yet.

Interrupting her reverie, Maggie runs into the living room, Corey sauntering behind and James bringing up the rear. Maggie throws herself on Sally's lap and wraps her arms around her neck, "Goo'night mom!" Sally laughs and hugs her daughter close for a moment, then reaches up to grab Corey's hand, pulling him down with them. "Oh, Mom!" he says, rolling his eyes, but reaches his arms around both Sally and Maggie for a moment in a quick hug. Sally kisses them both. "Good night, love bugs," she says. James herds them toward bedtime, saying, "Go brush your teeth, and Mags I'll be there in a minute to read a book." The kids untangle themselves, Maggie bouncing from the room as usual with boundless energy, Corey following. Turning to Sally, James says, "You look a bit more relaxed. Have you been thinking through things?"

"Yes," Sally says, "I'm getting in touch again with how much I'd like to be a good wife and mom, take good care of myself, and also be fulfilled professionally. I don't have the way through yet, and it's so easy to lose focus and only see giving up as a possibility when I'm so tired. And when I do something, like being late for the meeting today, I get so down on myself." James nods as Maggie yells from her room, "DAAAAAd-dy, I'm REAAAAA-dy!" They both chuckle as James shrugs. "To be continued, after another installment of Harry and Hermione, as Mags calls it."

——⁓——

BENEFITS OF INTERNAL CONVERSATION

Learning a new way to be in conversation with yourself instead of acting out of habitual patterns of dealing with internal conflict brings many benefits. Let's take a look at a few.

BEING AT CHOICE

Using this model facilitates becoming more conscious of your thoughts, which is incredibly powerful in and of itself, since most people go through the day unaware of their thoughts. For example, if you have thoughts of judgment you aren't conscious of, those thoughts run you nonetheless, and you react without being aware of why you feel or act that way. In other words, even if you are not aware of self-judgments—notions such as "I'm a screw-up," "I'm hopeless," or "I'll never be able to do it well"—you still release neurotransmitters consistent with having those thoughts that may make you feel alternately resistant and angry or hurt and depressed.

When you make these thoughts conscious, however, you can begin to shift this cycle—through inquiring into the needs that particular aspect of you is trying to meet in articulating that judgment. For example, judgments of yourself often reflect needs for care, consideration, competence or mastery, or ease in being able to do something. When you focus on the needs, you are able to think of strategies that might meet the need better than ruminating on how terrible you are. You are then at choice; instead of being run by the thoughts and reacting unconsciously, you are aware of the thoughts and the needs behind them, and you can choose how to respond.

LEARNING AND SELF-KNOWLEDGE

If you'd like to travel to Las Vegas, it helps to know whether you're starting from, say, Los Angeles or San Francisco; the way to get there is distinctly different. Similarly, if you would like to create your dreams, it's helpful to know where you are right now. Because becoming more aware of thoughts and what is driving you gives you insight into yourself, it allows you to act more effectively to get where you want to go in these ways:

+ It gets you closer and closer to what is in your present situation.

+ It aids you in understanding why you act the way you do.

+ It helps you discern what needs you're seeking to meet.

+ It uncovers what your dreams and goals are, and what needs you'd be meeting by achieving them.

+ It allows you to decipher what resources, skills, and capacities you possess, and what contribution from others would support you to reach your dreams.

SELF-JUDGMENT TO SELF-CONNECTION

When you judge yourself harshly for your actions, you often don't end up learning much. You might think you need that judgment in order to do better or be better the next time, but when you truly look into your experience, you can see that all judgment does is sensitize you to punishment and blame. Nobody wants punishment, so instead of learning to shift actions or their way of being, people learn to avoid taking responsibility and thus try to avoid being blamed.

What's great about working with internal conflicts is that it helps you learn how to better meet your needs instead of simply avoiding punishment. This gives you a way to shift out of guilt, shame, and anger, or even depression, to a kind of self-connection that allows for optimal learning. When you learn how to meet your needs in this way, you stand a much better chance of effectively changing your behaviors and ways of being in the world.

CONNECTION TO SOURCE

If you are in internal conflict, you are not present and not connected to the life within you. Internal mediation is a way to transcend the thinking that blocks you from being fully connected with the source of life, the source of creative energy. Using the tools in this book will help you get back to that connection, and from there you can live with a more compassionate way of relating to yourself and others.

LESS STRESS, GREATER ALIGNMENT, INCREASED ENERGY, AND CONFIDENCE

Different voices arguing within you about what you ought to do creates stress, and it can feel as if you are driving with one foot on the gas and one on the brake, or like you are split with different parts of you trying to go in different directions. You start and stop, start and stop, and then become frustrated with yourself for not taking the action you (or at least one part of you) desire.

When you can hear and integrate these different voices, and therefore meet the needs that are being expressed through your doubts and fears, you stop fighting with yourself, bringing all parts of yourself into alignment. As you would expect, people typically prefer the outcomes they create when they are in alignment rather than in conflict. Ending the internal conflict also tends to unleash a lot of energy that is no longer caught up in trying to ignore or manage the discord within. That energy can give a welcome boost to taking action on your dream.

—∿∿—

After James leaves, Sally sits back down on the couch and asks herself, *What would it take to have all of these needs met? To be moving ahead professionally, while taking care of myself and my family?* Asking the question helps Sally see that she is clear on what taking care of her family means, since she's been doing that for years—organizing schedules, making sure kids are picked up, handling household tasks, and so on. But she's much less clear about what taking care of herself means. *I guess before I was working, I just did what I needed naturally, but now with spending so much time on work, I'm getting lost. What would more self-care look like, specifically?*

A few ideas jump into her mind.

Getting enough sleep, that's up there for sure. Eating well and getting some physical activity, of course. But it's also something about having a different relationship to myself and what happens. Like today, being able to recognize what's going on sooner so I don't suffer so

*much like I did this afternoon. I'd like more allowance of these differ-
ent parts of myself and to hear what's really going on without necessarily buying into what they're saying on the surface. Also noticing
earlier when I'm stressed so I can do something about it before it gets
too bad. That would be nice.*

Sally ponders these self-care ideas and a few requests start
to emerge.

*I'd like to start moving bedtime up, maybe slowly so that I can
adjust. Scheduling in some of my self-care might be a good idea. I
schedule my work meetings, but I can also schedule in when I'm going
to work and when I'm going to exercise, even if it's just a few minutes,
and of course family things. That way I'll be less likely to let work over-
ride what I need to do for me.*

She feels a niggling doubt from the part of her concerned
about becoming run-down and exhausted, that even scheduling it won't be enough, that self-care will be fit in around the
edges and then pushed aside easily. Sally recalls an article that
suggested when creating a schedule to start with the necessities
like self-care (sleep, exercise, etc.) first, then add in work and
other commitments. *I'll try that this week and see if that helps. I
know it's about making time for what's most important to me, not
finding it, and this is important. I am important. I'm not going to help
my family or my business if I'm not in good shape.*

Sally smiles, feeling her strong resolve to make sure she's
taking care of herself as well as her family and business.

—◦◦◦—

NEXT UP

As you become more aware of your thoughts, you may also
become more aware of how often internal barriers show up and
stop you. Perhaps even thinking about what you'd like to create in

your life has already brought up a few sabotaging thoughts. In the next chapter, we'll take a look at what a dream is, the common internal barriers that can stop you from even knowing your dream, and how to move through those barriers so you have a clear vision of what you'd like to create.

2 | WHAT'S YOUR DREAM?

CREATING CLARITY AND CONNECTION WITHIN

You have to dream before your dreams can come true.
—A.P.J. ABDUL KALAM

———

JAMES AND COREY PULL UP TO MAGGIE'S SCHOOL JUST AS she comes bursting out the front doors. Corey shakes his head watching her run full tilt toward the car. "She has two speeds, fast and faster."

James chuckles. "Three if you count 'off' when she's sleeping."

Corey shrugs. "Yeah, I don't really see that one." Then he turns to his dad. "Have you found the off switch?"

James playfully punches Corey's shoulder, gently admonishing with a smile. "Corey, she's your sister!"

Corey shrugs again and returns to the iPad in his lap, ignoring Maggie as she clambers into the back seat with a "Hiiiiiiii Daaaaaaad!" James reaches back and ruffles her hair, then pulls away from the curb as Maggie says, "How come Corey always gets the front seat?"

"'Cause I'm bigger than you," Corey shoots back.

"So what?" counters Maggie.

James's mind wanders as the two continue in the background. Since he was gone the previous couple of days, he'd agreed to pick up the kids even though it meant leaving work a bit early. Truth be told, he was glad to leave.

The trip had been good—training staff at a new urgent care center opening a few hours away. James reflects on how much he enjoys his job and the team he manages. Yet he's felt dissatisfaction lately, a sense that something isn't quite right, that maybe he'd like something more. He hasn't taken the time to think much about it, but it's been a niggling thought at the back of his mind.

Maybe seeing Sally go for her dream with her business has me wanting to stretch myself too, James thinks. *But where is there to go? This is my job, what else is there? It's not like I can quit and go chasing some vague idea right now . . . not that I even know what that would be for me. Besides, I have to be responsible. Family life is disrupted enough. I certainly can't do something big that would disrupt it even further.* James feels the heaviness in his limbs at these thoughts, and then his reverie is interrupted by a loud squeal from Maggie. "OWWWWW! Daddy, Corey just pinched me."

"Well, she keeps kicking the back of my seat," Corey reasons.

Between his kids bickering and the discontent within, James snaps. "All right, that's enough from both of you," he barks. Immediately he regrets the harshness in his voice as both kids clamp down into silence.

—⁓—

A dream is the starting place for all conscious change in your life and in the world. It's the first step in a process—short or long—

that may twist and bend on the way to the satisfaction and fulfillment of creating the life you'd like to live.

Do you know what your dream is?

Before you can begin to create your ideal future, you have to
know what it is you desire. What would you like to accomplish or
experience?

In using the word "dream," we are not talking about a pie-
in-the-sky notion, an unobtainable outcome, or a nebulous idea
in which you have no vested interest. We're talking about identi-
fiable states of the world or inner states that you would like to
create or experience that do not currently exist.

In this chapter, we address what a dream is and how to work
through any internal barriers that arise to knowing and formulat-
ing your dream. If you can already name what you desire clearly,
then you likely have no barriers arising in your internal conversation in the stage of creating a dream. If this is the case, feel free
to read this chapter just for fun, or simply move ahead to the next
chapter and begin to plan.

Perhaps instead of clarity, however, you experience one or
more of the following when you think about this stage:

+ You're not sure what we mean by a dream.

+ You feel stuck or uncertain about what your dream may be.

+ You're not sure if you should be dreaming.

+ You feel tight, heavy, angry, confused, distressed, or
   anxious when you think about creating a vision, or other
   feelings arise that divert you from fully forming your
   dream.

+ You have difficulty naming what you desire.

+ You don't even want to dream.

If so, then this chapter will provide a tool and ideas to help you have the internal conversations that will allow you to move through these barriers and gain clarity.

DREAMING BIG AND SMALL

Numerous types of dreams exist. There are big dreams and little ones, outer visions of what you'd like to see in the world, and inner visions of what you wish to experience. All dreams count, and all dreams can benefit from what is in this book.

> **dream** n.
>
> a vision of what you would like to create

Here are some examples of big dreams:

+ Peace in the Middle East

+ Gandhi's dream of independence from Britain

+ Martin Luther King's dream that "my four little children will one day live in a nation where they will not be judged by the color of their skin but by the content of their character"

+ A world where consciousness, compassion, and care prevail

+ Change the disease-care system into a health-care system

+ End abuse or hunger

Some examples of more local-scale or personal dreams:

+ Create a community known for cultivating resilience in children and young people

+ Live a healthy lifestyle

+ Change the culture of my child's school to one of respect and acceptance for all kids

+ Heal a chronic illness

+ Bring a mindfulness program to the prison in my community

+ Buy a home

+ Write a book

Some examples of dreams more contained in scope:

+ Speak up at least one time in a meeting at work

+ Have a conversation with Mom that doesn't end in a fight

+ Do something fun on my next day off

+ Ask a new friend to have tea

+ Clear the clutter from my workspace

+ Plan a weekend trip

And examples of inner, experience-based dreams:

+ Experience less anxiety and more well-being each day

+ Stay calm and centered when I talk to my boss

+ Be aware more often of my thoughts and feelings

+ Focus when I'm working

+ Develop greater self-compassion

+ Bring a sense of play to everything I do

PRACTICE PAUSE

Now that you've read some examples of dreams, see if you can name and write down a few dreams you have, from small to large, inner to outer. What comes up for you when you try this?

A dream and a goal are not necessarily the same thing, though with smaller dreams they might be; a dream as we're using it is more along the lines of a vision for what you desire, which may entail setting many goals in order to reach it. Still, similar to a goal, it helps to think of a dream as something concrete. In other words, it's measurable and definable in some way, even if not quantifiably, and even if you think it is unlikely to be achieved in your lifetime, you will clearly know if it's been accomplished.

A simple example would be clearing the clutter out of your workspace—you can visually see that dream fulfilled. Similarly:

+ You can define what a healthy lifestyle would look like for you, and then set a whole series of small goals to aim toward living that way.

+ You can imagine the culture of a school that has respect and acceptance for all kids and how people would act in that setting.

+ You can envision being calm and centered while talking to your boss, and assess after each conversation the degree to which you experienced that dream.

Dreams that encompass larger concepts, such as a world characterized by the arising of compassion, or a political system that functions from true dialogue, can also be clearly delineated and described. Once you define your role in the dream, you can take steps to seeing it fulfilled, however that may look for you.

BARRIERS TO DREAMING

Before we outline the common barriers to creating a dream, let's hear from our three companions, Chris, Dawn, and Kevin, on what came up for them when they were asked to name their dream.

CHRIS

"I suppose my doctor is right and I should lose some weight, but I've tried so many times before and it just comes back. So why should I even set that as a dream for myself? I'm probably not going to be able to reach it, and if I do formulate that as my dream and can't do it, I'll just experience the pain of not being able to reach it yet again. Why bother?"

DAWN

"I don't know what I would like for myself. I've been taking care of everyone else and supporting their dreams for so long that somehow it just doesn't feel right to me to dream something for myself. It actually seems selfish. I guess I took on others' dreams and never thought about having any of my own. I was always taught to put other people first, and that's what I've done for my family. Maybe my family and raising great kids was my dream all along, but now that I'm no longer needed there in the same way, I'm not sure what I would like to achieve, or whether I even have the right to dream for myself."

KEVIN

"Dream? I'm not even sure what you mean by 'dream.' I don't dream—I'm all about doing. Sure, there are things I'd like in my life, but I don't have time to sit back and dream because I have to put food on the table and pay the mortgage."

Chris, Dawn, and Kevin are each stuck in a different way in thinking about what they desire. In addition, you read how James, too, has a sense of dissatisfaction and uncertainty at work but isn't clear what his options might be within the constraints of his job and home life. You may be experiencing similar thoughts and feelings.

Take a look at some of the interfering thoughts that may arise to keep you from being able to create a dream, even when you know you wish for something different in your life:

- If I formulate a dream, I'll experience the pain of not having it.
- Dreaming is unproductive.
- I'm too [old, young, etc.] to dream.
- I don't know what a dream is.
- I don't know what my dream is.
- I'm a doer, not a dreamer.
- I won't be able to make it happen anyway, so why bother coming up with the idea?
- I never follow through on ideas, so what's the point of getting started?
- If I go for my dream, I'll just be setting myself up to feel disappointed.

✦ If I try to do it I'll fail, so I don't want to be clear about what I desire.

✦ It's too big, and I'm overwhelmed even thinking about what I'd like to have or do.

✦ I'm just a [woman, man, kid, housewife, etc.].

✦ I'm not [smart, wealthy, competent, experienced, etc.] enough to dream.

Some thought barriers are a little less obvious, especially those that are predominant in your culture. In Australia, for example, the "tall poppy syndrome" describes how people who stand out will be cut down to size. In the United States, you might have heard, "You're getting too big for your britches." Japanese and Chinese cultures have the saying, "The nail that stands out gets hammered down." Along similar lines are:

✦ "The chicken who sticks his neck out gets his head chopped off."

✦ "It's the whale that spouts that gets harpooned." (attributed to Denis Thatcher)

✦ "The bigger they come, the harder they fall."

If you heard any of these or similar sayings growing up, you likely internalized them and may find that there's a deep sense of resistance to creating a dream that might have you stand out in the crowd.

Similarly, your family, in a misguided effort to protect you, may have sent messages about what is and is not possible for you based on the family's level of income, where you lived, where you were from, your gender, or your ethnicity. These messages of being from the "wrong side of the tracks" or not having the education or financial resources to be able to accomplish something in the world become internalized, and rather than seen as an obstacle to overcome or go around, they become an enduring statement of inability. You might even find that you don't feel you have the right to dream at all.

If any of these internal barriers come up when you begin to think about your dream, even those where it seems like knowing what you'd like to create is impossible, take heart! Wherever you are starting from, you can shift the internal conversation. Remember, every invention that exists today—cars, computers, television, the light bulb—began as a dream that was actualized into the world by the dreamer.

> ## PRACTICE PAUSE
>
> Which of the barriers mentioned above or in the examples of James, Chris, Dawn, and Kevin are familiar to you? How do they tend to show up in your life and stop you?

THE PATH TO NAMING YOUR DREAM

When barriers arise, many people simply stop. Why? Because they don't see a way through the barrier, and their dreams therefore languish. Yet there is a way through, and it lies in understanding that the thoughts are there for a reason—some part of you is speaking to ensure that certain needs are met. Remember, needs can always be met by a variety of different strategies; each voice you hear in your mind tends to advocate for a single strategy to further its ends.

Thus, each part of you is striving to meet a need for you, but it is typically single-minded in doing so, meaning that it doesn't consider other needs you may have. For example, a voice that seeks to protect you is often in conflict with the part of you that wants to explore, discover, and learn. A safety-focused voice can, by generating fear and anxiety, sabotage your attempts to grow and explore the world. But when you can listen closely to what is coming up, you become aware of what you can do to take care of yourself while still allowing yourself to have a greater vision for your life.

A tool that can help you hear what an internal voice truly desires is Self-Empathy. This tool uses the four components of communication from Nonviolent Communication—observations, feelings, needs, and requests. In the explanations below we will briefly describe these (if you are new to this work, see the first book in the Mediate Your Life series, *Choosing Peace*, for a thorough exploration of these components and techniques to practice them).

Here are the steps of Self-Empathy:

1. Identify Observations

2. Feel and Name Your Feelings

3. Find Your Needs

4. Make Requests

IDENTIFY OBSERVATIONS

Pinpointing observations requires stepping outside of the tendency to be caught up in your experience to look at it as an observer. Observations can be what happened in the outer world— what was said or done that a video would capture. They can also be aspects of your internal experience—whatever you notice about what's happening inside, such as sensations, thoughts, feelings, beliefs, attitudes, or assumptions.

> ### PRACTICE PAUSE
>
> When you focus your attention on the question of naming your dream, what happens? What thoughts or beliefs come to mind immediately? What happens in your body? Write down your observations.

FEEL AND NAME YOUR FEELINGS

Feelings are the sensations that arise in the body as you hold the observation in mind. You can experience what is going on in your body in a few different ways:

1. You can simply be present with your experience without trying to name or describe it with language, feeling the sensations that are arising in this moment.

2. You can describe the sensations in your body. For example:

   a. "I'm feeling heaviness and a sinking feeling in my stomach."

   b. "My shoulders and neck feel tight and I'm really hot."

   c. "My whole body just felt like it froze."

3. You can name what you are feeling. Use a list such as the one in Appendix A if it helps to identify the feeling associated with the bodily sensations.

To connect most completely with your feelings, play with all of these in sequence; first simply experience what is happening in your body, then describe it, then identify what you are feeling. If you are having trouble creating a dream, you might be feeling uncomfortable emotions like agitation, overwhelm, disheartenment, or apathy.

PRACTICE PAUSE

When you read over the observations you listed, what do you feel? Go through each of the three steps listed above in order, and end by listing your feelings.

FIND YOUR NEEDS

Needs are the fundamental qualities that support all humans to survive and thrive. They describe the underlying drivers that motivate your actions throughout the day—everything you think or do is a strategy to meet your needs.

If you're having trouble being present with what you'd like to create in your life, your feelings will presumably be ones you don't enjoy, which are typically connected with unmet needs. To connect what you are feeling with your needs, you might ask yourself the question, "If I'm feeling this way, what need of mine is not met?" In this way, feelings can be a gateway to your needs.

If this part of the process seems confusing to your cognitive mind, that makes sense! The interpretation that needs are not met is made by the non-verbal part of you, and your thoughts and feelings are therefore alerting you to that interpretation. Hence, if you allow the question of what those needs might be to percolate, certain ideas will arise (you can use the needs list in Appendix B to help you). When you name a need, let the reaction in your body tell you if it hits the mark. In other words, finding the need isn't necessarily an analytical process. Your cognitive mind comes up with a possible need, and then your physiological reaction tells you when you've guessed correctly. When you name the need accurately, your whole physiology will respond.

When you're just beginning to inquire into your feelings and needs, it may take some time to learn how your body gives you feedback, so simply pay attention when you name a need, check in with your body, and then name another one, and check in again. You may notice some sensation in your body such as relief, or warmth, or a sense of something falling into place. You might simply experience knowing when you've hit on the right one. In performing the process repeatedly, you'll learn your particular physiological state that corresponds to naming the need.

Also in this step, you can imagine that need being met. Since you've identified an unmet need that is prompting uncomfortable feelings, what would it feel like if that need were met? Get in touch with that feeling and savor it for a few breaths before moving on in the process.

PRACTICE PAUSE

Look back at your list of feelings, and identify one or more needs that are not met. For each need, imagine what it would be like if it was met.

MAKE REQUESTS

Once you uncover your needs, a natural next step is to try to meet them, and you do that through making requests of yourself or other people. Requests are positive (stating what you want instead of what you don't want), present-tense (stated as present-time agreements, not future ones), and in action language (stated in doable and concrete terms). It also helps to make sure you are not actually making a demand of yourself or another person—meaning if it is a request, you are open to hearing a "no." If you do hear a "no" and you respond with an attempt to punish, induce guilt, or in other ways coerce the other person to say "yes," that indicates you made a demand.

Now that you have one or more needs in mind, consider if there's a request you have of yourself or someone else. If you'd simply like to request that you again return to inquiring into your dream, see if you can now be present thinking about it after using Self-Empathy. Or, it may be clear to you at this point that you would like some more information, and your request is to take the steps to gather that information.

PRACTICE PAUSE

What request of yourself or others would
help you meet your needs?

———

After arriving at home, both kids disappear into their rooms, and James sits at the kitchen table. Knowing he'd like some relief from the discontent, he decides to try Self-Empathy and see what happens.

What's my observation? he asks himself as he grabs a pad of paper to document his process. As he ponders, he writes in four columns across the top: "Observations" "Feelings" "Needs" and "Requests." For the first column, he immediately thinks, *Well, I'm dissatisfied at work.* Although that's a feeling as well as an observation, he writes it under "Observations."

What is it I'm dissatisfied about? he asks himself. For a few moments, he muses about the different aspects of his work and what else he might be able to do. *My job is what it is, there's no-where to go with it.* He believes this thought for a moment as it seems true to him, then realizes, *Oh, wait, that's what I'm thinking about it, so I can include that as an observation.* James writes down: "Nowhere else to go in job." He is also aware that Sally is spending time building her dream. *She's doing her thing, but it's just beginning, so I have to be responsible. I can't do something radical like leave my job right now.* He writes down: "Sally's pursuing her dream so I have to be responsible."

As he considers his feelings, he checks in with his body. The weight he'd felt earlier is there, feeling like his limbs are being pulled downward. He also detects some energy in his stomach and solar plexus, like something is churning there. Continuing to feel into these sensations, he asks, *What am I feeling?* The first word that comes up is "restless," so he writes that down. "Confused" also arises pretty quickly as he taps into his sense of not knowing what it is he wants. He looks back over the observations and as he focuses on the final one about Sally and being responsible, he notices some heat in his neck and head. *What do I feel about that?* he asks. It takes a moment and then he hits on it: "disgruntled." The heat dissipates slightly as he names this feeling. He adds dissatisfied to the list since that was where he started the process.

Though these feelings are uncomfortable, James remembers that they are arising from unmet needs. *So what are my needs?* he asks himself, turning his attention to the Needs column. *I'm dissatisfied because I'm pretty comfortable in this job and I'm not learning as much anymore. The challenge is not as high, so growth and learning are definitely needs not being met.* James pauses to write these down. *There's also something about achievement and contribution . . . I know I contribute at work, but I'd like to contribute beyond the company. And of course I'd like to be more fulfilled at work.*

James considers the feeling of confusion from not knowing what he really wants and writes "clarity" under his other needs. As his eyes go back to "disgruntled" he pauses, thinking of Sally and the responsibility he feels with his family. As he probes into what that sense of responsibility is about, he comes to recognize that in part he wants some predictability and security in their home life. *I think that's important for the kids too,* he thinks. *There's something more behind this feeling of being disgruntled . . . maybe seeing Sally go for her dream. I'd really like some consideration that I have dreams with my work too, and I'd like to be moving on those like Sally is.*

Reviewing his list of needs—growth, learning, achievement, contribution, fulfillment, clarity, predictability, security, and consideration—James feels a settling in his system, a bit of relief from the discomfort of the earlier feelings.

Standing up to stretch, James looks down at the sheet and says out loud, "Okay, what now?" The empty Requests column draws his attention and he wonders what he might do next. *This is going to be a process . . . I'm not going to have all the answers or know how to meet these needs right away,* he acknowledges. *Still, I guess one next step would be to brainstorm what might bring me more fulfillment in my career.*

Writing that down, he thinks of his buddy. *I should call up Steve . . . he may be able to help me with some ideas.* Steve was a kind of mentor to James early in his career—they worked at the same company before both moved on, but they've remained friends and still speak occasionally. James writes "Call Steve" under "Brainstorm."

Reviewing the list of needs, James decides another request of himself is to revisit his needs as he considers his options for moving forward. *And, of course, I'd like to talk to Sally.* Thinking of Sally, he remembers the kids, and knows another request of himself is to clean up the mess he made when he reacted out of his own frustration and unmet needs and snapped at Corey and Maggie in the car.

James's List

Observations	Feelings	Needs	Requests
dissatisfied at work	restless	growth	brainstorm what might bring more fulfillment in career
nowhere else to go in job	confused	learning	
Sally's pursuing her dream so I have to be responsible	disgruntled	achievement	call Steve
	dissatisfied	contribution	revisit needs when considering options for moving forward
		fulfillment	
		clarity	
		predictability	talk to Sally
		security	
		consideration	clean up mess with kids from earlier reaction

—*m*—

Let's look at what happens with our three companions as they go through Self-Empathy with their barriers to dreaming.

CHRIS

When considering taking steps to be healthier, Chris notices first the observation, *I'll be disappointed again in myself*. He identifies that he feels powerless and hopeless about being able to make any changes, and he feels disappointed in himself for past failures. Needs that come up are for safety, protection, and a kind of self-care—like wanting to be in a cave and pull the covers over his head. He would also like to have a sense of accomplishment and pride in setting and reaching goals with his health. He comes up with the request of himself to think through what he tried in the past and to ponder what worked and didn't work. Ultimately, he determines he will strive to find a way to articulate his dream such that it truly reflects what he wants in his life, instead of focusing on what he doesn't want. He resolves to also call a close friend who lost weight years ago and maintained it.

DAWN

The observations that stand out to Dawn are the thoughts that she doesn't know what she wants, that it's selfish to dream, and that she doesn't have any right to have a vision for herself. She recognizes the role her history plays in those patterns of thinking: the example her mom set was to sacrifice all for the kids and family, plus Dawn grew up on a struggling farm. Money was often lacking and Dawn had been frequently told growing up that she couldn't have or do things she wanted. When having these thoughts, Dawn notes that she feels a bit overwhelmed, confused, dejected, and afraid, as if something terrible would happen if she allowed herself to dream. She pinpoints the need for trust, both in herself and that everything will be okay if she allows herself this step of creating a vision. Other needs include support, clarity about what she would truly like for herself, and a sense of aliveness and discovery. Her requests for herself are to come up with all the ways she does have trust in herself, and think through what helps her feel alive and where she might find some support. She thinks maybe she could brainstorm some ideas, and if the fear comes up, she'll return to Self-Empathy.

KEVIN

Kevin becomes aware just how resistant he is, actually feeling disgruntled about even the idea of dreaming, and realizes it is coming from his needs for sustainability and stability in providing for his family. He feels responsible for keeping up the standard of living they are used to, and he begins to understand how much he ties his sense of self to being seen (and seeing himself) as a good provider. He is also weary of that seeming like it's his main purpose and desires some balance, not only in his outer life, but also in his inner world. He wants some freedom to act to meet other needs, like enjoyment of his life and what he has created with his family. His wife has said for quite some time that it would be nice if he was around more, and he'd always agreed but continued to make work a priority. He decides his requests are to take a good look at the whole situation—his career and his home life—and talk to his wife about what he's thinking.

SELF-EMPATHY IN PRACTICE AND IN LIFE

Self-Empathy is a wonderful practice to do regularly throughout your day to begin to embody the four components of communication and to have the skill of listening for them readily available. While it's commonly used in situations where needs are *not* met, an enjoyable way to practice it is when needs *have* been met. Perhaps you feel great after a work event, or have a family dinner that you truly enjoyed. In this case you will simply follow the same steps:

+ Identify the observations—what happened outside of you or your thoughts and feelings.

+ Connect with what is happening in your body and name the feelings.

+ Find the needs that are met, and imagine them being met even more.

+ See if any requests arise.

You may find it easier the first few times to have someone else support you as you go through the steps. In fact, a practice you may like is to set up a regular time with a friend and support each other in using Self-Empathy to shift how you feel about a current situation. It doesn't have to take long, and it can make a huge difference in how you feel.

PRACTICE PAUSE

What could you do to help remind yourself
to practice Self-Empathy each day?

If you are new to the process of Self-Empathy, and especially if you have little practice with finding observations, feelings, needs, and requests, we recommend you go through it as outlined above until you feel adept. Once you have embodied it to some extent, there are shorter ways to use it if you don't want to take

the time to do it in depth in the moment, yet would like to connect with what's going on for you. We find that most people,
through practice, generate their own alternative paths to connection, and we encourage you to do the same.

Here are two ways you can use Self-Empathy without going
through the full-length process. One is a medium-length path we'll
call "condensed" (if, for example, you can take a few minutes
away from what you're doing), and another is a "quick" path (if,
perhaps, you're in the midst of an interaction and would like to
do something in that moment to connect without stepping away).

Condensed Path

In this shortened process, you can go through the steps more
quickly by simply identifying one observation as a place to start,
and then follow through with a feeling, need, and request for that
one observation. (In a full practice you might have a list in each
category, as James did, but if you only have a few minutes, start
with the observation that feels the most compelling, and then follow the process from that starting place.)

Perhaps you finish a phone call with a coworker and realize
you're a little unhappy about it. You have a few minutes to spare,
so you identify an observation, such as the thought, *I shouldn't
have told him about the proposed changes.* Checking in with your
body, you notice a slight churning in your stomach and identify
that you feel uneasy. You ask what need is not met, and you realize that you'd like more awareness in the moment of what to tell
your colleague about future possibilities. As such, you come up
with a request to ask yourself, *What information does this person
require right now?* before talking with colleagues. You could also
have a request to revisit this situation and go through a longer

Self-Empathy process when you have more time, as there are likely to be other aspects to explore and further requests that would help mitigate the undesired consequences of what you said.

QUICK PATH

If you're in the midst of a situation and would like to shift how you feel, you can also view any one of the components as an entryway. For example, maybe you identify an observation (either what is happening outside you or the thoughts in your mind) and then skip the feeling and go straight to a need. Or perhaps you notice that you're feeling afraid or discontent, so you name your feeling and then find the unmet need. You might even be able to go straight to the need itself without identifying either an observation or feeling, if that's clear to you. Finally, your request could be the starting place, and identifying that may be the aspect that shifts you quickly in relationship to the situation. Overall, remember that identifying needs, met or unmet, tends to be the most connecting, so you want to be sure that's one of your touchpoints in the quick path.

For example, you walk into a meeting and see a coworker you have disagreed with in the past. You notice a tightness develop in your chest and remember in past situations associating this feeling with the need for respect. When you state this need to yourself, you notice a lessening of constriction and a softening of your belly that signifies you have accurately identified the need related to the tightness. You take a couple of somewhat deepened inhales while imagining this need being met. Having done so, you turn and greet your coworker, choosing consciously how you want to behave.

MORE ABOUT DREAMS

If your dream has to do with an internal state you'd like to experience more consistently, be careful that you do not hold that dream in a way that creates judgment. Sometimes people take on a dream such as, "I'd like to be more at peace" and use it to stifle their experience, judging anything that arises that isn't peace as "bad" and pushing it away.

Ask yourself if there is some other way to be the person you want to be that is *inclusive* of all your experience instead of *exclusive*. For example, one way to experience more peace is to notice and pay attention to all that arises in your experience—including distress or difficult emotions—being present and naming them. This basic mindfulness practice results in more peace in your internal experience.

The other option is to tie your state of being to something specific, such as experiencing peace while in a conversation with your ex, or joy while doing mundane chores. You can then plan (see the next chapter) what to do before and during that situation to make it more likely you can experience what you desire.

When you have a big dream you are working toward, smaller dreams arise to support it, and you may find that you need to go through this same process at both the big-dream and small-dream levels. For example, perhaps through Self-Empathy you identify a big dream of a world where people live free of addiction. When you name it clearly, it brings excitement, but also numerous ideas—smaller dreams—about what you could do to work toward creating it. You could write articles about overcoming addiction, give talks to local groups, offer workshops, or work through a local recovery center. Self-Empathy can assist you in clarity about what smaller dreams would most meet your needs.

Not all of these smaller dreams have to be initiated from

within, either—other people may present you with opportunities. Perhaps you write an article for a local paper about addiction, and a community group contacts you about putting together a program for them. If the opportunity matches what you would like to accomplish, it may become your dream too. For us, when people ask if we would be willing to offer training in their country, doing that training often becomes a new dream of ours.

EMBRACING THE DREAMER IN YOURSELF

While working on this stage of articulating your dream, you'll want to focus your attention only on your dream itself. Why? Because different parts of you play different roles in the realization of a dream, and you don't want the parts that plan and then implement to interfere with the part that dreams and imagines and puts yourself in the future having accomplished it. In other words, you don't want to think about how it will all come together just yet; right now, you're simply the dreamer. This is similar to the idea that when you're brainstorming, you want to simply come up with ideas, not criticize or analyze or make decisions. When you allow this part of yourself to come out and play without distraction, you silence those parts of yourself that can put a damper on the dreamer.

So how long should you stay in dreamer mode? We suggest until you're satisfied, at least to a certain extent, that this is an idea that resonates with you, meaning there's a sense of it feeling right, exciting, or harmonious when you imagine bringing it to life. While thoughts may arise in this stage about what it will take to make this dream happen, or about your ability to accomplish it, you can jot them down, but don't entertain them—not yet. It's best to simply record the thoughts and appreciate that they have shown up, but not let them dissuade you from pursuing the dream. When you get to later stages of the journey, those thoughts will be your starting point and you'll use the tools we offer to have those conversations with yourself. For now, however, it's crucial to stay only in the conversation of what it is you'd like to create.

While this stage may simply involve naming your dream, it may also be a much longer and more involved process of doing Self-Empathy, gathering information, sharing ideas with others, receiving feedback, and refining your dream, especially if it is more complex. It may require going through cycles of those elements punctuated by numerous sessions of Self-Empathy before you can clearly articulate what you'd like to achieve.

In fact, the whole process of actualizing your dream is iterative, and you may likewise revisit your dream down the road when you are in other stages of planning or actualizing it. You may learn more as you begin to take action and have the necessary conversations with yourself and others to bring your dream into existence, possibly finding it necessary to revisit and refine the dream. If you ever begin to feel uncertain, disconnected from your dream, or that something doesn't quite fit, return to the stage of dreaming to once again clarify your vision.

We've introduced Self-Empathy in this chapter as a way to work with barrier thoughts that get in the way of knowing your dream. At times, you may find that you have more than one voice speaking up, and you may even have an argument between them that keeps you from dreaming. In these cases, you can use the process in Chapter 4, the Internal Mediation map, to support you to work through that internal conversation to find your dream. In Self-Empathy, you are in mediator mind, empathizing with *one* voice to find the observations, feelings, needs, and requests to connect with what that voice is telling you. The Internal Mediation map, however, will support you if you have *more* than one voice and would like to mediate between them.

CONNECTING TO YOUR DREAM THROUGH NEEDS

The goal of the conversations you have in the dream stage is to be connected to your dream, meaning that when you bring it to mind, the emotions you have are consistent with needs being met, such as anticipation, exhilaration, hope, or a calm certainty. This is a great sign—in experiencing feelings you welcome, you will stay present with your dream while you articulate it, write it, or tell other people about it.

Once you have identified a dream, you can use Self-Empathy to connect with the needs that you hope will be met through actualizing it. Perhaps you'd like to give a dinner party for a few friends. As you think of this dream and imagine it happening the way you desire, what do you feel in your body? What needs do you hope to meet by gathering with your friends over a meal? Go through the same steps of identifying observations, feelings, needs, and requests.

> PRACTICE PAUSE
>
> Take a dream you would like to work on
> during the reading of this book, and go
> through the steps of Self-Empathy to connect
> you to the needs you hope it will meet.

When you're connected to the needs that you hope will be met by the dream, whenever you plug into the dream, you're also plugging into those needs. This clarity can help at all stages of bringing your dream to fruition, especially when communicating with others about what you'd like to create. One of the most powerful ways to foster collaboration is to connect people to the needs you're seeking to meet through the building of your dream. When you "enroll" people in those needs, they are more likely to want to support you because they, too, would like to feed into those needs (since needs are universal). Plus, if you meet resistance from other people, being clear about your own needs helps to be able to listen for theirs (see *From Conflict to Connection* for more).

Let's return now to our three companions and their process of articulating a dream.

CHRIS

Chris follows through on his requests to himself, and through both his call with his friend and looking at what happened before, he thinks that the key might lie in how he approached the whole issue. "I always thought about it like a diet, and maybe that's why it didn't work. What I'd really like is to have healthy choices be the way I live all the time, not for just a few months so that I can lose some weight." As he considers how he would describe a healthy lifestyle, he begins to see the connection between all areas of his life. "I'd like to be around for a long time for my wife and kids and eventually my grandkids. I used to enjoy being active in college, and I'd like to feel good in my body and be able to go hiking or play some team sports and feel strong doing those activities. If I can make some changes in how I eat, my activity levels, and in some other areas like sleep and taking more time off work, and I make those changes in a way that they become how I live, then I'll set myself up to be healthy in the future."

Dream: Create a healthy lifestyle that allows me to enjoy today and be around for many tomorrows.

DAWN

Over the course of a few weeks, Dawn keeps returning to her needs and requests. Initially, as she brainstorms ideas, she has to keep returning to Self-Empathy. "The overwhelm and fear kept showing up, and I'd go through the process again. Each time I found I connected more to my needs." She finds support in a close friend and in her husband, both of whom acknowledge how much she has given to her family. "With their help, I see that it's okay for me to now want to create something for myself, and the world won't fall apart if I do. What a relief!" As the fear comes up less frequently, she finds excitement emerging as she thinks about what might be fun and interesting for her. In looking back at all she did as a mom, one experience stands out: "When I was PTA president, a lot of cuts were happening in the schools and all the arts were the first to go. I was so angry, and I felt like I was beating my head against the wall trying to change it. The situation has only gotten worse in the years since. Kids are missing out on all the benefits that participating in music, visual arts, and theater can give them. I'm going to do something about it."

Dream: Create a nonprofit to bring arts programs to children in the community.

KEVIN

When Kevin reveals to his wife his thoughts about work and providing for the family, but not feeling like he's enjoying their life, they enter a deep discussion about how things have been working. "We ended up diving into our finances and commitments, looking closely at what we have versus what we need, and even bringing the kids into the discussion at one point to find out their perspective. I also considered what's going on at work, and whether the pressure I put on myself about what I need to do there is real, or if I'm actually spending more time there than necessary. It felt like taking the blinders off, being honest about what was actually true about my life and work instead of continuing to unconsciously live out of these unexamined points of view." In taking a closer look at his reality, Kevin acknowledges his desire to continue providing well for his family, but also create better harmony between work and home life so that he can enjoy both. "It's not that I don't like my work, I very much do. I'm not interested in quitting and having us go live in a cave. But this working to the exclusion of everything else is not something I'm willing to keep doing."

Dream: Create balance in my life so I can enjoy both work and my family and lifestyle.

Ultimately, this stage is about being able to envision the world and the life that you would like to live. Far too many people would like to experience a different world, and they get stuck in a sense of hopelessness about ever seeing it happen, or powerlessness about their capacity to create it. If this describes you, know that you do have the potency and capacity, and it all starts with being willing to listen when the barriers arise so that you can move through them to find your dream.

What is your dream?

—⁓—

"I think that's a great idea, hon!" Sally says, putting a casserole into the oven as James finishes chopping veggies for the salad. "Yes, I'm a little concerned about what it might mean around here, but it's fun to see you so excited again about something at work. Seems like it's been awhile."

James grins. "I *am* excited! I don't know why I didn't think about this before."

Over the past couple of days, James has been thinking on and off about what he might do to meet more of his needs at work. Talking with Steve was a huge help. James had a few vague ideas going into the call, and through their conversation he hit on a possibility that made his heart sing. It also scared him, which he took as a good sign. He was going to begin positioning himself as a leader in his field through writing a couple of white papers and presenting at industry conferences.

"And I know you're concerned," he says to Sally, "but I don't anticipate it having much impact around here. I certainly don't want it to. It feels like we're starting to get to a better place with working out our schedules. There are only two conferences coming up in the next six months that are possibilities, and I still need to go through the process of applying to present. Thankfully, Steve is on the committee of the first one, so I'm hopeful about that coming through."

"Seems like your conversation with him really opened things up for you," Sally says.

"Absolutely," James agrees. "It felt like all these puzzle pieces just started falling into place. We talked through what I've been doing, and I saw how much I have to offer. I can bring a different perspective on best practices in training in this field, and that gives me such a sense of purpose and meaning . . . it's like pulling together so much of what I've been doing and learning over my career. Steve really helped me understand what I've been doing in a new way."

"That must be very gratifying—that you've been able to get clarity on what you'd like to do and how in touch you are with the needs you hope it will meet."

"It is . . . thanks for reminding me. And it's not only the needs I came up with when I did Self-Empathy the other day— the ones I shared with you—I think it will meet those and a few more besides. And being enthusiastic about work again is wonderful."

"And so fun to see! How do you think Scott will respond?" Sally asks, knowing that James and his boss don't always see things the same way.

James shrugs. "I can't imagine he'd have any problem with it. I mean, one of his people out there being a leader? It will reflect well on him and the company. I kind of hope it'll give me a little more negotiating power there too, make me seem more valuable."

Sally nods. "So, you've had the conversations with yourself and others to move past your confusion and be able to name your dream—what now?"

James sets the salad on the table. "Well, I have a few next steps with writing and sending proposals, and I'm also going to start mapping out the thoughts I'd like to share. I'm so looking forward to getting to work on both of those!"

—m—

NEXT UP

Now that you are clear on your dream, it's time to work on planning, a stage that can similarly bring up unbidden thoughts and feelings that stand in your way. In the next chapter, we'll take a look at how to work through the barriers that arise to creating a plan to actualize your dream.

3 | FORMING YOUR PLAN

CONVERSATIONS TO ACHIEVE YOUR DREAM

As for the future, your task is not to foresee it, but to enable it.
—ANTOINE DE SAINT-EXUPÉRY

———

JAMES SEARCHES FOR A TOPIC TO TALK TO HIS SON ABOUT as he and Corey work on cleaning out the garage. James was pleased that Corey didn't give him much attitude about it when he enlisted his help during breakfast, and so far they've made good progress with organizing and are now sweeping out all the dirt and leaves. Casting around for something to say to connect with Corey, James realizes that he's always been so caught up in thinking it's wrong for Corey to be playing video games, he's never thought to ask what sparked Corey's interest in them.

"So Corey, what do you like about these games you play on the computer?"

"I don't know, they're fun," Corey says.

"I didn't grow up with those, you know," James says, "so they're not something I really get."

"Seriously? You didn't play any video games?" Corey stares at his dad, incredulous.

"Well, you've met your grandpa . . . you know how he is." James rolls his eyes.

"Oh, yeah," Corey responds with a short laugh. After a pause, he adds, "I guess I'm interested in the graphics, so I play a lot of them to see how they create the art, but also how they put it all together. I think there's so much more that could be done with these games."

"Like what?" James asks, his curiosity piqued.

"Well, kids like playing them, but so many are just about entertainment . . . and they could be used for learning. It would be so much more fun to learn some of the stuff they try to teach in school if it was in a video game instead, you know?"

James gives an interested nod.

"It could even be kinda like, I don't know . . . covert learning. Instead of trying to shove something down our throats, if it was in a game, kids might take it in without even realizing it."

James is so astonished hearing all of this that he stops sweeping. "It sounds like you have some great ideas. Have you thought more specifically about what you'd like to see taught that way?"

Corey shrugs and hangs his head, as if embarrassed to say any more. "Yeah, kind of."

"Cor, I'm really interested. I'm realizing that I was so in my point of view that you were slacking off by playing them that it never even occurred to me to ask you about your interest in them. I regret that. I'd really enjoy hearing your ideas whenever you're ready to share them." James returns to sweeping, giving Corey space.

After a brief pause, Corey says, "There's all this stuff about bullying, not just at our school but in the earlier grades too, like at Maggie's school. They do these stupid assemblies and class discussions where they're talking about it and that we should accept others and their differences, but those don't ever really create change. It just seems like they go about it the wrong way. But as a video game . . . you can start shifting attitudes about understanding how we're all different in some way, and having tolerance for those differences, and then these preachy tactics that don't work anyway wouldn't even be necessary. Kids would just take it in through the game." As Corey goes on to describe his vision, James finds himself drawn in, excited about Corey's ideas.

As Corey pauses to take a breath, James interjects, "Cor, this is a really cool idea! You've got me all interested and en-rolled in it and I don't even know much about video games. Where'd this idea come from? A personal interest of yours? Or more from experience with this idea of being different?"

"From experience, I guess. Everyone's dealt with it in one way or another. Remember Maggie last year having trouble with that kid? His older brother is in my year. They're . . . not so bright, and Maggie's really smart and interested in science, so it sets her apart. Makes her a target for a kid like that."

Once again, James is surprised. "I didn't know you were paying any attention when all that happened, much less had such a sophisticated analysis of what went on there."

"I didn't really then. I've just been thinking about it more this year. There's a lot of ways I feel different from other kids, and it makes me feel alone sometimes. But then Mr. Loewen said something to me at one point and I realized that most of us feel that way, but we just keep it to ourselves."

"And you'd like to contribute to changing that?" James asks.

"Sure, maybe we don't have to feel so alone. Seems silly for everyone to be hiding that we're all really feeling the same way."

"That's really powerful, Cor. So what's next, how are you going to create this game?"

Corey shrugs, palms up. "Yeah, I don't know about that. It's just an idea really."

James pushes a little. "But it's a great idea . . . you've got me interested. What would it take?"

"Well, I don't have all the programming skills, so I'd need other people working on it with me. I can't do it on my own and I don't know who else would be interested." Corey pauses and looks down. "Besides I'm just a kid. Who'll listen to me? No one will pay attention. Plus I'm sure it would require some money to get it made, so . . . I don't know . . ."

———

At this point, if you've come up with your dream and connected to the needs you anticipate will be met by it, you may have a feeling of excitement, hope, and eagerness. In order to begin taking steps to eventually create your dream, though, first you require a plan.

Most people think of a plan in terms of steps, or actions to take to reach a goal. If you have a dream to give a dinner party, for example, the steps might include something like the following:

+ Decide on the guest list
+ Set a date
+ Create the menu
+ Invite people
+ Shop for food
+ Cook and prepare the space
+ Eat and enjoy

When we talk about the plan, however, we mean more than simply these kinds of action steps. Each one of these steps is actually a conversation you have with yourself and possibly with others.

> plan *n.*
>
> the action steps to take and the conversations to have, with yourself and others, to actualize your dream

This may seem like an overly complicated way to look at it, yet you'll find it becomes useful when the barriers to planning show up. For example, let's say that this is your conversation with yourself about the dinner party:

I'd love to have a few people over for dinner. Jae and Sam got back from their trip recently, and I'd like to see them and hear about it. And I know Ken and Beatrice would enjoy it as well. I'm going to invite them all over.

In this case, deciding on the guest list is a straightforward conversation—after a brief chat with yourself, the guest list is decided.

But what if your internal conversation sounds more like this:

I'd love to have a few people over for dinner. Jae and Sam got back from their trip recently, and I'd like to see them and hear about it. I know Ken and Beatrice would enjoy it as well. I'd like to invite them all over . . . except that Beatrice's sister is staying with her now, and I really don't like her. When we were over there last, she dominated the entire conversation and I really couldn't enjoy being with Beatrice and Ken. But if I invite them, I might have to invite her too.

Now there's an element of uncertainty about what to choose, a barrier showing up in your planning process that could stall you. Your conversation isn't smooth, and without a new way to consider this barrier, your dinner party idea may well stay an idea. Likewise, in the example of Corey, he has an idea for a video game and is connected to the needs that it would meet for him, yet he has plenty of thoughts that stop him from moving forward.

If you think about the steps necessary to reach your dream and you can easily list them (as in the first example), then this chapter may not be necessary for you. If you get stuck, however, or feel any heaviness enter the picture that takes you away from the positive feelings of being connected to your dream, then you likely have some barriers. In this chapter, we'll help you identify those barriers and learn a process to help you move through them.

BARRIERS TO PLANNING

There are probably an infinite variety of barriers that can arise when you think about what would need to happen to reach your dream. In the case of planning, any thought that arises that creates a hitch in you or takes away the positive feelings of being connected with your dream is a barrier. Here are some of the common categories of barriers that show up at the planning stage.

OVERWHELM AND DESIRE TO SEE THE WHOLE PATH

If you have a big dream, it will likely require many steps in order to reach it, and two related feelings may arise: overwhelm and a strong desire to see all the steps immediately. The magnitude of the vision can bring up overwhelm, as can knowing that it will take many steps.

People often deal with overwhelm through control, by trying to see the entire pathway to their desired outcome and knowing how the whole process is going to unfold ahead of time. If they can't, they think they don't have a plan and can't start, and if they do manage to lay out many of the steps that are clear from the outset, it can reinforce the feeling of overwhelm. This catch-22 situation is enough to keep anyone from moving forward. Even with smaller dreams, some aspect might intrude to create similar feelings, such as the sense that you don't have the time it would take to work toward your dream.

Let's take a look at Chris and his healthy lifestyle dream. As he thinks about planning, this barrier arises for him:

"I felt really good about my dream, but now I'm feeling swamped by everything I would need to change. There's what I'm eating, how I'm eating, that I know I'm not getting enough exercise and probably not enough sleep either. There's what to do about how much I've been working and the stress from that, not to mention how to even begin fitting in some of the things I might enjoy. Where do I start? I see all of these puzzle pieces in front of me, but not how to put them all together to end up where I want to be."

RESISTANCE TO MOVING FROM DREAM TO PLAN

For many people, dreaming is fun. It's the "building castles in the sky" stage, where the imagination gets free reign and you envision the amazing things that *could* be. It's exciting and invigorating.

But then comes planning. If dreaming is fun for you, planning—putting nitty-gritty action steps to bring your dream into reality—may feel painful. You might experience resistance to this stage, seeing it as boring, mundane, or tedious. Or, you might want to simply skip over planning altogether and go straight to action, without thinking through the appropriate way to get where you desire.

Let's revisit Dawn and her dream. When she starts to plan the creation of an arts nonprofit for children, this is what comes up for her:

> "I'm so excited about my dream! I can already see a local center and hear the children's laughter as they explore different arts, and I have so many ideas of programs we could offer in the schools. As soon as I start to plan, though, all of that excitement goes away. It's mind-numbing and wearisome to think through all the steps needed to get to that vision."

SELF-DOUBT

It's probably no surprise that one of the quickest dream-killers is to doubt yourself. We saw this happen in the beginning of the chapter for Corey as he explained his dream to James and then named his barriers:

+ He's just a kid.
+ No one will pay attention to him.
+ He can't do it on his own and isn't sure he can get others to help.
+ It will require money.

Once doubt in yourself or your abilities begins to take hold, it becomes increasingly difficult to plan or take any action.

EXPECTATIONS

When a dream requires significant change, another barrier that can arise is resistance to change based on expectations. These can stem from what has happened in the past, from the way you've been living, or from other people. In other words, as you contemplate the steps to take, you may find that you get stuck not knowing what to do because of past ideas and beliefs about who you are and how you do things, in addition to what others expect of you.

As Kevin contemplates what his work/life balance could look like, he finds this barrier surfacing for him:

"Though I feel solid about what I'd like my life to look like, I keep running up against these ideas about what I should be doing. Some are from me—the expectations about what it is to be a man and bring home the bacon—and some are from other people. Even though I've talked to my family, I still sense an expectation about the kind of life we have. I also anticipate pushback at work, from what people have come to expect from me there. Plus I'm used to being fully committed to my job, and this feels like I'll need a major personality adjustment to move ahead on creating more balance in my life."

PRACTICE PAUSE

When you think about planning to reach your dream, do any of the above barriers (or others) arise? Name any barriers you have to planning for your dream.

REMOVING BARRIERS THROUGH SELF-CONNECTION

Everything that arises, including your barriers in the planning stage, is information about what is going on for you. As you learned in Chapter 2, your feelings can alert you when a part of you is interpreting that needs are not (or will not be) met. As such, Self-Empathy helps you learn to identify all the components of what is happening—observations, feelings, needs, and requests—so that you can make a new choice. Now that you are familiar with and have begun to practice Self-Empathy, we'd like to introduce another foundational process that can also uncover your needs so you can more effectively learn to meet them.

The Self-Connection Process (SCP) is a key practice to help you focus your attention (bringing awareness and presence) so that in the next moment you are more at choice in the actions you take.

> **self-connection** *n.*
>
> the ability to be aware of and present with what is
> happening within you—physiologically,
> emotionally, and mentally

Below we walk you through the SCP, and we recommend that you treat it as a guided practice as you are reading through it—or rather, read each step and then do it before moving on to the next one. Through our examples of Corey, Chris, Dawn, and Kevin that follow, we'll see how SCP helps them connect with their needs and discover a new way through or around the barrier, instead of allowing it to stop them.

SELF-CONNECTION PROCESS (SCP)

1. **Breath**

    a. Focus on your breathing. Deepen the inhale as you breathe in, and extend the exhale longer than the inhale.

    b. Repeat this several times while staying aware of your breathing.

2. Body

    a.   Focus on what you are feeling. Feel the sensations and emotions, the aliveness and energy, by being in your body and experiencing it fully. At this stage you are solely being present with and experiencing sensations, scanning your body and noticing your sensations and where they are located. As much as possible, take in what you are experiencing without talking to yourself about it.

    b.   Describe what you're feeling, using whatever language you are comfortable with to describe your sensations.

    c.   Name the feelings you are experiencing (use the list in Appendix A to help).

3. Needs

    a.   Now that you're aware of your feelings from Step 2, look into what is prompting you to feel that way. Connect with the needs that are met or not met in your current situation. (Typically, when barriers arise, you will most readily identify needs that are not met; however, you can also look for the needs met by the voices speaking up.) A way to do this is to ask yourself, *If I'm feeling this way, what need is the unconscious part of me interpreting as met or unmet?* The idea here is that your unconscious is communicating to your conscious mind that needs are being met or not met by prompting feelings to arise in you. In short, you use these feelings to uncover your needs. (Refer to Appendix B for a list of needs).

b. Check in with your body as you consider the needs.
    Though it's not a cognitive process of "figuring out"
    what they are, when you name the need that most
    closely fits, your body will respond. It may take some
    time and practice to learn your particular physiological
    response that signals you are naming the need that is
    met or unmet—it may be a feeling of warmth,
    relaxation, a sense of something falling into place, or
    simply a knowing and certainty.

c. "Deepen into" the needs you've identified. Imagine what
    it would feel like for those needs to be fully met. Savor
    what that would be like, and how your life would be.

www.mediateyourlife.com/self-connection-process-video/

———

"Do you want to try something?" James asks.

"Try what?" Corey says.

"Just a process you can use anytime you feel blah or yucky."

"Oh, one of those weird things you and Mom do?" Corey
looks sideways at James with a slight smile.

James grins. "Yeah, one of those weird things we learned. It
sometimes helps to see things a little differently."

"Sure, I'll try it," Corey says with a shrug.

"First, just take a couple deep breaths. I'll do it with you."
James pauses as he takes a couple breaths and Corey mirrors him.

"Now, notice what's going on in your body. What sensations
are there? Things like light or heavy, temperature, pressure,
tension..."

"Um . . . I don't know, I guess my shoulders are kind of

tense." Corey pauses. "Everything just feels, like, dense, as if I'm trying to move through molasses."

"Great." James says. "And if you could name your feelings, what would they be? Are you scared, discouraged, angry, bummed out, insecure, or something else?"

"I guess I'm afraid that I'd try to do something and it wouldn't go anywhere. Seems easier not to try."

James reflects back what he's heard. "So you're reluctant to start when you're not sure what will happen?"

"Yeah, I'm not comfortable talking to people about these things. I'd be embarrassed."

"So you're uncomfortable and embarrassed when you think about talking with others about your ideas. Is that because you'd like acceptance and respect and you're not sure you'd get it?" James begins to guess what needs might be motivating Corey.

"Sure, I'd like respect," Corey affirms. "If others got the idea and we could work on it, that would be awesome."

"It sounds like you'd like some movement on the idea, to see it starting to be created. And it also sounds like you'd just like to know that it's safe to talk to others about it, and you'll be okay whatever their response is. Is that right?"

"Yeah. Someone at school said, if you knew you couldn't fail and things would work out somehow, what would you do . . . and I'd do this." Corey stands a little straighter as he says this, his eyes flashing with certainty.

> ## PRACTICE PAUSE
>
> Bring to mind again the barriers that arise for you when thinking about moving ahead on your dream, and then go through the Self-Connection Process.

Here's what happens when our companions use SCP on their barriers to planning:

CHRIS

Chris practices SCP, starting with a few deeper breaths and checking in with his body. He identifies a jittery feeling in his solar plexus, and notices that he feels like he jumps out of his body as he thinks about creating a plan. He also describes tension in his neck and forehead, as if he is scrunching his entire head trying to figure it all out. He names his feelings as frazzled, desperate, and confused. As he ponders what needs are prompting these feelings, many unmet needs come up from the way he has been living—needs for relaxation, play, vitality, and well-being. Deepening into those needs and imagining what it would be like if they were met, he feels happy and begins to understand that those needs not being met is contributing to his sense of overwhelm. He also feels the need for a sense of clarity and ease in moving ahead with making the desired lifestyle changes.

DAWN

As Dawn takes a few deep breaths and checks in with her body, she feels heaviness in her limbs and a sinking feeling in her gut. The image that comes to mind is that she is being pulled down into the ground. She labels her feelings as lethargy and indifference, and she also notices how discouraged she feels to have encountered these barriers after feeling so much excitement about her dream. This recognition leads her to see her need for inspiration throughout the process, and she also desires a sense of congruence across all aspects of creating her dream, giving her confidence that it's actually possible.

KEVIN

It takes Kevin some breaths before he can even deepen the inhale and extend the exhale when he tries SCP. He immediately notices the pressure he feels in his body and how it constricts his breath. As he focuses on the sensations, the pressure settles in his muscles, and he feels tension throughout his body. He senses dread over whether he would make a mess trying to make changes, while also impatience to already be where he wants to be. He also perceives irritation at all the expectations. The need for integrity, and for living according to his values and from intrinsic motivation instead of from other's expectations comes up. As a result, he desires some relief from the pressure of who he is supposed to be, wanting to be allowed to "just be himself," whatever that may mean.

SELF-CONNECTION PROCESS IN PRACTICE AND IN LIFE

SCP is a wonderful practice to do throughout your day as a way to repeatedly return to connection with yourself and your needs. All of our Mediate Your Life maps start with some form of self-connection, and in many cases we recommend doing SCP first so that you can choose which map to use next. Think of SCP as the entryway to being aware, present, and at choice. It is a means to access the mediator mind—that state in which you can hold all that shows up in your experience, including different voices, without being locked into one perspective.

As with Self-Empathy, it's good to practice the full version above, taking some time when first learning it to become familiar with the steps and how your body responds. In practicing you will begin to learn what most helps you become self-connected. Then, you may find ways to organically bring that practice into a situation when it would be helpful to you to focus your attention on your needs and act from them. Below, we give two possible ways that this process might unfold in shorter variations.

CONDENSED PATH

Integrating SCP into your daily life is fairly straightforward. If you don't have time for the full process, the practice can easily be condensed by taking a breath as described above, then checking in with your body through any of the suggested ways (feeling your sensations, describing them, or naming a feeling), and then naming the need that is prompting your feelings.

QUICK PATH

If you become aware that you are no longer in a calm, present state and would like to self-connect quickly, start by taking a full breath, deepening the inhale slightly and slowly exhaling. Then go straight to identifying an unmet need.

The more you have practiced SCP in the long form, the more successful you will be bringing it into the midst of your day. Why? Because when first learning to identify needs, it can take some time to become familiar with what needs are, which ones you tend to interpret are unmet, and what your body feels like when certain needs are met or not, as well as when you've named the need that hits the mark. Remember: the physiological shift in naming the need is most important, however quickly you are trying to return to self-connection. Without that, it is simply a cognitive exercise that is less likely to result in prompting you to make new choices to meet your needs.

PRACTICE PAUSE

If you wanted to regularly practice SCP in order to more frequently connect to yourself and your needs, when would you practice? How would you remind yourself?

There's another variation on Self-Connection Process that can be helpful in understanding and accessing mediator mind. To use it in this way, think of SCP as a mindfulness practice relating to observation, feeling, and need, and mirror the same basic steps as follows:

1. **Breath**: Observe your breath, as well as any thoughts or sense perceptions (sight, sound, touch, taste, smell) that are in your awareness.

2. **Body**: Feel what is happening in your body, including internal sensations and feelings.

3. **Need**: In focusing on need, find the inner place of well-being that is not tied to what is happening externally, where you already know that you are safe, loved, cared for, accepted, and connected. You might use the phrase "I am . . ." to tap into this knowing, repeating to yourself: I am safe, I am valued, I am connected . . . The focus is not

as much on the words as it is on finding the place within that experiences the inner knowing of them.

When you can practice this regularly, you become more adept at activating mediator mind, calling forth the part of you that is not caught in any specific point of view, but that can be aware of all that is going on and be okay. Accessing this part of you also has a calming, reassuring effect, especially in times of difficulty.

THE PLANNING STAGE

The goal of the planning stage is to identify the conversations you can have that will move you ahead in reaching your dream. This does not mean you need to map out all the steps in advance; it can simply be naming the first one or a few actions you'd like to take. When you have a plan (or the beginnings of one) you feel good about, you are ready to move on.

It's important to recognize that this stage can look very different depending on your dream and any barriers that come up in planning. If your dream is to declutter your living space, you may have no barriers to planning and merely come up with a simple list of what to do.

However, let's return to the example of holding a dinner party. In the scenario we mentioned at the beginning of the chapter, you are planning a small dinner party with a few friends. If a barrier comes up in any area, such as whether to invite your friend's sister whose company you do not enjoy, then you know there's a conversation to have, with yourself and maybe others, about that part of the plan.

Now, instead of the party being a simple one at your house, perhaps you're in charge of planning a dinner event for fifty people. Each of the steps we mentioned earlier—including the guest list, menu, location, invitations, preparation, and so on—is now a more complicated undertaking. Planning in this case requires a complex process of organizing a whole series of conversations you'll have, with yourself and other people, for each of those steps. Identifying the conversations to have and the outcomes you'd like from those conversations becomes even more important.

Some of your conversations may be with other people, such as the chef or those involved in who should be invited, and the desired outcome is an external result: the menu, or the list of invitees. Some of the conversations, on the other hand, may be internal, such as how to handle any intrusive thoughts that get in the way about your own ability or judgments about how others are behaving. In this scenario, your plan would include the conversations you will have and the outcome you'd like from each one.

Sometimes, a dream involves fewer outer steps and more internal barriers. Take a more complex scenario, for example. Perhaps your dream is to reconcile with your mother, who has been ill and may not be around for much longer. If you've had a long, troubled history with her, many barriers may arise in planning how you will reconcile, including expectations based on past interactions, doubts about your ability to maintain your calm, uncertainty about whether reconciliation is even possible, and fears that you and she don't have sufficient time left. With all of these barriers, you may be strongly tempted to let go of the dream.

Planning for this dream will include anticipating all the conversations to have with yourself and others so that you can entertain hope that your attempt to reconcile will have an outcome you desire. For example, you may have a conflict within you about whether it's even worth it to try to reconcile, and you plan to have an internal mediation with yourself (see the next chapter) before any further planning. If you're clear that you do want to reconcile, you can plan all the conversations to have with yourself, bring in support people you want involved, and even plan and practice a conversation with your mom. (Since this is an interpersonal situation, see *From Conflict to Connection* for all of the conversations before, during, and after that you can plan to include.)

When you identify a conversation to have with yourself or others, it's important to identify the outcome you'd like from that conversation. In this case, the outcome you'd like from the conversation with your mother is to reconcile with her (and you may want to more clearly articulate what that would mean for you). Perhaps to prepare, you'd like to enlist a support person to help you become less sensitive to the things she says that trigger you, with the outcome that you will be able to stay calm in a conversation with her regardless of what she says.

During the planning stage for this dream, you can use SCP to continually reconnect with your needs and come up with a plan that you feel good about to prepare for your conversation with your mother. That doesn't mean you may not still have trepidation about having it, or even that you know entirely how, but merely that you feel good about the next steps you will take.

In this stage, you plan in the greatest detail that part of the dream you have the most difficulty with. (Note here that a dream such as clearing clutter may have little difficulty associated with it in your mind, so detailed planning may not be necessary.) Here are some ideas of the types of conversations that may be helpful to achieving your dream.

Conversations with yourself:

+ Healing and tending to the parts of you that resist or seek to sabotage the dream
+ Preparing yourself for conversations with others
+ Recovering and learning from conversations you have had with others

Conversations with others:

+ Enlisting their emotional support to help you be resilient in response to challenges you may face
+ Seeking guidance, advice, and wisdom
+ Making the agreements that will be necessary for your dream to be completed

Regularly checking in with yourself through using SCP gives you two different types of information. First, you know what your needs are so you can come up with strategies and requests that will meet those needs. Second, when you know what it feels like to be connected to yourself, it's easier to then be aware when you are disconnected, which alerts you to attend to what is going on. When you have uncomfortable feelings arising, it's likely you have a barrier coming forth that could sabotage your efforts.

Chris, Kevin, and Dawn have used SCP to connect with their needs, so let's see how that impacts their capacity to move ahead with planning.

CHRIS

As Chris sits with his needs for clarity, ease, relaxation, play, vitality, and well-being, an idea starts growing in his mind. Here's how he describes it: "It was like there was this little seed that sprouted in my mind about how related everything is, and that it doesn't matter where I start. The question I had earlier about where to start—it's not relevant, really. I can start anywhere. And I wanted to see a whole path but there isn't a path, or maybe there is but it's not relevant right now either. All I need is the next step. The later ones will become clear, and right now I couldn't know what they are because I will be different when I get there. Connecting with my needs and really diving into what it would be like to be living with that kind of vigor and fun, I feel ready to take the first step, and I even know what it is. I just found out about a program they're offering through work to help people be healthier through lifestyle change, and it's free. I'm going to join that program so I have some support with all of these changes."

DAWN

When Dawn reflects on how her dream of creating a non-profit is different from anything she has done before, she realizes that it is a matter of scale. "When I did things before, like as PTA president or in some of the work I did, I could jump straight into action because the plan was always really clear. So now that I have this vision, I want to go straight into action, but what action to take is less obvious than in those smaller projects. I'm not used to planning so much and so I'm actually impatient about it. The problem is that it's showing up as 'I just don't want to do it,' because I don't really know what to do. Now that I'm aware of it, though, I know I can figure it out. Plus I've always enjoyed the process of things, not just the end result, and I can apply that to the process of planning too. I do know how to go about creating at least the start of a plan for this arts center. The first thing I need is some more information, so my first steps are to talk to a few people I know in the community who know more about setting up nonprofits than I do. And I'm also going to talk to two friends I can think of who may be interested in being involved. I like working with others to get things done, so I'm going to make sure this is a collaborative effort."

KEVIN

When Kevin deepened into his needs to be himself and live in integrity, imagining them fully met, he became aware how much he'd been living in the future, out of an unexamined fear of what might happen. He knew that to make the change he wanted required being more in the present moment. "If I keep living out of this fear of what might happen, I'll just keep creating the same scenario. So when I think there's an expectation, I'd like to catch it and then ask where that's coming from and whether it's real. I might need to have some more conversations with my family and people at work. What I'd like to do is really test all of these assumptions I have about what will happen or what people expect of me. In small ways, test to see whether these are accurate or whether I'm making it all up. And I know one place to start: I have two extra vacation days that are owed me at work from work trips I've been on in the last few months, and I'm going to take them soon and plan a short trip with my family."

James senses that Corey is connected to his needs and ready to move past his self-sabotaging thoughts, so he asks, "If you knew things would work out one way or another and you were going to take a first step on this, what would it be?"

Corey is silent at first, then says, "I don't know. Where would I start?"

James gently prompts, "Is this all in your head right now? Have you put the idea down on paper?"

"Oh." Corey half-chuckles. "Duh. No, it's just in my head."

"So that might be one step, to just write down your vision for the game so you have something to show people. Then who might you talk to about it?"

Corey ponders for a moment. "I could talk to Mr. Loewen at school."

James is confused. "Ben? But he's your English Lit teacher, isn't he?" Ben Loewen is the son of James and Sally's good friends Alicia and Sean, and he is in his first year of teaching at Corey's high school.

"Yeah, he is, but he's cool and I think he would get it."

"Oh, of course, you're right," James affirms. "It's a great idea to start with someone you're confident will be able to hear you and give respect and acceptance to you and your idea."

Corey adds, "Plus, he did tell us a story one day about how he and some friends way back when created a program to help them do something . . . can't remember what exactly, but it sounded like cheating in their classes somehow. So he knows something about computers, and he may know someone else I can talk to."

James recaps Corey's plan. "So you'll outline your idea in writing, and then talk to Mr. Loewen at school, and the out-come you'd like from that is to have some affirmation of the idea and see how he may be able to help you move forward?"

Corey nods thoughtfully. "Yeah, I can do that." He looks around the garage. "Hey, are we done here? I'd like to go work on it right now."

James laughs. "Sure, go ahead, I'll finish up. I appreciate

your help today, and I think you've got a great idea there. I'm excited to see where it goes."

Corey leans the broom up against the wall then turns to say, "Thanks, Dad!" before heading into the house.

—⁓—

NEXT UP

The tools in Chapters 2 and 3, SCP and Self-Empathy, are foundational skills and useful in a wide variety of situations, including when you find barriers arising to moving toward your dream. But it's possible that you will still find yourself stuck after going through these processes. This is because you have a conflict between different parts of you. Self-Empathy and Self-Connection Process can help you understand what's going on and connect with your needs, but to work through an internal conflict, you require a process to *mediate* that conflict. In the next chapter, we'll guide you in building on the foundational skills of Self-Empathy and SCP so you can apply those skills to mediate between two different parts of yourself that want different things.

4 | Taking Action

Mediating Internal Voices

The key to making healthy decisions is to respect your future self. Honor him or her. Treat him or her like you would treat a friend or a loved one.

—A.J. JACOBS

—⁓—

SALLY FLIPS THROUGH THE MAIL A BIT ABSENTLY, HER MIND on what James told her about his conversation with Corey, when one envelope catches her eye. Seeing the name of the largest community health organization in the country on the outside, she wonders, *What are they contacting me about?* Ripping the envelope open, Sally quickly glances through the contents, her jaw dropping. The letter invites her to present a session at the organization's national meeting, held once a year.

Oh my. This is really quite a coup, Sally muses. *How did I get so lucky? I'm still pretty new at all this. Now I have a chance to be a presenter at this meeting, in front of so many people in the field? What a huge opportunity!*

Despite the seeming serendipity of this news, Sally knows it's more than that. She had met the founders of the organization at a conference, and they'd shared a meal over a great conversation in which they'd discussed some new and welcome ideas. The memory brings a smile to her face.

Of course I'll do this! she thinks. But as she starts imagining what she'll talk about and how to prepare, her momentary excitement gets derailed by another thought.

Whoa, wait a minute. Am I really ready for this? I don't have nearly the credentials or experience in the field, not to mention the experience as a public speaker. Why would anyone listen to me? What are the chances I can give a good talk, much less one that's new to these people who have more knowledge in this field than I do? If I don't give a good talk, that could be even worse for my reputation! Plus, there's no guarantee it will move my business forward. If I spend time away from my business to prepare, and then it doesn't yield anything, maybe it's not the best use of my time.

Sally walks to the window, still holding the paper. *But how fun it could be! This is exactly the kind of chance that could help me establish myself. All the people I'd meet there . . . who knows what might come of it!*

Just then, another contradictory thought springs to mind. *What happens if I do succeed? I could end up overwhelmed with business or opportunities, and I barely feel like I'm managing things now. How would I be able to deal with even more possibilities? Especially when I'm trying to find a way to be there for my family and myself, in addition to my business?* With a sigh, Sally places the letter on the pile of things to do and proceeds to go through the rest of the mail.

―⁓―

As you move toward your dream, you'll take many—perhaps even hundreds—of action steps. Choosing some of those steps may be straightforward and simple, while some may tie you in knots and cause sleepless nights. After all, creating a dream is likely to come up against constraints that already exist in your life. How to manage your time and other resources, what opportunities to pursue, and how to proceed to bring your vision into reality will all require choices.

When your action is obvious or uncomplicated, you simply make the choice and move on. For example, prior to opening the invitation to speak, Sally took numerous actions: she contacted a client to respond to a question, finalized a report, responded to an inquiry about her work, and planned what she would do the following day. All of those choices were easily made, and she had no need to approach them as a conversation with herself.

As soon as she opens the invitation, however, she quickly becomes embroiled in a difficult internal conversation. The barrier to taking the next action shows up, causing her to put the invitation aside. You, too, may have experienced the same type of trepidation in a similar circumstance.

In this chapter, we will outline the ways this barrier can arise in internal conversations so that you can not only more readily recognize it, but also move through it using a key map—the Internal Mediation (IM) map—that will allow you to be in complete alignment with your choice.

BARRIERS TO TAKING ACTION

When faced with potential actions, you may come against a barrier that feels like being caught between parts of yourself that each desire something different. In other words, instead of a clear path ahead, you feel pulled in two different directions, or pushed in one direction and pulled in another. As a result, instead of feeling aligned internally to take action in a particular direction, you have two or more parts of yourself that have a different point of view about the proper way forward. Whether they simply disagree or are in a flat-out argument, you are in conflict. This internal conflict, without a method to mediate it, can cause you to take actions that are less than ideal—or even stop your forward momentum altogether.

Internal conflicts can occur with any type of choice, whether large and life altering or small and common; they may reflect possibilities further in the future or those concerning an action to take in the next moment. Regardless of their content, the barrier of conflicting internal voices appears in different ways, creating varying types of internal conflict. The four ways these conflicts arise follow the Practice Pause below.

PRACTICE PAUSE

Before reading the four types of internal conflict, can you recall an internal conflict you've experienced?

EQUAL CHOICES

The first type of internal conflict is when there are two possible choices you could make and you feel conflict over which one to choose. You might be conflicted over whether to take a certain job or stay where you are, move to a new place or not, or marry a certain person or stay single. The mundane choices of daily life, such as what to eat for dinner, how to dress for an event, or whether to work out or rest, can create internal conflict as well.

This conflict inside of you may sound like:

+ I'd really like to try this new job, *and* there's a lot of benefit to staying where I am.

+ For my vacation, I want to go to this retreat, *and* I would also love to visit my friend abroad.

+ I'd prefer to move someplace with a more affordable cost of living, *and* I really like the area I live in now.

Here's how this type of internal conflict shows up for Chris as he works toward his dream of creating a healthy lifestyle:

Chris starts on the new program that offers support to make healthy lifestyle changes, and just a week in, his old buddy Mark calls, reminding Chris about the weekend gathering of college buddies coming up the following month. This group of friends, now spread around the country, meets every couple of years in some part of the country. "I really enjoy these guys. We go way back and it's always such a hoot to see them again. We have a great time when we get together, and I really don't want to miss it. But I also know that these events tend to involve a lot of alcohol and foods like we ate in college, which weren't the healthiest. And this one is in Vegas! That's guaranteed to be a raucous weekend, and most of it completely against the goals I now have for my health and lifestyle. I really don't know what to do. I want to go, but I'm also committed to my new plan for my health."

Typically, people resolve these types of conflicts through some habitual pattern they have developed, maybe by making lists of pros and cons of each choice, flipping a coin, or soliciting other people's opinions.

Equal Choices Conflict	Typical Responses
I want . . . I also want . . .	Making lists of pros and cons of each choice Random method of choosing (flip a coin) Soliciting other people's opinions

UNEQUAL CHOICES

You may also face a decision in which you do not hold the two choices equally: you expressly want to choose one option but the other is the one you feel like you *should* do, or even *have to* do. In short, two choices are in front of you, but you resist the less desirable option. Internally, this conflict may sound like:

+ I want to take the day off work, but I really should go to the office.

+ I should go to the dentist and get my teeth cleaned, but I'd rather not.

+ I'd like to chill out, but I know I need to work out.

+ I want to get started on this new work project, but I should finish the report that's due tomorrow.

+ I want another beer, but I really ought to stop now.

Here's how Kevin experiences a similar conflict:

Shortly after Kevin defines his dream to create more balance so he can enjoy his lifestyle and time with his family, he is offered a promotion at work to a more prestigious position. It involves more responsibility and more money, not to mention some status. Kevin finds himself torn. "I should really take this position. It's higher paying and since we're looking at lowering our expenses, taking it means we can be financially independent sooner. Plus, I've worked so hard in my career that it's the next step up, and turning it down might actually hurt me—sending a message to the company and my boss that I'm no longer serious about my work. But then that kind of thinking is how I got here in the first place! I don't want to keep putting off the time when I can really enjoy spending time with my family or doing things outside of work. And since this position is more responsibility, it may require more time as well. Do I accept the position, or turn it down?"

Again, people deal with these conflicts in some habitual manner, and often the choice comes with a certain emotional reaction. "To hell with it!" you might think, "I'm tired, I'm going to pick up dinner instead of cooking." Or, you might feel resigned: "Though I really want to take the day off, I have to go to the office and finish that report." Because you carry the emotional reaction forward into the action you take (such as resenting having to go in to work), it affects what you do, usually in a negative way. As such, finding a way to reconcile the two points of view, instead of merely choosing one over the other, makes a huge difference in how you move forward into action.

Unequal Choices Conflict	Typical Responses
I want . . . but I know I should . . . I should . . . but I really want . . .	Bully ourselves into a decision "To hell with it, I'm going to . . ." Carry emotional reaction into action

DESIRE–AVOIDANCE

Another way internal conflict shows up is when you want something but a part of you is avoiding it, frequently out of a strong emotion or underlying belief. While the previous two examples of equal and unequal choices are often easily verbalized and occur readily in our minds, this type can be subtler, whether manifested in words or in actions.

For example, you have entered into your to-do list the task of calling someone about funding a project you'd like to get off the ground. But when it comes time to make the call, you think, *I'll do that next, after I check my email.* Thirty minutes later, you move on to another task though you still haven't made the call. Your avoidance occurs not quite consciously, and despite knowing the task is something important for you to do.

Sometimes, the internal conflict is so intense that your mind seems to instantly skitter away when you view the task on your to-do list, and next thing you know, you've spent thirty minutes on your preferred social media platform or reading the news online. You may not even remember the moments that immediately followed noticing the item on your list because you jumped away from it so fast.

Another nonverbal cue that shows you're in a desire-avoidance conflict is that while contemplating the task, you notice your heart pounding or you begin to sweat. That physical reaction is indicative of an emotion or belief that's causing you to avoid the task, and therefore the feelings of discomfort.

When this type of internal conflict does show up in thoughts, it often sounds like an argument between the voices in your head, as exemplified by Sally as she contemplates the invitation to speak at a significant meeting in her field. As is common in these cases, she finds herself ping-ponging back and forth between the two perspectives, not even realizing that some of her fears are directly opposed to each other (I'll fail . . . I'll succeed). The voices in her mind chase themselves in circles: "Of course you're going to do this, it's a chance of a lifetime!" "Wait a minute, you shouldn't do this, you're not (ready, able, etc)." If she doesn't recognize that she is in conflict, her concerns and fears could overwhelm the part of her that is excited about the opportunity, which will result in her putting off acting until it's too late (which is another way of making a choice).

With Desire–Avoidance conflicts, a part of you interprets that some needs won't get met if you do the task and therefore pulls you in a different direction. If you can put this internal conflict into words, it might sound something like:

+ I want to have this call with a prospective client, but I'm feeling uncertain how they will respond.

+ I'd like to go to that doctor and find out what's going on, but I'm afraid of what he'll say.

+ I need to call and get this insurance problem straightened out, but I'm dreading dealing with the bureaucratic bull.

+ I want to contact this organization about doing a talk for them, but I'm concerned about how I'll come across.

Though avoidance may arise from any interpretation of potential unmet needs, doubts about your ability or how you will be perceived by others, especially if it's a new arena for you, are perhaps the most prevalent in stopping you from taking action. If any task in front of you raises thoughts like the ones below, you can likely frame it in terms of Desire-Avoidance.

+ I'm not capable of doing that.

+ I don't have the skills.

+ I'm too shy/stupid/inexperienced.

+ I don't have the credentials.

+ They'll reject me.

As with the other internal conflicts, the typical response tends to favor one side of the conflict and ignore the other. In this case you may continue to:

+ avoid the task until it eventually falls ever lower on the to-do list

+ decide you're not going to do it at all, favoring the avoidance side

OR

+ favor the desire side and power through the task, forcing yourself past the thoughts, beliefs, or emotions that come up in thinking about taking action

Desire–Avoidance Conflict	Typical Responses
I want to, but I'm . . . [afraid / nervous / anxious / worried]	Continue avoiding and not get the task done Decide you're not going to do the task Power through or force yourself to do it

OBLIGATION

The final type of internal conflict can show up much like any of the previous types, but it has its own distinction. In this case you've said you would do something, and when the moment comes to do it, you find you'd rather do something else. The "rather" can be out of desire, or out of avoiding what you said you'd do. This may show up in any of the three previous forms we've discussed:

- **Equal Choices**: "This conference I signed up for sounds interesting, *and* I'd also like to have a weekend for myself."

- **Unequal Choices**: "I should go to this conference (since I did pay for it), *but I'd prefer* to use that time to take care of other things in my life."

- **Desire–Avoidance**: "I said I'd go to this conference and it could be great, *but I'm apprehensive* about not knowing anyone else there."

When you commit to doing something in the future, you may then turn it into an *obligation*, which easily leads right back into an internal conflict between the part of you saying you *have* to because you said you would, and another part that is seeing some needs that might not be met were you to go ahead. In other words, even though you made the choice sometime in the past to carry out the commitment, until you actually do it, the choice point may still be in front of you.

In her journey to create a nonprofit arts organization, Dawn faces this conflict in the following situation:

One of the first things Dawn wants to do is set up a board of directors. One day, while chatting with Marge, an old friend whose kids went to school with Dawn's, they start talking about Dawn's idea. Marge is enthused and interested in helping out, and in her excitement of sharing ideas, Dawn suggests that perhaps Marge can serve on the board of directors. Marge appears pleased about that idea, but then Dawn has second thoughts the more she thinks about it. "I was so excited she was interested in the nonprofit that the idea of her being on the board just popped out of my mouth, but now I'm not so sure. She might have the interest, but I don't know if she has the skills or experience I'd really like members of the board to have in terms of helping build the organization. But I said she could, so although there are other people I'd prefer to have on the board, I feel like I have to offer it to her."

Obligation Conflict	Typical Responses
I said I would . . . but now I . . .	Cave in to the obligation Depending on how this conflict is showing up, typical responses can include any of the previous ones.

PRACTICE PAUSE

Think about which types of internal conflict sound most familiar to you. Can you write down examples from your own life in each category? How did you respond when these examples came up?

When people don't know of a different way to work through these conflicts, it's easy to conclude that the typical reaction/response is the only way forward. If they do try to consider both sides, they may feel hopeless about how to reconcile seemingly opposing viewpoints. The typical responses are understandable, and if they work for you, then use them. If you find, however, that ignoring or discounting some part of you leads to consequences you don't enjoy, consider that how you make these choices affects the actions you subsequently take. If you desire to take action from connection with all parts of yourself, take heart—the map we provide in the next section will help you do just that.

MEDIATING INTERNAL CONFLICT

Distinguishing different internal voices and keeping them separate may be difficult if you are not practiced at identifying and listening to them. The Internal Mediation (IM) map provides a simple structure that makes it easier to navigate these conflicts.

In the Mediate Your Life approach to conflict resolution, we have an inherent structure that underlies all types of conflict. If you've read *From Conflict to Connection*, covering interpersonal conflicts, you'll recognize the underlying structure of Connection and Resolution: in the Connection phase you empathize with both parties, and in the Resolution phase, you consider the strategies that will meet the needs of both parties. In the case of interpersonal conflict, one party was you and the other party was another person. In the case of internal conflict, however, the two parties are both within your own mind. Hence, when you mediate between them, you seek the needs behind what each voice is saying, and then consider how you might meet the needs of both parts of yourself.

While this may sound like a foreign concept to you, the goal of internal mediation is incredibly beneficial: to have the different parts of yourself understand and hear each other so you can find a way to move forward that is congruent with both parts of you. The best part is that resolving the conflict through an understanding of the needs of both voices leads to experiencing a sense of ease, peace, and self-connected awareness that affects your choices and behaviors in a positive way.

The process we outline in this chapter is a way of applying the skills learned in the previous chapters to empathize with internal voices so you can learn to better meet your needs in subsequent choices.

INTERNAL MEDIATION (IM) MAP

	CONNECTION		RESOLUTION
Mediating Between Two Parts of Yourself	**A's Needs**	**B's Needs**	**Synthesis/ Strategy to Meet All Needs**
Process	Empathize with A: surface A's needs	Empathize with B: surface B's needs	Consider what strategy might meet the needs of both A and B
IM Steps	1. Empathize with A 2. Empathize with B 3. Ask B to empathize with A 4. Ask A to empathize with B		5. Make Solution Requests and Agreements

Here are the five steps in the Internal Mediation map:

+ Step 1: Empathize with A
  o Allow A to speak unedited
  o Empathize to uncover OFNR (Observations, Feelings, Needs, Requests), focusing on needs

+ Step 2: Empathize with B
  o Allow B to speak unedited
  o Empathize to uncover OFNR, focusing on needs

+ Step 3: Ask B to empathize with A

    o B repeats A's needs

+ Step 4: Ask A to empathize with B

    o A repeats B's needs

+ Step 5: Make solution requests and agreements

www.mediateyourlife.com/internal-mediation-process-video/

One of the tools that can help you speak from each voice is to set up different chairs for each part of you. As each one speaks, physically move to that part's chair. If you don't have two chairs, you can move from side to side on a couch. As another alternative, you can merely think about physically embodying each voice. In other words, as you try this, you'll notice that each part may have a distinctive posture, tone of voice, or way it uses language. Allow that part of you to "take over" for a few minutes so that it can be fully heard and understood.

For purposes of our example, we'll assume you're using two chairs, but if you're using a couch or physical embodiment, simply substitute your method of switching voices with ours.

After you've set up your two chairs, choose one voice to begin the process with; if one voice is louder or more insistent, start with that one. As you go through the sometimes confusing mediation process below, it's helpful to have a "name" to refer to each part of you. (By "name" we don't necessarily mean an actual name —oftentimes the name will refer to their main role or what need they're trying to meet.) Thus, as you talk to each part of you, elicit what name it would like to be called. It's important to allow the part to tell you its name, rather than giving it a name that may upset it and hinder the conversation.

If this is sounding confusing already, not to worry—it will become clearer as we walk through the process below.

STEP 1: EMPATHIZE WITH A

The first two steps you'll recognize encompass Self-Empathy, meaning you are empathizing with each perspective in the conflict, listening for the four components of communication (observations, feelings, needs, and requests). However, at the initial stages, it's helpful to maintain a focus on needs. As you move to Step 5 in the Resolution Phase, you can bring in requests.

To empathize with the first voice, observe what that voice is saying, and identify the feelings that arise in you with those thoughts. Then inquire into what needs that part of you is seeking to meet.

You might approach empathizing with this part of you the same way you empathized with yourself in Chapter 2. However, since it's important to step into this voice, allowing it to speak so that you can listen closely to it, you can think of this step as a conversation between Voice A and mediator mind.

Let's witness Chris beginning his internal mediation.

Chris decides to start with the part of him that wants to meet his buddies, and when he asks that part what it would like to be called, he hears, "Vegas, Baby!" He sets up two chairs to move between as he mediates his conflict. Here's how Chris (Mediator Mind) empathizes with Vegas, Baby!

Vegas, Baby!: "I love getting together with these guys! We have a great time catching up and just being guys for the weekend."

Mediator Mind: "It sounds like you'd like to have some fun, is that it?"

VB: "Yep. These trips are like being in college again, pre-responsibilities of work and mortgages and being a husband and father. I can let go of that for a short time, blow off some steam."

MM: "Like reconnecting with a time when you had fewer worries and felt more free?"

VB: "Freedom, yes, and it's about these guys too. We go way back, we know each other well, and even if we aren't constantly in touch, it feels like time just melts away when we get together. It's about maintaining those relationships. Being with them reminds me of *me*, of who I can be, or maybe who I really am."

MM: "So friendship is important to you, and being reminded of who you really are?"

VB: "Yeah, there's something nice about just being able to *be* for that time."

MM: "I'm hearing that going to Vegas would meet needs for fun, freedom, friendship, and being you. Anything else?"

VB: "No. That sounds about right."

STEP 2: EMPATHIZE WITH B

When Part A feels heard, switch to the other perspective, and do the same thing. You might start by asking Part B what it wants to be heard about. It will likely have some things to say (if it hasn't tried to break in already) based on what Part A said. Identify any observations, feelings, and needs while having a conversation with Part B so that it can be heard to its satisfaction.

Now that the part of Chris wanting to go to Vegas is feeling heard, he notices that the other side of him, concerned about his health goals, is chomping at the bit to speak up. He moves into the other chair and allows that part to speak.

MM: "What would you like to be heard about?"

Voice B: "I'd really like to stick to the goals we've just committed to and started working toward. This is how we've gotten off track before . . . something comes along that conflicts with our health goals and we let them go. If we want to make this a lifestyle, we need to stick to it."

MM: "So you're concerned about this pattern repeating itself again. These health goals are important to you, and you'd like to find a way to stay with them long enough to become the way we live, is that it?"

Voice B: "Yes. And if we go to Vegas, we're putting ourselves in this situation where we're not going to be able to."

MM: "It sounds like you're really trying to make sure all the needs that we're trying to meet in setting these goals—to thrive, be around for family, enjoy life—are represented?"

Voice B: "Well, yeah. We've made a commitment to this dream, and someone has to protect it . . . make sure we don't forget it when something exciting comes along that might take us away."

MM: "What would you like to be called? Dream Protector?"

Dream Protector: "That sounds fine. We've been so disappointed before when we lose weight and then don't keep it off, so I'd like to make sure that this time we don't go there again."

MM: "Are you trying to meet needs for integrity and continuity in setting and reaching these goals?"

DP: "Absolutely. And there's power too in finally achieving what we've said we want to achieve."

MM: "Right, so also empowerment to achieve what we want."

If some other part of you wants to step in while you're empathizing with Part B, simply acknowledge that part of you, note "who" it is (it may be Part A with more to say in response to hearing Part B), and let it know that you will listen to it shortly. Stay focused as much as possible on hearing and empathizing with Part B.

STEP 3: ASK B TO EMPATHIZE WITH A

The goal of Steps 1 and 2 is to allow both A and B to express themselves and for you to empathize with them—in other words, for both sides of the conflict to be heard. In Steps 3 and 4, the goal is to get them to hear *each other*, to in a sense have the two parts of you that have been in conflict start communicating so they can collaborate on a strategy that will meet the needs of both.

Since both voices are inside you, it may seem strange to have each one reflect the needs of the other. You might be thinking, "Well of course they heard each other, it's all inside me!" But surprisingly, when you actually embody the voices, it can be challenging for them to hear each other. It's no different from when two people are in conflict and each is entrenched in their own point of view; even if person A has just heard what person B said, including their needs, the more distressed they are the less likely they will even remember those needs, much less be able to reflect them back. The same thing can happen within your mind. But the goal of conducting Steps 1 and 2 is to hopefully allow A and B to be heard enough that they can actually hear the other's perspective. This is also where writing down the needs that come up can be helpful.

In Step 2, you talked to Part B and helped uncover the needs it wants met. Now in Step 3, you ask B to reflect back what A said, focusing on feelings and needs.

MM: "If there isn't anything else you'd like to be heard about, DP, would you be willing to say what you heard VB wants?"

DP: "Okay. I heard that VB wants to go and have a good time with old friends, and let go of responsibilities for the weekend. I guess he sees health goals as another responsibility he'd like to forget."

MM [Though DP has reflected, it's clear from the last remark that DP is still feeling put off by VB's perspective, so MM chooses to empathize more]: "Are you feeling frustrated because you'd like some support from other parts and not be the only one advocating for this dream?"

DP: "I guess so. I mean this dream is for Chris, to have a level of wellness far into the future."

MM [Continues empathy, then reiterates request to reflect VB's needs]: "So support and maybe some understanding about these goals being important for Chris's future. Whether you agree with VB's strategy or not, would you be willing to just say that you heard his needs for fun, freedom, friendship, and being himself?"

DP: "Yeah, I heard he has those needs to have fun with friends, have some freedom, and be himself for the weekend."

As Chris finds with DP, sometimes when one part reflects it becomes clear that it needs a bit more empathy, and a round or two of guessing its needs (as in "Are you feeling frustrated because you'd like some support . . ." and "So support and maybe some understanding about these goals being important for Chris's future.") can help it reflect the needs of the other part ("Yeah, I heard he has those needs to have fun with friends, have some freedom, and be himself for the weekend."). Mediator mind, as the holder of the process, can make these choices based on what the voices are saying, tracking the needs and the steps of the process to ensure each voice gets heard by the other.

STEP 4: ASK A TO EMPATHIZE WITH B

In Step 4, return to Part A and ask it to reflect back the needs identified by Part B.

> **MM:** "VB, would you be willing to say what you heard DP would like?"
>
> **VB:** "Sure, I get that DP wants us to stick to the health plan we set out. And I'm not against working toward that, but the point is not to put off all fun until some future when we're healthy. One of the needs for the dream was fun and to enjoy life! How is turning down this weekend enjoying life?"
>
> **MM** [Again, MM notices that while VB has reflected a bit, mostly it has responded to what DP said, indicating that empathy may help]: "So I'm hearing you're not against the health goals . . . in fact, you see that going is a way to meet one of the needs behind the dream—to enjoy life—and you'd like to be able to do that without waiting for some distant future."
>
> **VB:** "Yeah, what's the point of the dream if we can't live on the way there?"
>
> **MM:** "I hear it's important to you to not put aside living while working on health goals. I also heard DP's needs for empowerment, integrity, and to protect the dream. Would you be willing to let DP know you heard those too?"
>
> **VB:** "Yeah, I heard that DP would like the empowerment of achieving these goals, protecting them, and sticking to what we said we'd do."

It's quite likely that you will go through multiple rounds of Steps 1–4 for A and B to hear each other. How the process typically unfolds after an initial round of hearing A and B and asking them to reflect back is that it becomes a conversation between A and B. However, it helps them hear each other if before they say what they'd like to be heard about, they repeat what they just heard from the other part. Mediator mind may take a less direct role, ensuring that each is reflecting and hearing the other, and focusing on needs, stepping in only if the voices start arguing. Each time you switch roles, simply make sure you restate what the other part said, then what you (as the other part of you) would like to be heard about.

> As Chris continues the conversation, DP and VB communicate more directly. Chris moves between chairs as each voice speaks, and each voice reflects back what the other says before responding:
>
> **DP:** "I hear that you'd like to enjoy life while working toward health goals. And I'd like you to hear my concern that certain situations, like Vegas, might go too far toward enjoyment and leave health in the dust."
>
> **VB:** "I get it. You think that being with the guys, especially in light of past trips, is a recipe for disaster when it comes to the dream. I see the challenge of it, I just don't want to give it up because it might be a bit difficult. It seems like you want to protect the dream to the exclusion of all else, and that won't work. I'd like these other needs met too."
>
> **DP:** "You'd like to not give up the trip, just because it might be difficult to make healthy choices. And from my point of view, when the desire is for fun and to enjoy life, health goals are nowhere in consideration. I'm fine with having those needs met, I just want to ensure that we find a way to meet all our needs, not just a few of them."
>
> **VB:** "Yes, I hear that you're responding to those times when enjoyment overshadowed everything. I'd like to find a new way too."

STEP 5: MAKE SOLUTION REQUESTS AND AGREEMENTS

You'll want to stay in the first four steps of the Connection Phase until the two parts of you have uncovered the needs motivating each of them and are hearing each other. Once you reach that point, you'll often find that you naturally begin to move into the Resolution Phase and Step 5. Chris is now at that point—VB and DP have both acknowledged that they are willing to find a way to meet all of the needs they've uncovered. So the obvious next question is, "What do we do now to meet all of these needs?" This is where the two parts can begin to collaborate to find a strategy.

It may help to think of mediator mind facilitating this step of the process, because that is the part of you that can hold all needs simultaneously and be outside of any particular point of view. They are all *your* needs, after all; each part of you is simply in touch with and advocating for particular needs from its perspective of concern. From mediator mind, you can imagine what it might be like to have all needs met and ask for (or suggest) strategies, checking with both parties to see whether proposed strategies would work for them. The two parties may also make requests of each other. (The next chapter will go into more detail on the elements of requests and making agreements with yourself.)

Since it's quite possible to get re-triggered in the process of making requests, sometimes you may find more empathy is required—and even a return to the first four stages—before continuing with requests and agreements.

Let's see how Step 5 unfolds for Chris:

MM: "So it sounds like you're both okay with trying to meet the needs for fun, friendship, freedom, being, health/wellness, integrity, and protection of the dream. Do you have any ideas about how to meet these?"

VB: "I think we should just go to Vegas and make sure to eat healthy and get some activity in while we're there. Probably won't be perfect, but I think it can be done."

MM: "So you'd like to go and aim for incorporating your health goals into the trip. DP, would that met your needs?"

DP: "On the surface it seems like it would, but I know it seems easier in advance than it actually is in the moment. I would suggest not going on the trip and connecting with the guys another way. I say we have some fun with the family that weekend instead."

MM: "So you're concerned with VB's ideas about being able to follow through on the intention while in the moment?"

DP: "Can you blame me? Remember the last trip when you said, 'Yeah, I'm not going to drink as much and I'll eat better this time," and you drank yourself silly and gained eight pounds over the weekend!"

MM: "So you'd like some trust that this time would be different?"

DP: "Yeah, I'd like VB to be realistic about the likelihood of being able to do that, and maybe put some safeguards in place."

VB: "You know, that last time really didn't work. I remember being miserable after. I think these trips have been about going back to a time that was so much fun in the past, but it's no longer really me. Funny, I know I said it was about being me, but it's really more of a nostalgic me. If I look at what being *me* is now, it includes all aspects of my life. I guess this is helping me realize that our normal way of spending time together isn't so great for me, so I'm not sure I want the same kind of trip anymore."

MM: "I'm hearing that you might be open to not going—or to asking the others whether they are open to a different kind of trip?"

VB: "That feels a bit scary. I can imagine some ribbing or the guys not getting it and thinking I'm raining on their parade, but yeah, I'm open to it. Maybe I can reach out to Mark and see what his thoughts are."

PRACTICE PAUSE

Take a small internal conflict you are currently experiencing. Identify the two parts of yourself, and work through the Internal Mediation map.

Here's a summary of working with a present/future internal conflict:

Identify the different voices in your mind and set up a chair for each.

Decide which voice to begin the process with.

Step 1: Allow Voice A to speak. Empathize with Voice A by observing what that voice is saying, feeling the emotions generated by those thoughts, and then inquiring into the needs that part of you is seeking to meet

Step 2: Allow Voice B to speak. Empathize with Voice B in the same way—observing the thoughts, feeling the emotions, and inquiring into the needs that part of you is seeking to meet.

Step 3: Ask B to empathize with A, reflecting back A's needs.

Step 4: Ask A to empathize with B, reflecting back B's needs.

Step 5: Explore strategies that will meet all the needs uncovered. Make requests or agreements with yourself and/or other people to support you in putting your choice into action.

Since we've heard how Chris works through his internal conflict to stay true to himself, let's hear from Dawn and Kevin about how they fared when they applied the Internal Mediation map.

DAWN

Dawn used the IM process with her ambivalence about feeling obligated to offer a board position to her friend Marge. Starting with the part of her that said she had to offer Marge a position, she uncovered a few needs. "I like to honor my word and be in integrity, and I did suggest it to her. I also don't want to hurt her feelings, as it wouldn't meet my needs for care and kindness, plus I really do want her involved in some way. I'd love her contribution and the collaboration of working with her." Dawn also listened to the other part of her that had some concerns. "I'm thinking that I'd like people on the board to have experience building a nonprofit, since I don't, and Marge doesn't fit that profile. I planned to only have a few people to start with, so with limited spots, I'd really like to do right by the organization and create a structure that will be more likely to lead to success." As she mediated between these two parts of herself and they began to hear each other, Dawn realized that being caught in the polarity of the two had her stuck in all-or-nothing thinking. She arrived at an agreement with herself about considering all options, including both what the board might look like and what other roles Marge might play in helping form the organization.

KEVIN

Kevin felt heavy about his job promotion, completely torn about whether to take it. He decided to try the IM process and see if anything new emerged. "I knew starting out that I had a part of me saying I should take the position, and another part arguing for my dream." He started with the part of him that was saying he *should* take the promotion, as he suspected that it wouldn't listen until it could have its say. "As I sat in that chair, I realized that part of me was speaking out of hope and fear. It saw this other dream of retirement being a few years closer if I took the promotion, so it has the hope of reaching that dream, regardless of the dream I've identified to enjoy my life outside of work now too. And, it speaks to protect me from possible negative consequences of not taking it.

And while I was empathizing with that voice, another one showed up that I didn't expect. Another part of me *wants* to take the promotion. It's a higher status and responsibility, and it meets my needs for achievement and challenge. After setting up a third chair and empathizing with that voice, the part of me saying to turn the promotion down became the "should" voice—telling me I should turn it down because of the commitment I made to the dream of balance now, not later. As I listened to that part of me, it's really speaking up for my needs of enjoyment of my life and what I've been able to create—connection with my family— which is so important to me, and to have some balance.

I felt for a bit like I was going in circles, with each of these three parts of me taking turns being the 'you should' voice, and it made me realize how much that sense of 'should' for me is a clue that some part of me is afraid some needs won't get met. Understanding that in the way I now do made this process worth it, even as I continue to mediate between these parts to resolve the conflict."

—〜—

As Sally goes through the next couple of days, the invitation niggles now and then at the back of her mind, and each time, she pushes it aside. When she realizes she hasn't even mentioned it to James, she knows she needs to address her uncertainty. Recognizing the signs that she's conflicted, she sets aside a little time to go through the Internal Mediation process.

Sally sets up two chairs opposite each other and gets paper and a pencil. She draws two wide columns and a thin one down the middle labeled "Needs," then she labels the left column "A-" and the right column "B-". Wondering where to start, she decides it might be easier to begin with the part of herself that wants to accept the invitation, so she fills in the word "Excited" next to "A." She sits in one of the chairs and feels the anticipation of going, then internally allows this part of her to speak. (We'll illustrate here in columns to demonstrate the movement from chair to chair.)

Mediator Mind

Excited

"This is such a great op-portunity. A chance to present my ideas and meet more people, net-work, and maybe get some more business."

As Sally thinks this, she jots down key phrases and words on the left quarter of the page. Pondering them, her mediator mind considers what needs Excited is trying to meet.

Mediator Mind	**Excited**
"You'd like to meet people so you can grow your business, meeting needs for sustainability?"	"Yes, but more than that, it's the connections themselves—you never know where they'll lead, and the more people I meet, the more I'll feel a part of this field."

Sally jots notes as her mediator mind empathizes.

"So that's also about a sense of possibility for creating more in the future, and belonging in this field?"	"Yeah, I guess I still feel a bit on the outside since I'm just getting started. The more I can meet people, and meet them in this setting where I'm presenting—as if I already belong—maybe I'll start to feel more connected."

Sally's mediator mind returns to an earlier idea expressed by Excited.

"I also heard you'd like to present your ideas. Is that about contribution?"	"Well . . . I'd like to share some thoughts, and I definitely hope it would be a contribution. Plus there's getting the experience of presenting."

Mediator Mind   **Excited**

"So experience, and maybe growth are both important to you?"	"Yes, I'd definitely like to keep growing and learn-ing. And it would be fun! I think I'd really enjoy it."

As Sally talks herself through this internal conversation, she jots the key pieces of the dialogue in the two left columns on the page, with Excited on the outside, and Mediator Mind on the inside.

Excited	MM Empathy			
Opportunity	Grow business – sustainability			
Present my ideas				
Meet people	Creating more in future			
Connections leading to ?				
Feeling part of field	Possibility			
	Belonging in field			
Experience				
Fun presenting	Contribution			
I'd enjoy it	Experience / growth			

Feeling complete with Excited for now, she moves to the other chair and taps into the part of her that's not so sure about going.

Sitting in this chair, Sally feels her body stiffening with tension.

Mediator Mind

Voice B

"You want to go running right into this without thinking about it and all it means, all it would take, and what could happen. What if you don't give a good presentation? It could hurt you in this field instead of helping."

Again, Sally jots down what this part of her wants to be heard about and considers what might be motivating it. She stumbles a bit as she empathizes, finding this voice harder to hear.

"So you'd like some certainty that the presentation will be good and people will receive it? Is that about being seen a certain way in the community?"

"Yes. I'm concerned how much doing a bad presentation will impact how people see you. I know you want business out of it, but there's no guarantee of that, regardless of how well you present. Maybe you'll get no business, and then what?"

Sally feels Excited trying to jump in and argue that it wouldn't matter, that the connections could be valuable anyway, but she stays with empathy for this part of her.

Mediator Mind	Voice B
"I'm hearing your concern about going in with an expectation of getting business and wondering how we'll feel if that doesn't pan out, is that right?"	"Yeah, I would hate to see all the time spent and have it not build the business."
"So you want to make sure the efforts we make are effective in growing the business?"	"Absolutely. The best way forward is to take the action that's most likely to lead to our goals . . ."

Again, Sally feels Excited waving arms in the air to respond, and she internally lets Excited know that she will get back to her, while she allows this voice to continue.

	". . . And what happens if too many opportunities come from this and we end up overwhelmed? That could stop everything in its tracks too. Just when you're attempting to be there more for your family in addition to your business, having too many things coming in could throw all of it off."

Sally pauses, confused. As she looks over her notes, she notices all the "what ifs" this part of her is throwing at her, and that empathizing with the needs each time doesn't seem to shift this part of herself. This leads her to wonder what need is underneath all of it.

Pondering and coming up empty, she remembers how she used to deal with "what ifs." Her father always told her, "What's the worst thing that could happen? Imagine what that is, and then envision surviving it." His words had encouraged her to make many choices she might not have made otherwise, but she recognizes how she had always steamrolled over this part of her that brought up the "what ifs." Looking back over her list of all the points raised by this part now, it finally occurs to her to simply ask, "What is your job? What are you trying to do for me?"

The response, delivered with a huffy attitude, is immediate.

Mediator Mind

Voice B

"Hello! I'm trying to get you to think about things! You're so ready to just jump right in to the next new exciting thing, without considering what will work and whether that path is the best one to take to get to the top of the mountain!"

Sally laughs, noticing that while embodying this voice, she is rolling her eyes, reminding herself of Corey when she doesn't understand something obvious to him and he's particularly annoyed. Mediator mind then empathizes.

Mediator Mind   **Voice B**

"You'd like some
thoughtfulness around
these choices, considera-
tion of all aspects and not
just the fun or adventure
of it, and to make sure
that all needs are taken
into account, is that it?"

Even as she asks this, Sally feels emotion rising and knows she hasn't quite reached what's really going on yet. Dropping deeper into the feeling, she asks, *What is it you'd really like me to hear?* The response is quiet, but unmistakable.

"I'm trying to protect you.
You're putting yourself
out there with this pres-
entation. I don't want you
to be embarrassed or
shamed in front of these
people. You could be . . ."

Her internal voice falters, and Sally senses the fear of anni-hilation that this part of her is trying to avoid. Her hand on her heart, she asks, *You're trying to protect me from being annihilated, aren't you? So you're saying all these things to try to keep me safe?*

Merely asking the question makes her feel lighter, and she knows she has finally reached the core of what this part is striving to contribute. *What would you like me to call you?* she asks herself. *Perhaps "Safety"?* The voice responds, *Yes, call me "Safety."* She sits for a minute, breathing into the sweet feeling of this part of her finally being heard, and then fills in the columns on the right with her observations.

A - Excited		Needs	B - Safety	
Excited	MM Empathy		MM Empathy	Safety
Opportunity	Grow business – sustainability		Being seen in a certain way	Give bad presentation
Present my ideas			Effective in efforts to grow business	No guarantee of business
Meet people	Creating more in future			Too many opportunities – could get overwhelmed
Connections leading to ?			Thoughtfulness about choices	
Feeling part of field	Possibility		Consideration of all needs	What path is best
Experience	Belonging in field			
Fun presenting	Contribution		Safety / protection	Plan to move forward
I'd enjoy it	Experience / growth			Shame / Annihilation

Sally senses that Excited is a little calmer, not clamoring quite as much, but would still like to respond. Before switching back to Excited's chair, she asks Safety if she's willing to restate Excited's needs.

Mediator Mind

Excited

Safety

"Yeah, I know she's all about the adventure and fun of it."

Sally's mediator mind prompts a bit more.

"I also heard Excited would like to meet needs for sustainability, belonging in the community, contribution, and growth. Would you be willing just to let Excited know you heard those?"

"Okay. She would also like to grow, contribute, belong in the community, and create a sustainable business."

Sally switches back to Excited's chair and asks if she would be willing to say that she'd heard Safety's needs for thoughtfulness and consideration of all needs, and of course, safety.

Excited reflects a little grudgingly, then responds.

Mediator Mind

Excited   **Safety**

"Safety would
have us stay safe
and consider eve-
rything until the
end of time, and
nothing would
ever get done. I
say take the risk
and act! We can
change directions
if it seems like that
path isn't the best
route."

Now it's Safety who attempts to jump in and respond, but Sally's mediator mind keeps the process on track by empathiz-ing first with Excited.

"You would prefer
to go ahead and
take some risks,
and change course
if it seems it's not
right?"

Mediator Mind

Excited   Safety

"Yes, because you can't plan and think your way through these things forever. You have to take action to know whether you're on the right path or not. If you try to think your way forward, there are always endless considerations and trying to second-guess what will happen, which is a good way to never move forward at all. And we're just talk-ing at a conference, not going off into the wilderness."

"So you value learning through doing and move-ment as a way to know the path forward."

At Excited's affirmation of this statement, Sally moves back into Safety's chair and asks Safety to reflect Excited's needs, only to find that Safety needs a bit more empathy.

Mediator Mind

Excited		Safety

"Excited thinks it's important to take risks and not ponder things so long that we don't take action. I'm not against acting. I'm not saying let's not do this presentation, or anything else. I just would like some thought put toward how to do it so we're taken care of, especially emotionally. Of course we're not going off into the wilderness, but if this goes sideways, people can be really harsh and demeaning. I always have to keep the brakes on to make sure we stay protected, and I'd like for us to be prepared for any emotional fallout that might happen."

Mediator Mind

Excited

Safety

"So you'd like to
be protected from
hurt and criticism,
especially emo-
tionally. Would
you also like to
trust that you're
being heard and
your concerns
taken into ac-
count?"

As mediator mind reflects this to Safety, Sally notices a
shift in herself. Sitting in Safety's chair, she feels sadness at
trying to contribute something of value that took a long time
to be heard (protecting Sally and her emotions) and relief at
finally being heard. Sally is also aware that Excited truly heard
Safety this time. As she feels the two parts of her at last listening to each other instead of simply arguing for their viewpoint, mediator mind can sit back a little and be less involved
as they speak directly to each other.

Mediator Mind

Excited

Safety

"You would like to contribute and be heard, and you're concerned about going into these situations where we could be criticized, so you want us to have some preparation and forethought about handling what might come up. Is that it?"

"Yes. I'd like to have some plans in place to make sure we're taken care of. I know you like to jump in and act, that it meets your needs for learning and movement, and that's fine, but sometimes when you do that we pay a price for it later. I don't want to not act, but can we please put something in place to take care of us in case things don't go as well as hoped?"

"I get what you're saying. I can see that acting quickly does meet some needs but not others. I'm willing to talk about how we can do what you'd like."

After going through Steps 3 and 4 and writing down the main points, Sally reflects on the page and writes down the needs in the central column before moving into requests.

A - Excited		Needs	B - Safety	
Excited	MM Empathy	Sustainabil-ity	MM Empathy	Safety
Opportunity	Grow business - sustainability	Contribu-tion	Being seen in a certain way	Give bad presentation
Present my ideas		Possibility	Effective in efforts to grow business	No guarantee of business
Meet people	Creating more in future	Effective-ness		Too many opportunities - could get overwhelmed
Connections leading to ?	Possibility	Belonging	Thoughtfulness about choices	
Feeling part of field	Belonging in field	Growth	Consideration of all needs	What path is best
Experience	Contribution	Experience	Protection from emotional hurt	Plan to move forward
Fun presenting	Experience / growth	Fun		Shame / annihilation
I'd enjoy it		Thought-fulness	Trust, be heard, and contribute	Be prepared
		Considera-tion	Safety	Take care emotionally
		Movement		
		Be heard		
		Protection		
		Safety		
		Trust		

Reflecting on this list, Sally asks herself, *What strategies would help meet all of these needs? What can I do to make sure that I'm both prepared for the presentation and can handle any emotional fallout?*

Sally is surprised when Excited responds first.

Mediator Mind

Excited		Safety
"We can definitely plan and prepare for the presentation to make sure we feel confident going into it. Safety, what would help you feel comfortable with possible responses?"		

Sally moves back to Safety's chair, but feels blank, almost like Safety is struggling to stay in the conversation when the fear arises. From mediator mind, Sally gently asks:

	"How about doing Self-Empathy when this feeling comes up and you're concerned about taking part?"	
		"Okay, yes, that sounds good."

Mediator Mind

Excited

Safety

"And we could set up support with someone, like James, Alicia, or Shawn, for before and after the pres-entation to con-nect and to help with any difficult thoughts after-wards."

"Yeah, maybe knowing that there's someone to talk to will help."

Stepping out of both roles and back to mediator mind, Sally realizes:

"Self-care, too, might contribute. It's always easier to stay calm when we've had plenty of rest, exercise, and been meditat-ing on a regular basis."

With agreements in place to do Self-Empathy when she feels concerned about presenting, to enlist support from some-one, and to keep up her self-care, Sally notices that she feels more relaxed and comfortable with the idea of presenting at the con-ference. With a smile, she begins to compose her acceptance email.

—⌒⌒—

INTERNAL MEDIATION IN PRACTICE AND IN LIFE

If you are just beginning to distinguish what different parts of yourself are saying, we know this process can seem very confusing. What follows on the next pages are some ways to practice and integrate it into your life so that it feels more and more natural, and in the next section we'll talk about additional tips for working with the map.

As with all of our maps, it helps to practice it as laid out until it becomes more embodied and you find your own way to mediate between your internal voices. For example, though we still refer to this map in our own internal mediations, we rarely follow it closely. After becoming more accustomed to the internal conversations you have, the basic process is to simply empathize with whatever internal voices show up, moving to that voice's "chair" when it speaks, allowing each voice to be heard, and then helping the voices connect with each other so they cooperate to find a resolution.

If you're feeling overwhelmed merely reading through the process and examples, that's understandable. It can feel complicated at first, but if you give it time and a fair chance, the process is powerful and well worth the effort it takes to get to the result. It's also sometimes easier, especially when learning, to work with someone else. Regardless of how many times we have done the IM map, we still find it helpful to work with at least one partner, with the other person in a role-play or as a support person helping empathize with and keep the voices straight. In Chapter 10, we will discuss the various ways to practice with one or two partners.

INTERNAL MEDIATION (IM) IN DAILY LIFE

While it is important to practice the full IM process to learn to embody it, you may have times when you are aware of an internal conflict but can't take the time to do the complete map. Shortening the IM map may not be quite as effective as a full process, but it can still provide a way of relating to yourself that leads to a favorable outcome. If your typical method of interacting with an internal conflict is to shove one of the voices down or ignore it, simply listening and asking what needs it wants to meet interrupts that habitual response, opening yourself to new possibilities.

CONDENSED PATH

To resolve an internal conflict without going through the entire IM map, it helps to remember the goal is to explore new possibilities through surfacing the needs of each part of you and making sure they hear each other. Once you've gone through the full process a few times and are familiar with it, the process can go much faster.

If you have a conflict arise in the midst of a situation, you may be able to work through it by merely listening to what one voice says and looking for the need being expressed, then hearing what the other voice says, and uncovering the need being expressed. If you begin to feel different about the situation and new ideas arise, then you can be confident the voices are hearing each other. By being fully present (in mediator mind) with both voices, and not losing yourself in the points of view or resisting them but connecting with the needs they are seeking to meet, you can find a new way forward from that connection.

QUICK PATH

In some cases, you may be able to shift an internal conflict simply by empathizing with one of the voices. Oftentimes, one is quite familiar while the other is one you habitually turn away from. Sally experienced this with her conflict: her Excited voice was familiar but she tended to turn away from Safety. This is common with any conflict where one voice is saying "should"—many people will push this voice away instead of listening. But when you empathize with that voice first and discover the needs that part of you is trying to alert you to, you can sometimes quickly connect to that part of you and a new way forward emerges.

PRACTICE PAUSE

Schedule at least three times on your calendar to walk yourself through an internal conflict using the IM map.

BEING SUCCESSFUL WITH IM

The most important thing with internal mediation is to allow yourself to speak from—or as—each part of you. Rather than talking about the voice or speaking from the global "I"—i.e., the mediator mind aware of all the voices—you're actually embodying each part, allowing it to come out and have its say. In this manner, each voice will use "I" when speaking from its perspective and expressing what it wants, and it will use "you" when speaking to another part of you. It may even use "we" in talking about overall goals. The difference between talking about parts of you versus talking from a part might sound something like this.

Talking about two competing parts:

I know that I really should track my expenses and income so I know where I stand. One part of me wants me to be in control of my spending so I can start saving more, and yet I'm afraid it will mean a life of deprivation.

Embodying two distinct parts in conversation:

Voice 1: Come on, you know you should really take stock of your financial situation. You're just being lazy. You can't stay in denial forever about how far in debt you are. Get off your butt and do something about it.

Voice 2: I like being able to do what I want and have what I want. You'd be happy living in a cave, eating bugs! I have a life, and that involves needing to spend money on some things. I don't want to stop living now for some unknowable future.

There's value in talking about a part at certain times—it can be very helpful in identifying that you have an internal conflict—but the power of the Internal Mediation process lies in allowing the voices to speak, to listen and have a conversation with them, and to discern what they'd like to be heard about. As you can tell from the above example, the tendency when talking about internal conflict is to sanitize it, or to try to silence one voice, sometimes becoming defensive in the process. But when you allow the parts to speak, trusting they want to contribute even if they speak harshly, three benefits arise:

1. You uncover a more complete picture of the needs each part is seeking to meet.
2. You experience the emotional shift of each part being fully heard.

3. You are more likely to resolve the entire conflict through unanticipated ideas arising out of the connection to needs.

Ideally, as in a formal mediation, when your internal voices each get to speak, the two parties begin to communicate with each other and find a strategy that works for both. Again, it may be tempting to lapse into "talking about" mode instead of embodying the voices themselves, so if you find yourself doing this as you go through the steps, see if you can shift to actually speaking from each voice. *Listening to the parts of yourself is key.* Keep in mind that this process is not about treating one of the voices as a problem to be fixed, or about coming from the perspective that you'll listen to the voice but then it needs to toe the line and do what you say. That doesn't work. If a voice doesn't get heard, it will have its say one way or another, usually inflicting some level of stress.

PRACTICE PAUSE

Take a current internal conflict and talk *about* it, then talk *from* each part of you. Can you feel the difference between the two?

People frequently avoid seeing the perspective of the "judgmental" voice, yet the more you allow each voice to speak and can distinguish what the internal dialogue is saying, the more likely you are to shift the conflict. For example:

When Sally was first starting her business, she considered purchasing a training program to help her market her services. One part of her very much wanted to invest in it, and another part argued against it. The part of Sally that wanted to invest saw a possibility that could come from participating in the training. The other part was wondering whether she already knew enough and it was really necessary.

This second voice initially sounded fairly innocuous, and when she tried to mediate between the two, she became stuck, with nothing shifting in the conflict.

Then she realized that the part of her arguing against the training was far from bland. Since she had been talking to James about the decision and seeking his support, she had couched this voice in mild, acceptable language. When she tried embodying that part of herself, she realized the voice was actually saying, *You already know enough. The last thing you need to do is put things off and spend even more money on training. You just need to get off your lazy butt and do what you already know to do.*

Hearing it this way, the tone was harsh and blaming, the implication being that if she did purchase the training, she was wrong and bad. But recognizing what the voice was actually saying, difficult as it was, she was finally able to truly empathize with it, and she realized that it was empowering her—it wanted her to find fulfillment through taking action that would lead to success. Once she was able to empathize with that part of herself, including the judgments, she could hear beyond them and make a decision that served her well.

Journaling this process, instead of trying to keep it all in your mind, can also prove to be helpful. Writing down what the parts of you are saying keeps it all more clear, and it provides an easy way to track the needs that different parts of you are seeking to meet. Our internal voices often argue and talk over each other, just as two people will do in a disagreement. As such, it's easy to lose track and not realize you've shifted into another voice. But journaling allows you to listen to and empathize with each voice as a separate entity.

In journaling, you may write the entire conversation out as it occurs, or you might create a chart like Sally did, to keep track of the primary themes and note the needs each part of you is seeking to meet. As you play with different options, you'll find what works for you to follow the internal conversation.

Now, if the issue you are mediating is large and complex, be aware that you may not reach a strategy the first time you mediate it, and that is perfectly normal. It may take working with it little by little, uncovering layers to the conflict before you can see a new way to move forward. Because of this, when first learning this process, it's best to practice with smaller, day-to-day conflicts, such as which restaurant to choose for dinner, whether to exercise or rest, or what to do on your day off. These less enmeshed issues can aid you in becoming familiar with the process, as well as in practicing identifying observations, feelings, and needs, all of which will help when you face a more complex issue.

If you have tended to deal with internal conflict in any of the typical ways addressed earlier, it's important to realize that the voice you've been pushing aside may be in distress. That part of you has been trying to be heard and contribute to you for years, and when it's ignored, often the intrusive thoughts become more and more shrill. If someone hasn't been listened to, including a part of yourself, it may not trust that its message will be included in the current decision-making process. Because of this, it may take some time, and continued empathy, for this part of you to trust that you are now listening and taking its view into account. Best of all, you will likely experience relief when that part finally feels heard.

At the same time, there's also the part of you that has rejected or repressed that distressed and intrusive voice, seeing it as a troublemaker and stamping it down. When you can empathize with that part of you, and the distress it feels at hearing the intrusive voice, it's easier for that part of you to be able to listen and empathize with the voice that has been pushed aside.

At this point, we want to make it clear that since the examples in this chapter (and the book overall) were created based on real-life scenarios, they may give the impression that a little thinking and strategizing to find a "middle ground" between the perspectives is all that is required to mediate internal conflicts. This is not what we are suggesting. This approach is *not* about:

+ Choosing based on which side has more needs it's trying to meet

+ Caving to the part of you with the stronger argument

+ Comparing and judging the two parts of you and their viewpoint

+ Thinking the conflict through from an omniscient perspective to figure out the best way forward

It's difficult in short examples to convey—with all the nuances involved—how the process unfolds in any given situation. Because it's an embodied conversation you're having, it's far from being merely a cognitive process. Your goal, therefore, is to be compassionate with yourself and all parts who are speaking, knowing that when you uncover the underlying needs that each perspective is trying to meet, it creates an emotional connection to those needs—not only to that point of view within you, but *between* the different points of view that seem in opposition on the surface. As these parts connect, you begin to deeply understand that all internal voices—regardless of how they sound—are acting in what they perceive to be your best interest.

Connecting to needs tends to unleash creativity, which offers an entirely new way of seeing the whole situation that merely thinking about it cannot provide. As a result, the solutions that emerge were likely unimaginable when you first became aware of

the conflict. Yes, the same solution might occur in simply thinking it through, but when that solution comes out of a connection
to your *needs*, your choice carries a power behind it from the
deeper motivations with which you are now in touch. In other
words, the solution has a more profound meaning—and frequently
more calm and confidence—because you are fully aware of how it
impacts your needs.

While we encourage you to practice the IM map with "easier"
internal conflicts, or ones that seem to be more surface issues, we
actually find that there are no "surface" or "unimportant" internal conflicts. Even the so-called easier conflicts are uncovering
fundamental needs. For example, deciding what to wear to a
party may surface needs about being accepted by others if you
express who you are through your clothing. If you are truly engaged in the process, you will discover the needs that are motivating different parts of you (in this example, self-expression and
belonging). Whether or not you have ever listened to these voices
before, they are coming from a deep-seated place of care for you
and your well-being. When you shift from how the conflict is
showing up in your life and hear, often for the first time, where
these voices are truly coming from (especially if those voices have
been speaking in a way that's hard to hear), it can be highly moving. If you are willing to allow it, you can feel the overarching
care you genuinely have for yourself that you may not even be
aware of, and as a result, find ways to act on it that are far more
satisfying than the ways you've learned previously.

Don't take our word for it, though; try it out for yourself.

Let's now take a look at the outcome of the IM process for
Chris, Dawn, and Kevin.

CHRIS

The two parts of Chris came to the agreement that he would reach out to Mark about whether the guys were open to a different kind of trip, and if he didn't go, he would find other ways to meet his needs for friendship, fun, and freedom. With trepidation, Chris makes the call, and with transparency shares with Mark his dilemma and his desire for a different type of trip. To his surprise, Mark is quite open to the idea.

"He said he was thinking along the same lines, and wondering whether anyone else might not want a return to college days this time around. We started talking about other ideas that were more active and outdoors. Lake Mead is right near Vegas, and Mark thinks another friend knows a guy who operates an outdoor adventure company in the area, so we're approaching the rest of the group to see if they're open to more of a camping trip with some activities at the lake. I'm sure there will still be some food and drink involved, but if the focus is not exclusively on that, I'll be in much better shape to stick to my goals. Plus, just talking through it with Mark, I feel more confident that someone will be on my side and not pushing me to eat or drink what I'm not comfortable with. Maybe I can even enlist his help to keep me from indulging when I'm tempted."

Chris then reflects on the whole process of mediating his internal conflict and the unexpected change he notices along the way.

"Initially, the part of me I called 'Vegas, Baby' was certain that the only way to meet my needs for fun and freedom was to go, and Dream Protector thought the only way to meet my health goals and protect the dream was to not go. What was so interesting to me was how I began to see the whole situation differently after they connected. It's like the needs came to the forefront and the strategies receded into the background, and that created more freedom to explore different strategies. I feel so much better! I know that whatever happens, I'm actually okay with it. I'd love for the idea

Mark and I came up with to happen, but I'm clearer now about who I am and what will work for me. That feels great."

DAWN

To keep her agreement with herself about considering different possibilities for Marge's involvement, Dawn plays around with some ideas and also talks to Marge again.

"I still don't know what Marge might do for the organization, but I'm less concerned about it. Going through the IM process helped me see that I was caught in thinking things had to be a certain way, and afterwards I began to see other possibilities. That allowed me, when I talked to Marge again, to be more open and explore ideas with her about what she would enjoy contributing. We haven't made any decisions, but we keep bouncing ideas around and in the meantime, she's helping me stay on track with all the details of getting the organization incorporated. I trust that as things keep moving forward, we'll find the best fit for both Marge and the nonprofit."

KEVIN

Kevin continues to mediate between the three parts of himself that show up in response to his promotion. It takes more than one mediation, each time coming to some small agreement with himself—to talk with his family, to get more information on the new position and what might be possible— and then continuing the conversation from what he learns.

"The most surprising thing was that when I talked with the person who would be my new boss, we started exploring the idea of job sharing in the new role. Even though the position is senior-level, he has managed other job sharers, and he even floated the idea of a colleague I've worked well with in the past who he thought might be interested. Without really listening to all the different parts of myself, I never would have had the conversation that brought up this possibility, and now it's looking like a real one. It keeps me pretty much along the same track financially that I'm already on, but it means having more time with my family than if I was in it on my own, while still gaining experience in this new role. We're still working out details, but I'm excited to take it on."

NEXT UP

The final step of the Internal Mediation map is to make solution requests and agreements, which allows you to take action on your new clarity and internal alignment. As anyone who has tried to make a New Year's resolution has found, however, the path from what you choose in one moment to what you choose later is not always straightforward. Knowing how to make strong requests and agreements creates a smoother path to taking the actions that will produce the life you desire.

5 | BEYOND WILLPOWER

MAKING AGREEMENTS WITH YOURSELF

An agreement cannot be the result of an imposition.
—NESTOR KIRCHNER

———

P EG STEADIES THE SAFETY BAR AS JAMES MARKS WHERE to drill holes in the wall. "How are things going here?" he asks.

Peg sighs. "Mom's getting worse. It's slow, but it's pretty clear. It's taking a lot more time now to take care of her than when I first moved in."

James has come over to help Peg with a few chores at his mother-in-law's house, namely installing a safety bar in the bathtub. "How are you holding up?" he asks.

Peg reflects for a moment on the conflict that she, Sally, and their brother Gerry had when she'd first floated the idea, and how her siblings were opposed. "Well, I can say I have a new appreciation for how hard it is to be a caregiver. Until you've been in these shoes, you just don't have any concept of how difficult it really is, what all it brings up."

James nods as he secures the bar. "I can imagine."

"One thing I've realized," Peg continues, "is how important it is for caregivers to care for themselves. In fact, I actually came up with an idea for a product I'd love to create—care kits for caregivers—but now it's taking more time to care for Mom."

"It sounds like a great idea," James says.

"Thanks, but I've had all this internal conflict about it—I'd like to do it, but I don't have time. Then I remembered the process you and Sally did, so I tried it. It was so confusing! I had at least three different voices speaking up."

James chuckles, relating completely. "What were they?"

"Well, this is really embarrassing, but one part of me rails against spending so much of my time caring for Mom. This all came so soon after my divorce, right when I was trying to get my life together. It seemed perfect at the time. But now, that part of me wanting to move forward—the part that needs freedom to live my own life—feels on hold."

James nods in understanding.

"It was really hard to hear that part of me because another part is so in judgment of it, you know? Saying that I shouldn't want that when Mom has given so much for all of us. When I realized that voice was speaking up for helping Mom stay here in her house and providing a loving home for her during this difficult time, I really got in touch with what a gift it is to be able to provide that comfort and care for her. Plus, another part of me feels compelled to help others who are in this position and create some bigger meaning out of my experience as a caregiver."

"It sounds like you have a part wanting to move forward with your life, and another part in touch with the gift of caring for Mom, and then the third wanting some meaning to come from this, is that right?" James says.

"Yeah. And hearing from all those voices was helpful in understanding why I've been getting irritated at small things with Mom lately. That first part of me gets frustrated about not moving forward with my life, so the smallest things can set me off."

"So you identified your needs for freedom and moving forward with your life, as well as care, stability, and meaning. What are you going to do to get those met?"

"I'm not exactly sure," Peg says. "That's about as far as I got in the process. What do you think about helping me take the next step?"

James smiles. "Sure, let's try it."

———

Following the connection phase of the Internal Mediation map, the needs you would like to meet become clear. This clarity is a gift, a guiding force that opens the way for acting in new, more satisfying ways. When you reach that point, the final step of the IM map—making solution requests and agreements—provides the structure to take that clarity into making change in your life to reach your dream.

If, after doing the IM process, you simply take action on the strategy that the parts of you decided would meet their needs, you may not need an internal conversation for making agreements. For many people, however, trying to take action in a new way will conflict with their habitual ways of acting, making it easy not to follow through. In other words, without thinking through agreements to keep you on track, and how to respond when you don't, the idea of taking action may merely remain an idea.

Because most people aren't taught how to make solid requests and agreements with others, the difficulties are compounded when it comes to making requests and agreements with themselves. In fact, many people don't think to make agreements with

themselves at all, and therefore approach their desire to take new
action in the future in one of the following ways:

+ Hold a vague wish:

  - "Yeah, I'd really like to start an exercise routine."
  - "I think it would be great to find some time to meet
    new people."
  - "I know I should really plan my workday better."

+ Set an intention:

  - "I plan to work out this week."
  - "My intention is to make some new friends."
  - "I'm intending to structure my workday better."

+ Use willpower:

  - "I know I'll be tired after work, but I'm going to
    make myself go to the gym."
  - "I'm so shy, but I've got to go to this party so I can
    meet new people."
  - "I tend to get drawn into work, but I'm going to
    force myself in the morning to think through what
    needs to be done."

+ Set goals:

  - "My goal is to work out three times this week for
    thirty minutes."
  - "I'll find and attend five social events in the next
    month where I can meet new people."
  - "I'm going to schedule fifteen minutes at the start
    and end of each day for planning."

PRACTICE PAUSE

Thinking about your dream, which of these typical approaches to taking new action sound familiar to you? What benefits and drawbacks have you experienced in utilizing those approaches?

What you may or may not have realized at this point is that each of these typical approaches is a way of having a conversation with yourself. While one of these may be working for you—and if so, keep using it—it's been our experience that certain drawbacks tend to commonly arise in applying the above conversations.

For one, vague wishes and intentions often aren't strong enough to actually move people into action, and are hence easily pushed off into a future that never comes. Willpower involves a conversation where one voice is dominating another and forcing submission, which has all the downsides we've already discussed: one voice is not heard, solutions don't work or don't work for long, the unheard voice sabotages efforts, and so on. Finally, while goal setting is the most effective of the four, it still has some room for improvement, as it doesn't address your relationship to yourself or how to be most effective in reaching your goals.

When you have a conversation with yourself about *agreements*, however, you can improve the quality of the actions you take, increase the likelihood you will follow through, and enrich your relationship with yourself.

Before we get to the three types of agreements to make, let's look at making requests, since the requests you make become your agreements.

MAKING REQUESTS

Through the Internal Mediation process, you first uncover the needs you'd like to meet, and in the final step come up with what you would like to do to meet those needs. During the process, mediator mind—the part of you aware of all the competing needs—helps the different internal voices collaborate on requests that satisfy the desires of all. You may have already experienced how each of your internal voices can contribute strategies to help meet its needs, which leads to making a request of the other part of you.

Requests, as we use them, have three elements. They are:

+ **Present**: Requests are stated in the present tense.

+ **Positive**: Ask for what you want instead of what you don't want.

+ **Action Language**: The request is doable, specific, and concrete, meaning you will know if you've done it or not.

Let's take a look at each of these in the context of our internal conversation. (For more about requests in general and in an interpersonal context, see *Choosing Peace*.)

PRESENT

The present moment is really all you have, and this element of requests is acknowledging that even when you are saying something about the future, it's a commitment in present time. As such, it might help to keep in mind that you are making these agreements *now*, even if they are about something you would like to do in the future. (Note that this element tends to be more helpful when two people who have been in conflict are making requests of each other than it is in internal requests.)

POSITIVE

The most effective requests are stated in terms of what you want, not what you don't want. Yet it's sometimes initially clearer what you *don't* want, especially when it comes to your own behavior. In fact, you may have come to use the IM process because you noticed ways you act that upset you. In the previous chapter, part of your internal mediation may have included one or both parts telling the other what it doesn't like, which is completely normal. For example, Sally experienced this with Excited not liking that Safety considers everything for too long, and Safety not liking that Excited jumps in without thinking. The problem with creating requests or agreements focused on what you don't want, however, is that you will then stay focused on judgment in assessing your ongoing behavior, which is not the result we're striving for.

While we don't want you stuck in a pattern of berating yourself, uncovering what you don't like *can* be a helpful step in clarifying what you *do* want. Just remember that if you start with what you'd like to stop doing, be sure to take the next step and ask yourself what you would prefer instead. The answer to that question becomes your request.

Here are some examples of what you *don't* want and how they might be translated into what you *do* want:

+ I need to stop being rude to my mother-in-law. = If I feel upset when I'm around my mother-in-law, then I'll take a deep breath and silently count to ten.

+ I don't want to turn to food when I'm stressed. = If I notice I'm stressed and want to reach for food, then I'll take a walk.

+ I'd like to stop wasting my free time. = If I have free time coming up, then I'll plan what I'd like to do during that time.

+ I don't want to get angry and lash out at my partner. = If
  I notice the precursors to anger, then I will do the
  Self-Connection Process.

In these cases, you can see that there are two parts to the positive request—noticing when the behavior is happening or about to happen, and the new behavior you'd like to carry out instead. "If . . . then . . ." is helpful phrasing in these situations: "If [I notice behavior about to happen that I don't want], then I will [do something to interrupt my habitual pattern]."

ACTION LANGUAGE

If you create an agreement with yourself, you need to have a way of knowing whether you're keeping it or not. Let's take a common example: Perhaps your agreement is to take better care of yourself. That's a pretty vague agreement that could include any number of things:

+ Being in bed by ten p.m.

+ Going for a thirty-minute walk five times a week

+ Saying no to any invitations on Sundays

+ Scheduling meetings only between one and four p.m.

+ Eating only whole foods

Leaving the agreement as simply "I'm going to take better care of myself" is not in action language, whereas the individual agreements above are doable, specific, and concrete. It's easy to track if you were in bed by ten p.m., said yes to any Sunday events, or ate a donut. Hence, you don't want to leave an agreement in language that has a judgment or is unspecific. It not only makes it difficult to fulfill, but it's nearly impossible to assess later whether you did or not.

> ### PRACTICE PAUSE
>
> Name a request that will help you move toward your dream, and make sure it follows the elements of a request: it is present, positive, and in action language.

TYPES OF AGREEMENTS

As each part of you comes up with requests, ensure that they are present, positive, and stated in action language. When you find one or more requests that both parts of you are willing to try, you have an agreement about how to move forward to meet your needs.

Agreements are what turn the idea of new strategies into a reality in your life.

We recommend making three types of agreements. To introduce the three types, let's hear from Chris, Kevin, and Dawn about challenges they've faced in the past when they wanted to do things differently.

CHRIS

"In the past, I've tried to lose weight. That was my sole focus, and I didn't get specific about what I would change, or how my behavior and habits would shift, to get where I wanted to go. Even though at the time I thought I was clear, now I see that it was a pretty ambiguous and imprecise way to go about my health goals. I suspect that's why my results never lasted. I didn't really make any agreements with myself about what I was doing or how to do it."

KEVIN

"When it comes to work, I have no problem knowing what to do and doing it. In my personal life, though, especially when it comes to not allowing work to take over my life completely, I have a hard time following through. Countless times I've promised my wife, and even promised myself, that I would change in some way—whether it was about coming home earlier, or leaving work at the office, or unplugging on a vacation—and then I didn't fulfill that promise. It's embarrassing to admit, actually. It's no wonder my wife has trouble trusting that this time will be any different—part of me has trouble trusting it too. Following through on these kinds of agreements is my challenge."

DAWN

"I'm pretty good about making agreements with other people—I've learned that the hard way, through projects I've worked on with others, especially with my husband and kids. I found early on that being clear really helped, and I've been able to apply that to any change I'd like to make too. Where I struggle is when I'm not able to follow through. I just get so down on myself. It's important to me to care for others and to follow through on what I say, so when I don't, I tend to really beat myself up, and it's hard for me to get past that and move on. When it's an agreement I've had with myself, it's so painful to let myself down that I've sometimes ignored it completely, dropping what I wanted to do because I didn't know how to deal with my disappointment in myself."

In hearing from our three companions, it's clear that Chris's challenge with his health has been making strong primary agreements—agreements that follow the elements of requests and are a clear strategy to meet his needs. Kevin has more of a challenge with the second type of agreements we suggest making—supporting agreements—which help you follow through on your primary agreements. Dawn's tendency to beat herself up or drop an agreement if she doesn't fulfill it points to the importance of the third type—restoring agreements—wherein you choose ahead of time how you will treat yourself and what you will do in the event you don't complete your other agreements. Let's take a closer look at each of these types of agreements.

PRIMARY AGREEMENTS

> **primary agreements** *n.pl.*
> the strategies that all parts of you believe will meet the needs surfaced in the internal mediation

When one or more parts of you have made requests that all parts of you accept, we call these your primary agreements. Primary agreements may be about taking specific action or about changing typical patterns of behavior. While the lines may be blurry between the two, simply recognize that both options may arise after an internal mediation.

Examples of specific action agreements include:

+ Write an email to accept the offer to present at the conference.

+ Call a client about money they owe me.

✦ Go for a walk for thirty minutes five times a week.

✦ Meditate for at least twenty minutes daily.

✦ Talk to my boss about a raise next week.

✦ Do the Internal Mediation process about whether to ask my boss for a raise.

These agreements are all specific, doable, and you can assess whether you did them or not. Some may sound similar to goals, and if you're used to the type of goal setting that also stresses actionable behavior, you can use that method to make your primary agreements.

Changing a behavior pattern often entails first becoming aware in the moment you are beginning your typical response, then choosing to do something different. The awareness may come from particular thoughts, feelings, or sensations, which lead you to choose how you want to focus your mind differently, then act in a way that will lead to a more satisfying result than your typical pattern.

Here are examples of primary agreements aimed at changing a behavior pattern:

✦ If I notice I feel urgent to be heard, then I'll stop what I'm saying to do Self-Connection Process.

✦ When I feel tense during a meeting, I'll take two deep breaths into my belly before speaking.

✦ When I think, *I can't do that*, I'll ask that part of me what need it's seeking to meet in saying that.

With many dreams, even after performing the Internal Mediation process, it's likely you'll come up with requests and agreements that are still scary for some part of you, like Sally deciding to present at the conference. If you have made a primary agreement and still feel some dread, challenge, or discomfort in thinking about it, break it down into smaller steps. The one big agreement (present at conference) can be made into a series of small agreements, with your focus on, "Can I feel at ease and be present with my needs with each smaller step?" For example, Sally, in her plan to prepare for the presentation, broke down her commitment into these agreements:

1. Write the email accepting the invitation to present.

2. Schedule time to brainstorm points to cover in the presentation.

3. Brainstorm points to cover in the presentation.

4. Make travel plans.

5. Talk to James about planning for childcare while away.

6. Schedule time to write the title and description for the talk.

7. Write the title and description.

8. Send in the title and description to organizers.

9. Plan the talk.

10. Prepare any visual materials (presentation, handouts).

11. Practice the presentation.

12. At any point I notice Safety has concerns about being accepted, I will do Self-Empathy.

13. Ask James, Alicia, or Shawn to be available for support before and after the presentation.

14. Ask the organizers if I can have someone videotape the presentation so that I can use it for speaker clips and learn what I can improve.

As you can see, breaking down the overarching agreement into smaller ones makes it feel much more doable, as well as easier to plan in segments. Notice, too, that Sally includes on her list the agreements she made to take care of herself emotionally. As she takes action on each of these agreements, she can continue to check in with her needs, reassessing and adding any agreements that will support her in meeting those needs.

You may not require this level of planning with every agreement on the way to your dream; however, if you've had self-sabotaging thoughts arise and been through the Internal Mediation process, making these agreements with yourself can be instrumental in moving forward. They are also a way to help if you experience procrastination and overwhelm, though these are also opportunities to listen to your inner conversation and see if there's a conflict to mediate.

—⁓—

James asks Peg to set up three chairs to represent the different parts of her. "Do any of these parts of you have a request that it thinks would meet all the needs?" he asks.

Peg moves to Freedom's chair, and says, "I'd like it if we could get a little help with Mom so I can have a bit more time on my own. And to have that time really be off so I can focus on something else. Right now, it feels like I'm always on."

James suggests that Peg move to the chair of the part of her that would like to respond. Peg switches to Care's chair and first reflects back what was said.

"You'd like some help with Mom so we have a bit more downtime. My concern with that is feeling confident that Mom is cared for. I don't want some stranger in here doing things for her. I guess what would work for me is to have some help with all the 'extra' tasks that take up time, like grocery shopping and cooking, or handling some of the behind-the-scenes tasks like getting Mom's finances straightened out. It's great having you here today, James, to help out with these household things. I hate to lean on you and Sally any more, you both already do so much and are so busy, but maybe we could all sit down and brainstorm how I can get some help with these things."

James nods. "I'm willing, and I'm sure Sally will be too, but we can ask her when she gets back with Mom."

Peg then moves to Meaning's chair. "If we can find a way to create a bit more time, I'd love it if we could focus a bit on this idea I have and see where it goes, have that time be put to some good use."

Peg nearly jumps over to Freedom's chair again, saying "Yes! I'm in with that. I'd really like some forward movement on something that's our creation."

Realizing Care has a response to this request as well, Peg again changes chairs. "I'd like to speak up for care for us too, not just care for Mom. I get that spending time on something that is meaningful and moving our life ahead is one kind of care, and I'd like to make sure that our overall well-being is taken into consideration. That would include other self-care too, like more physical activity and doing something fun. Maybe we can combine those, like take a walk for thirty minutes or so a day and use that time to mull over ideas for the product. And how fun would it be to get together with someone for lunch to talk through this idea?"

Peg considers this for a moment, then looks at James. "That feels good, all voices in agreement. What now?"

James reflects what he's heard so far. "So you have an agreement to talk to Sally and me about how to get more help with some of the things that take time, and that when you do have time, you use it for self-care—especially activity and fun—and to start working on this idea." James grabs a pad of paper and jots it all down. "Any agreements about where to start with your idea?"

Peg moves back to Meaning's chair. "I see the two places to start as just getting the idea out on paper, brainstorm what all could be included, and do some research about how to go about creating a product like this. And I like the idea after that of sharing it with one or two people . . . I have a couple friends in mind who might be interested."

Peg's face lights up talking about what to work on, then gets pensive again as she moves back to Care's chair. "So we have an agreement to start with writing out the idea for the product of caregiver kits, brainstorm what might be included, and do research, then set up a time to share the idea and get feedback. I would like to bring up one other thing, which is about getting irritated easily. I'd like some agreement about not doing that, though I'm not sure what it would be right now."

Peg pauses a moment, then shifts back to Freedom's chair. "I suspect that if these other agreements happen, then it won't be as much of an issue. But just in case, how about something like, if I notice I'm getting irritated, I'll stop, check in with myself, and plan for when I can take a break?" Peg looks questioningly at James.

James suggests, "Maybe when you check in, look for your needs in that moment?"

Peg nods. "Yes, okay, so I'll stop, check in with my needs, and see when I can take a break."

Peg moves back to Care's spot to check in and see if that meets Care's needs. "Yes, that sounds good."

James finishes the list of Peg's primary agreements:

+ Brainstorm with Sally/James how to get more support with tasks so I have a little more time for myself.

+ Use extra time for self-care and working on new product idea.

  • Take a thirty-minute walk each day and use that time to think about product.

+ Write down idea, brainstorm what to include, and do research about creating product.

+ Set up time with a friend to talk through idea and get feedback.

+ If I feel irritated, I'll stop, check in with my needs, and plan when I can take a break.

PRACTICE PAUSE

What primary agreements can you create to help you move toward your dream? Do you have agreements for both specific actions and for changing behavior, if needed?

SUPPORTING AGREEMENTS

Have you ever made an agreement with yourself—perhaps to work out every day or stop eating candy at your desk—and then broken that agreement sooner than you expected? Often, making an agreement isn't enough, and you need some support to fulfill it.

> **supporting agreements** *n.pl.*
> agreements to support the fulfillment of the primary agreement

Though the agreement you're making is with yourself, and you may believe you'll keep it, it's still a good idea to assume that something may come up. For this reason, you'll want to think through what will support you to do what you desire. Definitely make these types of agreements if any part of you is suspicious that you won't follow through on the primary agreement for any reason.

Supporting agreements can come in a variety of different forms:

+ Agreements that help you keep the primary agreement
+ Agreements to check in later to see how the primary agreement is going and reassess if any changes might be necessary
+ Agreements with other people to help you keep the primary agreement or assess how it's going
+ Agreements with other people to give you feedback about how you're doing with your primary agreement

Here are two examples of primary agreements and what each of the above supporting agreements might sound like:

Primary Agreements		While working on my computer, I agree to change positions and stretch 2x each hour	I agree to respond to my daughter with empathy first, especially when I feel annoyed by her behavior
Supporting Agreements			
With:	To:		
Yourself	Help you keep primary agreement	Set alarm or use app on computer to prompt me to get up	If I notice I feel annoyed, then I will take a deep breath and connect with my needs
Yourself	Check in to assess and make changes	Schedule time on Saturday to think through previous week and plan changes for next week	After putting her to bed, I will note how many times I responded with empathy and what helped me do so
Other people	Keep or assess agreement	Ask my friend to text me at random time (when it fits in her day) to see whether I've changed position recently	Ask my husband, if he sees me react to her in a way he interprets as annoyed, to ask me, "Are you feeling annoyed?"
Other people	Provide feedback	Ask my massage therapist to tell me any positive changes she notices in my muscles	Ask my husband to tell me if he notices any changes in my interactions with our daughter

What you want to do is create agreements that will support you to do what you agreed to do in the primary agreement, and add any that emerge as you begin to take action. For example, as Sally moves forward on her list of agreements related to presenting at the conference, she finds that she could use some additional help. When she runs into questions in brainstorming her topic, she creates a supporting agreement to reach out to the meeting organizers and ask for a conversation to make sure she is on track with what they are planning. As she gets closer to the presentation date, she asks James, Corey, and Maggie to be her audience so she can practice. She also makes a supporting agreement with her friend Alicia that she can call her for empathy while at the conference.

When the primary agreement is about an ongoing behavior, supporting agreements can help you anticipate what might keep you from doing what you have committed to do. For example, let's say Chris decides that in order to get more sleep to support his health, he'll go to bed at 10 p.m. every night. After creating this primary agreement, he thinks through what tends to keep him up until midnight or later.

"Any number of things can get in the way of this agreement. After spending time with my wife and kids, sometimes I just want some time on my own, and that tends to come in the later evening after the kids go to bed. I'll stay up watching a movie or a TV show, even if it's not something I'm interested in, because it feels like just going to bed doesn't give me time for me. Or, if I have a project or deadline at work, then sometimes I stay up late to keep working."

Chris explains the supporting agreements he creates: "When I notice I want to watch TV, I'll do Self-Empathy first to connect with my needs. I want to be aware of why I'm watching, and if it's to meet needs for fun and entertainment, great! On the other hand, I don't want to watch a movie or TV show as a way to self-medicate or avoid difficult feelings. If I'm tempted to watch for any other reason than fun and entertainment, then I'll ask, 'What can I do that would actually meet my needs right now?' If I do watch TV, I'll also set an alarm that alerts me when to stop the program, and I'll stop it even if it's in the middle of a sentence so I can get to bed on time. I'll also use the alarm if I'm going to work in the evening to make sure I don't lose track of time. And, my wife is much better about consistently going to bed around that time, so I've asked her to pop in and ask, if she sees me still up when she's headed to bed, 'What's your plan for getting to bed tonight?' Since I've told her what question to ask me, it will prompt me to actually think about it rather than react out of my needs for autonomy or respect, especially if I've managed to bypass the other supporting agreements."

PRACTICE PAUSE

What supporting agreements might help you fulfill the primary agreements you named in the previous Practice Pause?

James asks Peg, "What would help you keep these agreements? Are there concerns that any part of you has about any of them?"

Peg considers it for a moment and then moves back to Freedom's chair. "I'm concerned that the time won't really happen. I know how these things go . . . it sounds like a good idea and then doesn't pan out in real life."

James asks, "What supporting agreements in your view might help make it more likely for you to have more time for yourself?"

"I guess a good start, even before talking to you and Sally, would be to list all the things that someone else could take on. I know a few were brought up, but a more complete list might be easier to work from. I think it may be important to set up a time, maybe weekly, to look back over how the week went and whether I had some extra time or not."

"Both of those are good ideas," James agrees, then seeks to clarify how Peg envisions checking in. "With the weekly check-in, would it help if that's with someone else, or would you do that on your own?"

"I think on my own to start, and maybe calling you or Sally if I have a question or need to troubleshoot a challenge that arises—if that's okay with you, of course."

James nods. "We can talk to Sally about that later too. Anything else that would help?"

Peg moves to Meaning's chair. "Just a silly one, but I'd like to put into the calendar for a couple weeks from now to send an email or call my friend to set up that lunch date. That will give a sort of deadline to have the idea written out and do some research."

"I don't think that's silly at all." James adds that to the list as Peg moves to Care's chair. "In that check-in time, I'd also like some attention to the self-care piece, whether there are any tweaks to make in that area. So maybe just add that check-in is not just about whether we had some extra time, but how we used it. Also, I know Freedom doesn't think the irritation will come up anymore, but I'd like some supporting agreement in case it does. I know how strong it can be, and it just takes over. If that happens, perhaps we could have a list of people to call. What do you think of that idea?"

"Sure," James says, "then if one person isn't available, you can try the next. Perhaps specify what to do on that call and the length. It would be easier for me, for example, if I knew it wouldn't be longer than five minutes, and what you'd need from me—*if* you wanted me on the list!" he adds with a chuckle.

Peg smiles. "Of course I do! I just hate bothering people . . . but having a list and a time limit would make it easier for me to follow through. So I'll ask at least three people if they're willing to be on this list, and if they'd be okay with me calling for no more than five minutes to empathize if I feel too irritated to discern my needs on my own."

James finalizes Peg's list of supporting agreements:

+ Create list of all tasks someone else might handle to free up time, for discussion with Sally and James.

+ Schedule weekly check-in time to look over week, whether I had some time for me, and also to check in on how I used that time, including both self-care and working on product idea.

+ If needed, enlist outside support for check-in time.

+ Ask three people to be on list for empathy call of no more than five minutes, when I feel too irritated to discern my needs.

———

RESTORING AGREEMENTS

Making an agreement with yourself is not about being perfect. Agreements will be broken; in fact, it's often easier for people to keep agreements with others than it is with themselves. That's why accountability partners can be so helpful when it comes to making change.

In hearing from internal voices in the IM process, one of those voices may express concern about being able to keep the agreement. In that case, supporting agreements can assure that part of you that you have a plan to meet its needs, and you also

may want to create a restoring agreement—one that says what you
will do in the event you don't keep the primary agreement.

> restoring agreements *n.pl.*
>
> agreements that address what will happen if the
> primary agreement is not kept for whatever reason

When people don't keep agreements, including internal ones,
the tendency is to go into blame and shame. The problem is, we
don't find that judgment helps us keep the agreement better next
time; instead, it tends to lead toward avoiding self-punishment,
which often means dropping the agreement entirely. Plus, it's
simply not enjoyable to be depressed, feel guilty, or beat yourself
up for not keeping an agreement.

One kind of restoring agreement, then, is about how you will
treat yourself if you don't keep the primary agreement. How will
you deal with your emotional response to not upholding the bar-
gain you made with yourself? For example, you might make an
agreement that says you will do one or more of the following:

+ Practice Self-Empathy.

+ Go through Self-Connection Process.

+ Acknowledge and celebrate the needs you were meeting
  in what you did instead, and mourn the needs you didn't
  meet by not fulfilling your agreement (see Chapter 6).

+ Remind yourself that you are human, that making
  agreements isn't about being perfect, and ask what you
  can learn from it to help you next time.

The other kind of restoring agreement to make is a practical one. If you don't keep the primary agreement, it's possible you may need to revisit it to assess if there's a way to change it that would make it more likely you will keep it next time. Or perhaps you need a different supporting agreement in place. Each time you do an assessment, you'll want to reconnect with your needs, not as "past" needs from the mediation, but needs you currently would like to meet. As much as possible, keep your agreements in the present, not a demand you're making on yourself now because you made the agreement earlier. When you're connected with the needs you'd like to meet, your action can flow from there.

It's important to note here that this is not about revisiting the primary agreement as a cop-out, as in *Well, I didn't keep the agreement, so maybe I shouldn't have it in the first place.* It's quite common for people to bite off more than they can chew, and revisiting may look like breaking down the agreement into smaller pieces, or otherwise shifting it so it's more likely to be kept.

In addition, when you first come up with a primary agreement, you may not have all the information to make the best possible agreement. Restoring agreements recognize the reality that as you move through your life, you will learn more. In other words, you start with an agreement that feels "good enough," and as you live with it and/or fail at times to keep it, you learn more about what will most help you make the change you desire.

If you are working with someone else—an enlisted support person or accountability partner—consider being very specific in restoring agreements about what role you're asking them to play if you report to them that you didn't keep your agreement. Typical mainstream roles of accountability partners include:

+ Coaching you
+ Advising you with solutions about how you can do it better next time
+ Consoling you: "It's okay, you'll do better next time."
+ Being a cheerleader: "You can do it! I know you can!"

For our purposes, we suggest that instead of the above list, you ask that your partner give you *empathy*. This involves looking into the need you were seeking to meet with the choice you made instead of keeping the agreement. If your partner is not well versed in empathy as we're using it, then request that they ask you a question to prompt you to reflect on this for yourself, such as, "What need were you meeting when you did _____ instead of keeping the agreement?"

After you receive empathy, you may find that you desire and are open to one of the more typical roles listed above. Likewise, if you find you'd like some more ideas about what you can try next time, you can ask for suggestions. It's rare that anyone wants coaching, solutions, or advice before they receive empathy, so with restoring agreements that include other people, always err on the side of requesting empathy.

PRACTICE PAUSE

What restoring agreements can you make in the event you do not fulfill your other agreements?

Peg turns to James, a concerned look on her face. "What if I don't do these things, though? Like if I don't use my extra time in a good way, or I don't call someone if I feel irritated, or I just snap at Mom?"

James says gently, "That's what the other type of agreement is for, because any of those may well happen. It helps to have restoring agreements in place for how you'll treat yourself and what you'll do in that case."

"I see."

"For example, what would you typically do if you didn't follow through on an agreement?"

"Hmm . . . I'd be upset with myself, even angry, and tell myself I've got to do better."

"Okay," James says. "What would you prefer to do instead?"

"I guess I'd like to understand what happened and be able to learn from it, so I can actually do it differently."

"That's great. A lot of the tools you already know can help with that," James explains. "You can do Self-Empathy or SCP, or you can go back to internal mediation if you need to. Finding and connecting with your needs is really the key to changing that relationship with yourself when you don't do what you said you would."

Peg has a realization and perks up. "I think what I'd like to try is asking myself a question, like when I've broken an agreement and I'm starting down that path, I can just ask, 'What tool can I use right now to help me connect with myself?' Then use it!"

"Great!" James writes it down. "And anything about the learning piece, like looking at the agreement to see if it needs to be changed?"

"Well, I guess I would use whatever tool comes to mind, and then ask whether the agreement can be changed or I can put a new supporting agreement into place."

James writes down Peg's restoring agreements:

- If I notice I'm upset or angry at myself for not fulfilling an agreement, I'll ask, "What tool can I use right now to help me connect with myself?"
- I'll ask whether the agreement can be changed or a new supporting agreement created.

—◦◦◦—

In summary, primary agreements result from requests that you anticipate will meet the needs uncovered in the mediation. Once you have your primary agreements, think through what will help you fulfill them by making supporting agreements. Then, decide how you will respond with restoring agreements, should you not keep the primary ones for any reason.

Supporting and restoring agreements serve as reminders that when you're making any change in behavior, it's likely that you won't succeed all the time, especially at first. As we've mentioned, people often react with self-judgment when they have made an agreement and then find they are still acting out the old behavior. But this is unhelpful and unnecessary, because behavioral change is not easy, and it takes repetition to make changes that go against habitual patterns. If you find that judgment and shame are common responses for you, you may want to create supporting and restoring agreements that help you connect with yourself and your needs instead.

Let's see what agreements Chris, Dawn, and Kevin come up with to support taking action on their dreams.

CHRIS

Even though Chris and Mark have reorganized the trip—with the blessing of all the guys—Chris still finds that his Dream Protector self is concerned about him making healthy choices while away from home. To increase his chances of success, Chris engages with this part of himself to devise some agreements. Here are the **primary agreements** he comes up with:

1. Stick to healthy foods—whole foods, focusing on protein and produce—but allow myself a treat food once a day.

2. Limit alcohol consumption to two drinks in the evening.

3. Engage in at least an hour of activity during each day of the trip.

"Based on my past experience, I can think of a number of scenarios that might keep me from making the choices that I'll be happy with later. Reflecting on these situations, I've come up with some **supporting agreements:**

1. Plan for my own healthy food, not rely on others.

2. Ask Mark for accountability support: check in with him at the end of the day to report on any treat foods I ate and my alcohol consumption.

3. Buy my favorite tasty non-alcoholic beverages to have on hand.

4. Start the evening with a non-alcoholic drink, then one alcoholic, then another non-alcoholic, then if I still want it, a second alcoholic drink.

5. Aim for seven hours of sleep each night, since making healthy choices is easier when I'm rested.

"Since the trip now revolves around some fun outdoor activities, I don't think a supporting agreement regarding activity is necessary. In fact, I suspect I'll get more during the trip than in my normal routine at home!"

Chris knows that even with his supporting agreements, he still may not manage to always keep to healthy choices, and comes to these **restoring agreements:**

1.   Check in about what need I was meeting when I indulged.

2.   Remind myself that every moment is a chance to make a new choice, including this moment.

"This last one will help me avoid the slippery slope I've run into in the past, where I make one unhealthy choice and then think, *Well, I blew it today, so I'll just start again tomorrow,* and then keep making unhealthy choices."

DAWN

As Dawn continues the process of creating the nonprofit, she recognizes that she both needs and wants to include others in the process. "In the past, most projects I took on were smaller, so I could be the main director. But this venture is much bigger, and I know I can't do everything myself. Plus I think the organization will be stronger overall if I can let go of total ownership and allow others to contribute. What I find, though, is that there's a part of me that has strong ideas about what to do and how to do it! That part comes into conflict with the part of me that would like others to be involved. I started to see this conflict in what happened with Marge, and since then I've been noticing it more. When I did an internal mediation between these two—the part that knows how things should be and wants to be in control, and the part that wants to include others—I found needs for excellence, empowerment, support, and cooperation. Here are the agreements I've made:

Primary Agreements:

1.   Notice when I have a strong point of view and want to take control, do SCP, and then ask myself, "Is now the time for control, or is now the time for collaboration?"

2.   If I react to a proposed course of action or reject it out of hand, I will do Self-Empathy.

Supporting Agreements:

1. Find a coach I can work with as I go through this process, someone who can work with me on how I'm being in the process of creating the organization.

2. Create a daily practice in which I use at least one of the Mediate Your Life tools with something that's going on in my work to create this nonprofit, so I'm more likely to think of them in the moment.

Restoring Agreements:

1. If I forget my agreements, I'll empathize with myself.

2. I'll talk to my coach about the situation to continue refining my understanding of when control is helpful and when collaboration will create better results.

KEVIN

As the possibility of job sharing takes shape, Kevin and his colleague, Rick, agree to take on the challenge. "I'm super excited about it, and at the same time I know that some agreements will help me stay focused on meeting all the needs the different parts of me were expressing in the internal mediation I did when considering the position. Especially the part of me concerned that I'll continue to focus entirely on work, when now I have the chance to have a bit more time away from it. Here are the agreements I've come up with so far:

Primary Agreements:

1. Do not work during non-work times—leave work at work!

2. Plan more activities with my family, friends, and on my own.

3. Create a list of things I'd like to do—projects outside of work I'd enjoy.

Supporting Agreements:

1. Make sure Rick and I have a solid agreement about when we each are working, when we are off, and communication protocols regarding contacting each other in respective off times.

2. When I am drawn to work in non-work times, connect with my needs and ask, "Is this essential now, or can it wait?"

3. Schedule time to check in once a week about my primary agreements.

Restoring Agreements:

1. If I don't do what I said I would do, then I'll empathize with the needs I met in what I did choose.

2. I will revisit all agreements and revise them as needed to continue tweaking for optimal balance as situations change.

NEXT UP

As you know, making strong agreements supports you in taking the actions to reach your dreams. Still, you will find that you mess up on your agreements, or you take action in a way that you don't enjoy. If you tend to resort to self-judgment in these situations while you're taking steps to reach your dream, it makes taking the next step even more difficult. In the next chapter, we'll show you how to hear that critical voice in a new way that will actually help you with future action.

6

STOP BEATING YOURSELF UP

BEFRIENDING YOUR INNER EDUCATOR

Each time you judge yourself, you break your own heart.
—SWAMI KRIPALUANANDAJI (BAPUJI)

———

SALLY CLOSES MAGGIE'S DOOR AND SIGHS WITH RELIEF. *I'm done! Mags on her way to sleep, and Corey in his room. He'll go to bed when he's ready . . . I've already said good night to him.* Walking out to the kitchen, she ignores the stack of dishes waiting by the sink and looks at this week's calendar hanging on the fridge. Seeing James's night out with his buddies marked on today's date, Sally moves their regular Friday evening pow-wow regarding household scheduling to the next day. Glancing back over the past week, Sally feels weary. *Why am I so tired?* she wonders. *This was a pretty normal week. Well, normal crazy.*

A voice chimes in to answer her question. *Well, all week, you really didn't get to bed when you said you would. You took Maggie to rehearsals for the school play on two nights, and last night you were up especially late finishing work after everyone was in bed. What hap-*

pened to taking care of yourself? Sally senses something inside her struggling against this voice as it continues. *And taking care of yourself means eating well and exercising too. And how did you do on those this week?* Sally hears the sarcasm clearly as she remembers how the week went. *Yeah, exactly,* her inner voice continues. *You stopped for fast food twice and also managed to skip a couple meals. As for exercise, well . . . nothing much to say there, since you didn't do any. If you can't even do the simplest things to take care of yourself, how have you managed to keep your family alive?*

Sally can feel herself closing off in the face of this onslaught and thinks she should probably just go to bed. However, she pushes the thought away as she grabs a pint of ice cream from the freezer and curls up on the couch. Flipping through channels on the TV, she finds a movie to watch and digs in.

—⁓—

You have your dream and plan, you've made decisions and have created strong agreements with yourself, and now you're acting on that plan to create your dream. Do you ever notice that you take action and then criticize yourself harshly for what you did?

Judging yourself for your actions is a key barrier that can arise, potentially stopping you from moving forward on your dream. For example, let's say your dream is co-creating a business with a friend. Your friend asks for your feedback about a decision she made, you candidly tell her your opinion, and she gets upset. Which of the following ways of thinking about what happened is more likely for you?

Wow, that didn't go too well. I like that I was open about what I said, and I said it with the best intention to respond and support my friend and our business. It didn't have the result I wanted—I met some needs, but didn't meet others. I'd like to think through how I could better meet all of these needs. It's important to me to be honest with myself about what happened and what I can change when what I do doesn't produce the results I desire.

Or

Oh wow, I really screwed that up. Why did she ask for my feedback if she didn't want it? She didn't get my intention or what I said at all. I probably shouldn't have said it . . . I should've known that she didn't really want feedback and anticipated that she'd be upset. And how stupid of me to respond the way I did when she did get upset. I should've done better. I'm awful at relationships. I'll never be able to do them right.

Some version of the second response is, for most people, a much more likely scenario. Instead of simply being able to look at what happened, many folks catastrophize, not only judging themselves, but taking those judgments to their logical end, which culminates in how awful they are as a human being. The conclusions included in the second scenario are:

+ The other person is wrong for interpreting what I said without caring about my intention (i.e., They're wrong for reacting to what I said.).
+ I'm wrong for saying what I said.
+ I'm wrong for not magically knowing what would upset her.
+ I'm wrong for not responding better when she got upset.

Intrusive thoughts about how you handled the situation revolve around how you might have done better, what you should have said or done, and what you should not have said or done. These kinds of thoughts are common and keep people from being able to shift out of judgment and into effective action moving forward.

If you grew up immersed in a culture of judgment, it might be difficult to even notice when you are judging yourself. The sense of wrongness about you and your actions can be pervasive and subtle, and it may take some time to notice how you typically make yourself wrong. You might notice that you're judging yourself from how you feel or the thoughts in your mind. Any of the following can provide a clue that you're in judgment:

+ Looking at what you did and finding fault with it, such as saying, "You screwed up."

+ Beating yourself up: "Why can't you . . ." or "Why didn't you . . ." or "You could have . . ." or "You shouldn't have done that!"

+ Feeling shame, guilt, anger, or depression

+ Comparing yourself to how others act or the results they achieve

+ Blanket generalizations or conclusions about yourself: "You're not good at this." "People don't like you." "You'll never succeed." "You're a _____ [loser, idiot, failure, etc.]."

These patterns of thinking and feeling can become habitual, which makes them more difficult to notice, because they seem to automatically arise, unbidden. What's more, you only become aware after the fact, sometimes much later. But there is an antidote for this—the process in this chapter will help you become aware of these patterns more quickly and transform your self-judgments into self-connection.

> ## PRACTICE PAUSE
>
> Think of a recent time you judged yourself in taking action to reach a dream. What did you say to yourself? How did you feel? What impact did these thoughts and feelings have on you?

The key here is that you are judging yourself for something that has happened in the past regarding your plan to move toward your dream. You might judge yourself because you:

+ didn't do what you said you would
+ executed on your plan but didn't like what you did
+ executed on your plan but didn't like how you did it
+ executed on your plan but didn't like the result

Let's see how these judgments show up for Sally, Chris, Dawn, and Kevin.

———

Saturday morning, Sally wakes up as James gets out of bed. "No, it's too early to get up," she groans.

James chuckles. "It's nearly eight o'clock. I better make sure Maggie hasn't taken over the world yet."

"Or at least the kitchen," Sally adds, remembering the morning Maggie decided to make pancakes on her own before James and Sally were up. Corey, somewhat gleefully, had come to tell them that the kitchen was covered in flour. They thought he was exaggerating. He wasn't.

"Exactly." James kisses Sally then leaves the room, shutting the door behind him.

Sally closes her eyes to try and catch a bit more sleep, but thoughts crowd out any chance of further rest. *Hellooooo, why do you think you feel crappy this morning? Staying up late and eating a pint of ice cream, what were you thinking? You made a stupid choice when you knew you should go to bed. Now you've ruined your weekend. You know you'll be tired and crabby, you won't be able to enjoy spending time with the kids, and you won't be able to connect with James. Who are you to think you can do all of this? You can't even take care of yourself. You're a failure, totally defective. I mean, really.*

Sally groans again. "I'm going to need help with this," she says out loud, reaching for her phone. She texts her friend Alicia.

Morning! How r u? Have any time? Could use some help.

Good! Shawn & I having coffee. Sure, what's up?

Let's just say, pint ice cream + movie = you FAILURE you!!!

LOL okay, talk in half hour?

☺

While Sally is judging herself for not taking care of herself as she promised—and her choice the evening before was due in part to judging herself for her lack of self-care the entire week—for Chris it's more about how following his plan to create a healthy lifestyle wasn't so easy in a particular situation. In fact, he didn't like the result of how he handled it:

CHRIS

"My family and I went to a wedding last weekend. I've been doing so well with all of my new healthy habits that I thought it would be easy at this event. Boy, was I wrong! I pretty much blew it. There were so many of my favorite unhealthy foods there. Between that and the social pressure of other people and fitting in with folks, I ate way too much. I thought I wouldn't want unhealthy foods, and if I did I would just take small portions of them. Well, I did want them, and all those small portions really added up. I actually went a bit unconscious about how much I was eating. I can't believe I did that because I should know better by now! I was stupid for assuming I would be able to make the same choices I would at home. It's been really hard since the weekend . . . I keep feeling like I'm a total failure, and I'm never going to be where I'd like to be with my health."

Now let's look at Dawn and how she falls into emotional self-recrimination based on judgments of how she carried out her choice.

DAWN

"I had a meeting with my new board of directors, and I've been feeling guilty ever since. We were talking about programs, and my vision is this center where kids can come and learn all different arts. I get that my vision is bigger than where we can start, but the board thinks that instead of that direction, we should just have a program that goes into the schools. I feel strongly about having a center, a place separate from the schools, even if it starts small. I remembered my agreements about asking whether this is a moment for control or collaboration, and I decided on control, and I'm fine with that. I just don't like how I did it. I did this heavy-handed, do-it-my-way-or-the-highway thing, reminding me of what I did sometimes as a mom trying to corral my kids to do chores or get into the car to go to school. I feel so bad about it. I don't know whether I can really run an organization. I can't treat people like they're kids when they don't do what I think is right. Maybe I'm just not cut out for this."

Kevin is struggling over making his desired choice and then not enjoying the result of that choice.

KEVIN

"It's proving trickier than I thought to stay away from work during my off times. Rick and I are still working out kinks in job sharing, and the other day, which was my day off, I felt pulled to take care of some work to make it easier on Rick and myself on my next workday. I asked myself the question about whether it was essential or could wait, and I decided it could wait. I spent the day with my wife and kids going through our garage, but the thing is, I didn't really enjoy it, since my mind kept going back to the work I thought I should be doing. The same voice that was judging me about not doing the work went into overdrive my next workday, blaming me for that day being more difficult and stressful because I hadn't taken care of things on my day off. So I chose to do what I wanted to, which was not doing work in my off time, but the fallout has been horrendous. I have no idea what to do from here."

JUDGMENT OF PAST CHOICES

At every moment, you are making choices about what to do or say, and a part of you evaluates these choices after you make them. This occurs with the hope that you'll learn from the choices you made so you can make better ones in the future. In other words, this internal Educator provides an inner feedback system so that you can consistently learn from your interactions with the environment. The problem is not that this feedback system exists; indeed, it is an essential part of the ability to learn. The problem is that the Educator frequently operates from the mistaken belief that punishment is the most effective way to grow, learn, and change. Thus, it often tries to educate through blame, criticism, and judgment, using demeaning language and a harsh tone of voice (generally, people don't have a voice evaluating them about all the ways in which they did a wonderful job). As a result, most people will tend to resist—whether blame and criticism is from someone else or a voice inside their head—as the need for respect for their autonomy is not met.

The typical response to this type of judgmental internal conversation may be to try to push it away or ignore it. Yet, as with all internal voices, this part of you is trying to contribute to you by educating you about what you did, however difficult it is to hear. And when this strong Educator voice shows up judging you for past actions, there's often another voice that wants to respond, essentially saying, "Yes, but . . ." and advocating for your choice. Thus, even if a part of you believes what the Educator says, you also have what's called an inner Chooser, and it will contend that it had good reasons for the actions taken. Thus, these types of internal conflicts are between the Chooser and Educator. As we've seen in examples of internal conflicts throughout this book, between a harsh evaluating voice and a defensive choosing voice, there's little room for connection and truly learning from each other.

In many people's experience, the Educator, or the judging

voice, is so strong that it's difficult to hear the "Yes, but . . ." voice. This quieter voice is often saying, "Yes, there's some truth in what you're saying, Educator. However difficult the message is worded and is unpleasant to hear, I do believe some of the judgment, but I had reasons for making the choice I made. I want to be heard too."

If you stay within the dynamic of the Educator judging what you did and the Chooser defending it, you might still find a way to move forward, but your focus will likely be on how to avoid the blame and punishment you are experiencing, rather than achieving internal understanding and resolution. This might involve shifting the blame onto other people, or it might mean you remove yourself from the situation altogether and avoid interaction with other people involved. In doing this, you relinquish a state of internal harmony and undermine your sense of confidence and ability. But when you can go through a process to hear both voices, it frees up your capacity to be present with what is and learn from what you did, instead of remaining in the turmoil of judgment.

When the Educator's voice is so strong that you have difficulty hearing the Chooser's, you might try Self-Empathy, yet miss empathizing with the voice that is quieter and less insistent. Both the part of you that chooses *and* the part of you that evaluates your choices need empathy. In short, framing these situations in terms of mediating the conflict between the Chooser and Educator more consistently and reliably helps you experience the full breadth of empathy.

PRACTICE PAUSE

How does your Educator typically talk to you?
How does your Chooser typically respond?

THE CHOOSER EDUCATOR (CE) MAP

The Chooser Educator (CE) process is the same as the Internal Mediation map, only we use different language for it because the situations arise differently. In IM, you have two voices that are at odds in some way about a situation in the present or future. In Chooser Educator, you have a harsh voice judging you for something you did or did not do in the past, and a voice defending its choice.

In IM and CE, the goal is the same—to identify the voices, find the needs, and help them connect so they collaborate to meet all of your needs. We suggest this map as a strategy to accomplish that goal, as the map will help each voice express itself, and then be heard by the other voice. As with IM, you may experience a lot of back and forth between the voices and feel the emotions well up with each, but keep the goal of connection in mind and you'll find the Chooser and Educator can collaborate.

CHOOSER EDUCATOR (CE) MAP

	CONNECTION		RESOLUTION
Mediating Between Chooser and Educator	**A's Needs**	**B's Needs**	**Synthesis/ Strategy to Meet All Needs**
Process	Empathize with A: surface A's needs	Empathize with B: surface B's needs	Consider what strategy might meet the needs of both A and B
CE Steps	1. Empathize with A (often Educator) 2. Empathize with B (often Chooser) 3. Ask B to empathize with A 4. Ask A to empathize with B		5. Make Solution Requests and Agreements

Here are the five steps in the Chooser Educator Map:

- Step 1: Empathize with A (often Educator)
  - Allow A to speak unedited
  - Empathize to uncover OFNR (Observations, Feelings, Needs, Requests), focusing on needs
- Step 2: Empathize with B (often Chooser)
  - Allow B to speak unedited
  - Empathize to uncover OFNR, focusing on needs
- Step 3: Ask B to empathize with A
  - B repeats A's needs
- Step 4: Ask A to empathize with B
  - A repeats B's needs
- Step 5: Make solution requests and agreements

www.mediateyourlife.com/chooser-educator-process-video/

Identify the Chooser and Educator within you—the part of you trying to educate you about the choice you made, and the part of you who made the choice. While in IM you name the parts, with CE it is often easier to simply stick with the names Chooser and Educator, since those are the roles they are playing in your inner drama.

In mediating a Chooser Educator internal conflict, we suggest starting the process by empathizing with the voice of the Educator, since it is often the one that is the most strident. The Educator is essentially saying some version of "You screwed up," "You did it again," "You should have known better," "You're a ____ (jerk, idiot, etc)." While the Educator frequently communicates in words, it may also communicate less verbally at times, conveying a sense of disgust with yourself, or a vague feeling that you've messed up again. You may also find the Educator speaking to you in mental images about your conduct, or in a demeaning tone. Due to the domineering nature of this voice, starting the mediation by empathizing with the Educator seems to help the process unfold more easily. This is because the voice of the Educator may not be able to hear anything else until it receives some empathy. You can, however, begin by empathizing with the Chooser if that voice is louder or more insistent.

To see how the CE map unfolds, we'll follow this scenario through each step:

> David is a father of two young children. One evening, out of the corner of his eye he sees his daughter playing with her younger brother, and it looks like she flips him over in a way that he ends up getting a little hurt. David's interpretation is that she intentionally threw her brother on the ground, so he says with some intensity, "What did you just do?" In response, she looks a little scared; David senses a wall going up in her, and she runs off to hide in her room. David thinks, *Oh, you so screwed up! Now she's going to be afraid of you. That's not how you want her to feel. You're such a bad parent.*

In the CE model, David's Chooser in the moment chose to react to his interpretation of what his daughter did, and then after he saw her response, his Educator judged him for the action he chose.

STEP 1: EMPATHIZE WITH A (OFTEN EDUCATOR)

In this first step, you allow the Educator to speak and then empathize using observations, feelings, and needs. What you'll find is that the Educator is trying to communicate that the choice you made didn't meet certain needs. The problem is that it does so in language that makes it hard to hear the Educator's underlying concern for your needs being met or what those needs actually are. In empathizing, therefore, you are translating what the Educator says into what that part of you wants—either for you or for someone else. It generally takes some work to translate these often harsh judgments of yourself, but it will become easier with practice.

> David sets up a chair for his Educator and one for his Chooser. Sitting in the Educator's chair, he looks for the observations first, and notices his Educator is saying, "You hurt her by doing that! You're wounding her in some way by getting angry with her—that was too harsh and mean and unkind. You're being an overbearing tyrant kind of parent. You know better than that! You shouldn't be acting that way when your goal is to communicate compassionately. What the hell is wrong with you?"
>
> Though David feels guilt and shame when he hears this, he realizes that his Educator is upset because of unmet needs, and begins to empathize from mediator mind.
>
> **MM:** "Are you angry because you'd really like to show her care and contribute to her well-being?"
>
> **Educator:** "Yeah! Did you see that look on her face? Plus she didn't learn not to be rough with her brother, she just learned to avoid you!"
>
> **MM:** "So it's also about making sure that we nurture her growth and development, is that right?"

Educator: "Yes, and I'd like to make sure she feels safe and secure; I'd like her to know she doesn't have to fear doing something wrong—that she'll still be loved."

MM: "Right, so care, contribution to her well-being, nurturing her growth, and for her to feel safe and secure. It sounds like there's also a desire to be connected to her?"

Educator: "Sure, I don't want anything to get in the way of being connected to her, especially not acting in a way that she feels scared."

When you can name your Educator's needs and be present with those, deepening into them and imagining them met, you will discover an antidote to the feelings of shame, guilt, and so on, that the typical language of the Educator generates. The best part is that you are now focused on what you want to create instead of what you want to avoid.

STEP 2: EMPATHIZE WITH B (OFTEN CHOOSER)

Allow the Chooser to say what it wants to be heard about and empathize by finding observations, feelings, and needs, again focusing on needs. The Chooser had reasons for the choice it made, and it likely wants to be heard about its motivation for the choice. When you switch to the Chooser's chair, your observation will likely be the choice you made and what your Chooser says about it.

As David thinks about the Chooser, he recognizes that his thoughts about how he acted carry the Educator's judgment (harsh, mean, unkind), and he looks for the *observation* about how he acted—what a video might record of the situation. He reflects on how in speaking to her there was a sharpness and edge in his voice, along with a forcefulness conveyed through his tone. The volume of his voice was higher than normal, and he looked at her with narrowed eyes, boring down at her with his stare.

Feeling calmer and less judgmental about his actions, David settles into the Chooser's chair and allows that part of himself to comment on the choice.

Chooser: "I thought I saw her flip her little brother in a way that possibly hurt him, so of course I reacted to it."

MM: "Were you scared because you'd like your son to be safe?"

Chooser: "Exactly. And she needs to know to be careful in playing with him because he's smaller than she is."

MM: "So you'd like her to be more aware of what she's doing around him so he doesn't get hurt."

Chooser: "Yes, that's it. I felt angry and scared, and I really want her to grow up aware of how her actions may be harmful to others, so everyone can be safer."

As David settles into these feelings and needs, he notices how touched he is by what his Chooser desires, and connects deeply with the desire for people to be aware and sensitive so that others can be safe.

Empathizing with the Chooser is one of the few times you are actually trying to discern what needs you were striving to meet in a past situation. Usually, when you think about a prior event, you think about it in terms of your needs in the present—the needs that are or are not met when you recall the situation. However, when you are working with inner conflicts about a choice you made, the Chooser wants to explain and be heard about the needs they were seeking to meet when they made the choice in the first place. In other words, if you look at what was going on in you at that time, you will see the needs the Chooser was attempting to meet by choosing particular actions.

A beneficial result of the first two steps in this process is that when you connect with your needs from the Chooser and Educator, you may notice compassion arising toward yourself. That appreciation of how you were acting out of these fundamental needs shows the care you have for yourself and others, allowing you to shift your negative perception of yourself to a positive one.

STEP 3: ASK B TO EMPATHIZE WITH A

As in IM, before moving back to hear more from the Educator, ask the Chooser to reflect back what the Educator said.

> Still sitting in the Chooser's chair, David asks the Chooser to reflect back the Educator's needs.
>
> **MM:** "Chooser, I heard that the Educator would really like to be connected to our daughter, to nurture her growth, contribute to her well-being, and for her to feel safe and cared for. Would you be willing to let the Educator know that you heard those needs?"
>
> **Chooser:** "Okay. Educator, I heard you have needs to support our daughter's growth, contribute to her, have her feel safe and loved, and to be connected with her."

STEP 4: ASK A TO EMPATHIZE WITH B

Back in the Educator's chair, ask the Educator to reflect back what it heard from the Chooser.

> Moving back to the Educator's chair, David asks his Educator to reflect the Chooser's needs.
>
> **MM:** "Educator, would you be willing to let Chooser know that you heard his needs?"

> **Educator:** "Chooser, you'd like safety and for people to be aware of what they're doing and when their actions might be harmful to others."

Then, if the Educator has more to say, you can repeat these first four steps of the connection phase until the Educator and Chooser are connected and ready to collaborate on making requests and agreements. As the conversation continues, each time you change from Educator to Chooser, remember to reflect back what the other said before going on, making sure that each is heard by the other.

STEP 5: MAKE SOLUTION REQUESTS AND AGREEMENTS

When you've been through the connection phase as many times as necessary for your Chooser and Educator to be connected, you naturally move into the final stage of finding the strategies that will meet all the needs. Your mediator mind, the part of you that wants all of the needs met without favoring the perspectives brought forth by either the Chooser or the Educator, can help facilitate the process of coming up with agreements about what to do moving forward.

This step can also include thinking about how you might have done something differently to meet all of the needs that surfaced. In essence, you do a post-hearsal, which also serves as a rehearsal for a similar situation in the future. This step can provide powerful learning from what happened as well as give you more options for acting in a desirable way in the future. It can also lead directly into the requests and agreements you'd like to make of yourself and/or other people to help you act differently. If the action your Educator judged is habitual, remember it may take some time to make the desired change, and you might need supporting and restoring agreements in place to help you make the change.

Now that David's Chooser and Educator have heard each other's needs, they begin to collaborate to find a way forward in the current situation, and in similar times in the future.

Educator: "I wonder if, in that moment before reacting from the fear and anger, we could have stopped and talked to her in a different tone, saying something more like, 'I'm really scared about your brother getting hurt, can you tell me what just happened?'"

Chooser: "I like that idea. Instead of jumping to conclusions based on the fear, we can ask her what happened and let her know the concerns in a way that is more likely to maintain a connection with her. I do get that while I'd like her to learn to play more safely with her brother, the way I reacted may have taught her more about protecting herself from anger and punishment. I do wonder about how to catch it before reacting . . . maybe just stopping to take a breath before responding."

Educator: "And would it work to remind ourselves of all these needs then—for safety, care, learning, awareness of how actions affect others, and connection?"

Chooser: "I think so. Since it may take a few times to be able to do this consistently, if it happens could you remind me in a more gentle way? Maybe even help catch it in the moment, rather than berate me afterwards?"

Educator: "Sure, I'd like to have these needs met too. How about we also go talk to her about the situation and what happened, and see about reconnecting now with this new awareness?"

Chooser: "I'd like that."

David sits with all of his needs in mind, realizing that in any situation where he sees someone acting in a way that concerns him, he'd like to respond to protect people's safety while maintaining connection with the person doing the action. Though he feels some sadness about not having been able to act as he would have liked with his daughter, he also now feels a new appreciation for how he can respond to similar situations in alignment with his values, and has hope that he can behave in new ways in the future. He looks forward to his conversation reconciling with his daughter.

"So what happened?" Alicia asks after they exchange pleasantries. Sally quickly fills her in on the week and the night before.

"This morning, I finally remembered that this voice is probably trying to help me out, but I'm having trouble hearing it, so that's why I texted you."

"Do you have a couple chairs set up?" Alicia asks.

Sally says, "Yeah, and I'm moving now to sit in the Educator's chair." She sits down.

Alicia	Educator
"So what would you like to say, Educator?"	"She just can't seem to get it together. I mean not that long ago we went through this whole process and she said she wanted to take better care of herself. But look how easily she forgets! ...

Alicia	**Educator**
	... First there was last week, and all the things she failed to do that she's said she wants to, but then to top it all off, she goes and binges on ice cream and a movie last night. That's not taking care of herself."
"You're really upset about this . . ."	"Yeah, I'm upset! This is the time when we need to make these changes, and I want to have some hope that it's going to work. I want Sally to be successful and to show that we can feel good and be fully engaged with work and family. But not only did she not get enough sleep or eat decently last week, she compounded it last night."

Alicia	Educator
"I'm hearing that you're angry because you'd really like Sally to be successful in her dream of having her business and family, and you'd like to work with her to be able to do that, is that right?"	"Yeah, but she obviously doesn't listen."
"Okay, you'd like to be heard, and to have some trust and hope that her self-care is actually going to happen."	"I'd like that, yeah. I mean, I don't get it—why is she making these choices that she knows aren't good for her?"
"That's a great question . . . let's find out. Sally, can we hear from the part of you that chose to eat the ice cream and watch a movie?"	

Sally moves to the other chair and settles in for a moment before speaking up.

Alicia	Chooser

| | "I wanted it. I was tired . . . it was a busy week. I wanted to have some time for me, to enjoy something, and turn my mind off and just have some space." |

| "So you wanted some space and enjoyment." | "Sure, and then Educator is harping on me about things I didn't do earlier. I couldn't take that in and was trying to get some relief from all that . . . I just wanted to *be* for a little while. And the ice cream just tasted good. It was actually soothing." |

| "You were meeting needs for relief too, to be able to not think about things for a bit, and to soothe yourself?" | "Yeah, and I admit that we ended up staying up way later than perhaps would've been best. I get that it didn't meet some needs, like rest." |

Alicia asks if Sally feels ready to move back to the Educator's chair. Agreeing, Sally moves and notices more tension. Alicia says, "I'm sure you have some responses to what you heard, Educator, but I'm wondering if before you go there, you'd be willing to let Chooser know that you heard her needs for care, enjoyment, space, and relief?"

Alicia

Educator

"I guess so. Chooser acted to meet needs for enjoyment, space, relief, and some kind of self-care. I just don't know what kind of self-care that is. 'We'll get so run-down that we'll then take care of ourselves by bingeing on ice cream and movies?' If the self-care we'd agreed on had taken place earlier in the week, then maybe we wouldn't have been at that point."

Now that Sally's Chooser has been heard a little, she can sense that part of her feeling angry at hearing Educator's words and wanting to jump in. But Alicia's next words help her stay in the role of the Educator.

"Are you frustrated because you would like some understanding from the rest of Sally about how all aspects of self-care work together and how each choice through the week is important?"

"Exactly. Yes."

Sally lets Alicia know that she's moving back to the Chooser's chair and speaks without waiting for Alicia's facilitation.

Alicia	Chooser

	"Would you stop treating me like a child? Why do you think I made that choice last night? Because you're harping on me and I can't take it anymore. I'm making my choices for good reasons."
"So, Chooser, you're feeling upset because you'd like respect and understanding for the needs you're acting to meet?"	"Yeah, respect. And care too. Educator says she wants care, but she doesn't treat us with any care at all. It seems like in some ways we want the same things, but when I get that judgment and wrongness coming at me, it doesn't work for me."
"You're hearing that you and Educator would like the same things, and you have a need for care. Is that in part about being seen for all that you're doing?"	"Yes, I'm holding a lot together right now, and trying to find my way through it. I'd appreciate more help in all of it, not more judgment."

Alicia	**Chooser**
"Okay, I'm hearing you'd like more support, as well as care, respect, and understanding. Would you be willing to let Educator know that you heard her needs for understanding about all choices being important?"	"Yeah, I get that Educator would like understanding and maybe some foresight about making each choice so that we don't get to the end of the week and feel exhausted."
"Thank you. Are you ready to hear from Educator?"	

Sally feels some relief already, having let both the Educator and Chooser speak and be heard. She moves back to the Educator's chair, and notices a lot of sadness arising.

Alicia	**Educator**
	"Chooser says we're on the same page about self-care, and that she needs care and support. I guess what bothers me is that she doesn't seem to listen about self-care and instead makes these other choices . . ."

Alicia	Educator

	". . . And because I'm not heard I use this harsh language to try to get her to choose differently, but I get that it isn't working . . . I just don't know how else to get these needs met. I don't want Sally to get to the point where she was last night. I'd rather she take care of herself regularly, so when she keeps making these other choices, I get frustrated and exhausted, so I push more. I guess what I'm doing isn't working, though. I can see it's not meeting the very need I'm trying to meet."
"So, Educator, you're noticing that your efforts to get needs met isn't achieving the result you'd like either. Do you or Chooser have any ideas about what might help you both get your needs met?"	"Knowing we're on the same page about self-care does help. I guess one thing I'd like is for there to be more forethought about it, or more consideration in the moment. It seems like what often happens is that the goal gets lost in favor of the moment's whim."

Alicia

Educator

"What would more con- sideration look like?"	"Maybe to have a more specific plan for some things, like exercise and sleep. And when it looks like we're choosing some- thing less healthy, maybe use some process to get clear about what all of our needs are and how to meet them with a little more awareness."
"Great, maybe do IM, since in that moment you'll be faced with a choice about what to do to meet all of your needs?"	

Sally moves back to the Chooser's chair.

Alicia

Chooser

	"I like the idea of a plan, and doing some process in the moment. I'm con- cerned about trying to do IM, since it can take awhile. Usually, if some- thing comes up in the moment, I feel an ur- gency to attend to it . . ."

Alicia

Chooser

	". . . So I'm not going to want to take a whole lot of time to do IM, unless we can find a quick way to do it. Maybe Self-Empathy would work. One thing I'd really like is if Educator wants to say something about what choices I'm making, to not do it in this patronizing tone."
"Since that's what you don't want, what would you like instead?"	"Maybe to empathize with me first?"
"Let's check in with the Educator and see if that works for her."	

Educator

Chooser

"Okay, let's try that. I guess another request I'd have is that if the end of the week comes around and Sally does feel exhausted again . . .

Educator	Chooser

". . . to find another strategy to get the care and relief, maybe something like a hot bath. And that if she does notice she's again drawn to behavior like eating ice cream, maybe to ask a question like, 'What can I do to increase my well-being right now?'"	"Yeah, I like those ideas. And you're also bringing up for me something else I struggle with. When I choose something, like staying up late to finish work, I tend to see it in isolation, like an impossible choice—I don't want to *not* get the work done, and at the same time, I don't want to go to sleep late. But nothing is really in isolation, is it? So, when that happens, I guess I'd like to reflect on what went on earlier in the day, to see if I can learn and change something to avoid ending up in the position of those 'impossible' choices."

Now that Sally's Chooser and Educator are in collaboration about getting her needs for self-care met, Alicia continues to support her to turn these requests into primary agreements and consider any supporting and restoring agreements.

—〰—

PRACTICE PAUSE

Take a current or recent Chooser Educator
internal conflict of your own and go
through the CE map.

Here's a summary of the steps of working with a Chooser Educator inner conflict:

Identify the voices of the Chooser and Educator in your mind.

Decide which voice to begin the process with (we recommend the Educator).

Step 1: Empathize with the voice of the Educator by first observing what that voice is saying, feeling into the emotions generated by those thoughts, and then inquiring into the needs the Educator is seeking to meet.

Step 2: Empathize with the Chooser in the same way—observing the thoughts, feeling the emotions, and inquiring into the needs the Chooser was meeting when it made the choice.

Step 3: Ask the Chooser to empathize with the Educator.

Step 4: Ask the Educator to empathize with the Chooser.

Step 5: Make solution requests and agreements. Consider how you might have acted differently to meet all of the needs that surfaced. Inquire into what you might like to do now or in the future. This might include actions to redress the situation you are working with, or it might be a more general inquiry and practice into what you would like to do should a similar situation arise. Make agreements with yourself and/or other people to support you in making the shift you would like to make.

Chooser Educator in Practice and in Life

It takes courage to begin this process and to empathize with the Educator. Most people's Educator is so unkind that they will do anything, even self-destructive behaviors, in order to avoid hearing it. It can take a few times through Chooser Educator to appreciate that this part of you is looking out for your best interests, and to trust that through the process you will be able to hear what it truly desires for you and find a different way to relate to it. Even then, sometimes it can be supportive to have someone else help you through this process. In Chapter 10, we'll discuss how to externalize the voices through role-playing with one or two practice partners.

The condensed and quick options for integrating CE into your daily life are the same as for IM. One of the easiest ways to recognize that you have a CE conflict is when you hear the intrusive voice of the Educator. When you've gone through the full process enough times, you can begin to trust that regardless of how hard this voice is to hear, it sincerely has some gift for you. As such, turning toward that voice with curiosity and inquiring into what it would like for you is sometimes enough to shift the whole structure of the conflict. How? Instead of resisting this voice and the emotions that it brings up, which tends to keep the conflict in place, you open to its perspective, and seeing the needs it's trying to meet can spontaneously bring up new possibilities.

One benefit of the Chooser Educator process is that it connects you to the needs on both sides—the needs the Chooser was seeking to meet, and the needs that weren't met in carrying out that choice. As Sally found, the Chooser often realizes that while it met some needs, others weren't met or the action wasn't as effective at meeting needs as it intended. At the same time, the Educator has needs it's trying to meet, and it may also recognize that how it goes about trying to educate doesn't meet other needs. By embodying both your Chooser and Educator through the CE map, they can each come to an understanding of what they are trying to contribute to you. Once all the needs are uncovered, strategies will come into your mind that are likely to meet these needs, a natural result of unleashing your conscious and unconscious creativity. Then, instead of judging or running from feelings that come up, simply be with them and learn from their messages so you will be internally aligned as you plan and move toward your dreams.

Here's how the CE map contributed to Chris, Dawn, and Kevin as they continue taking action toward their dreams.

CHRIS

"In using the Chooser Educator process, I see how the Educator really wishes for my well-being and wants me to succeed in making healthy choices. It is so concerned I'm going to repeat past experiences and let go of my goals that it is on the lookout for any signs of that—and if it sees any, it goes a little overboard trying to get me back on track.

"The choices I made at the event were from wanting to enjoy myself and trying to fit in—I don't want to stand out with my choices. I also realized that I don't want others to feel uncomfortable or like I'm judging their food choices, so I was meeting needs for care and allowance too. I've begun to question how else I can get enjoyment at these types of events separate from unhealthy foods, and how to make the choices I'll be happy with and still fit in. I've also made some agreements about planning ahead for these types of situations. I'd like to think through and make choices ahead of time so I'm not trying to decide in the moment, when I'm less likely to keep promises to myself. And if my wife is there, she also agreed to support me.

"Probably the most important thing I've discovered is seeing how much the Educator's harsh way of talking to me has contributed to giving up my goals in the past. When it tells me I'm a failure and I believe it, there doesn't seem much point in trying to succeed, so the way it communicates ends up having the opposite effect from what it wants to motivate. I've also made an agreement with myself that if I hear my Educator using this kind of harsh language, I'll look for the needs it's seeking to meet and ask it whether the language it's using is likely to create the desired result. Overall, I would like to learn how to speak more kindly to myself in evaluating my past choices."

DAWN

"My Educator so judged my behavior in the board meeting that I had trouble finding observations about what my Chooser did. Even when I tried to remember what happened as if I was seeing a videotape, I still had trouble. I think my Educator may be interpreting things in a way that isn't quite accurate. Still, I get that it is speaking out of needs for respect and collaboration when it evaluates how I acted, and also a need to honor those I work with. I spoke the way I did in the meeting because I feel strongly about my vision, and I want to be seen for that. I also get that I acted out of a need for power, and I really judge having that need. When I asked what need was being met in judging my need for power, I got that it was about equality, reciprocity, and gratitude, so I know the Educator is trying to make sure I'm not doing *power over* others. As a result, I became clear about how much I want to run this organization through *power with* others.

"My Chooser and Educator had some requests of each other. First, rather than jumping to a harsh interpretation of my own actions, my Chooser would like Educator to be open to inquiring with someone about how I did something, to determine if its (typically harsh) evaluation of me is accurate.

Second, my Educator would like Chooser to have a guideline for assessing *power over* versus *power with* when I decide it's a time for control. I haven't quite figured out how that will work yet, so that's an ongoing inquiry, but I feel good about the agreements I made, and I'm going to ask someone how my actions came across in the board meeting."

KEVIN

"In working through the Chooser Educator map, I saw that there's a part of me that still isn't quite on board with my dream, or maybe a better way to say it is that it has concerns about taking time away from work. My Educator was basically saying, 'See? Not doing work when you thought of it made everything more difficult and you didn't enjoy the time off anyway. If you'd just done the work, you could've enjoyed the rest of the time.' This part of me is so used to the way I've lived that it's having a hard time letting go to find a new way forward, of living life on different terms. Since I'm now sharing my job with someone else and am not solely responsible for the results we achieve, that part of me is speaking out of needs for integrity around work, achievement, productivity, and being a team player.

"Of course, my Chooser is also acting out of needs for integrity—to reach this dream that's important to me and to stick with the agreements that will help me reach it. Before, I've always simply continued to work, despite the voice saying that I was working too much, which is what kept me stuck.

"Through using this process, I see that it's a matter of continuing to listen, to tweak the agreements, and to keep trying things. One of the agreements I'm creating out of this round of Chooser Educator is a Time Out and Reality Check. When I notice that I've made a choice about not working and the Educator is already judging that choice, I will take a Time Out to check in with my needs, and also do a Reality Check about whether what the Educator is saying is accurate. I've noticed it tends to say that if I just get this bit of work done, everything will be smooth sailing. I first thought the need there was completion, but I then understood that there's a deeper need, to have the space and ease that comes with work being done. But I know there's always *more* work to be done, so I've realized that my Educator is trying to meet needs in a way that's not very effective. Because of that, I'll use the Reality Check to tap into the needs that surface and consider what will truly meet them. Even though I'd like to just have the quick answers that would allow me to live my dream right away, this process has helped me accept that as long as I keep using these tools as different situations come up, I'll be able to keep making the changes necessary to make my dream a reality."

NEXT UP

As you take action to actualize your dream, you may find that you feel like you're fighting against yourself in some way. In other words, it may feel like you have to change behaviors or ingrained ways of being such that you must shift an essence of yourself to actualize the dream. We've seen this in our example characters: Sally and Chris are both accustomed to putting their own self-care aside, Sally for her family and budding business, and Chris because he didn't believe he could be successful with losing weight and living healthier; Dawn has developed ways of interacting with people that she finds is limiting her ability to lead the nonprofit the way she desires; and Kevin is up against his tendency to put work ahead of everything else in his life, which is why he created his dream in the first place. In the next chapter, we'll talk about how to go about changing your habits—the ways you automatically think and act—so that they support you to reach your dream.

7

SMOOTHING THE PATH

CREATING AND CHANGING HABITS

Habit is notorious—and rightly so—for its ability to direct our actions, even against our will; but by mindfully shaping our habits, we can harness the power of mindlessness as a sweeping force for serenity, energy, and growth.
—GRETCHEN RUBIN

—⟨⟨⟨⟩⟩⟩—

SALLY IS READING AND RESPONDING TO EMAILS WHEN SHE comes across a newsletter. Scanning the article, she realizes that a woman named Betty she met at a networking event a few months ago would probably be interested in it. *I enjoyed talking with her,* she remembers. *She had some great ideas, and we were going to connect again and maybe collaborate. But I lost track of following up with her. Maybe this is the perfect way to reach out.*

Sally searches her email for Betty's name, only to come up empty. *What did I do with her contact info?* Sally wonders. *Didn't we email each other after?* She tries a few more name spellings and keywords but doesn't find anything. So she rummages through her desk drawer and scans a pile of business cards picked up at various events. *Nope . . . nope . . . nope . . . .* Sally searches her briefcase and each drawer of her desk but can't find the one she's looking for. When she glances at the clock, she realizes she's now spent a half hour searching. A spark of irritation flares as she takes a look at her list. Upon seeing the website tasks she wrote down, she thinks, *Oh, I'll do those, they're easy.* Turning her attention there, she gets to work on creating copy and images for her site.

After a few hours, she notices that it's almost time to leave for her late lunch with Peg. *I feel like I've been working all day but haven't gotten much done. I have too many days like this. What's going on? I'll never make this business work if I keep going like this.* Slightly frustrated with herself, Sally grabs her purse and leaves to meet her sister.

—⁓—

Achieving a dream often requires new behaviors and new ways of thinking. Especially when you have a larger dream, you may find that the ways you've done things in the past, even the beliefs and thoughts you have, no longer suffice. You begin to understand that you will have to change typical behaviors and thought patterns, as your dream requires a new set of habits.

A lot of what you do each day is dictated by habits. Studies show that you are acting out of patterns of thought and behavior as much as forty percent of the day. From how you get out of bed in the morning to how you prepare to go to sleep at night, as well as much of what you do in between, is likely the same from day to day.

> **habit** *n.*
>
> pattern of thought or behavior that has been
> followed regularly so as to become involuntary

People often think of habits as physical behaviors, such as how you tie your shoes, drive to work, reach for a cookie when feeling stress, or go for a walk every day after dinner. However, mental patterns can also be habitual. You might notice the same types of thoughts when you find yourself in similar situations.

✦ You dread family get-togethers when Uncle Tad will be there, anticipating his uncomfortable jokes and semi-drunken behavior. Even after he sobers up and stops telling off-color jokes, the dread still arises approaching any event where he will be in attendance.

✦ Anytime conflict arises with people around you, even witnessing others in conflict, you flee or freeze.

✦ Thinking about growing your business, you feel overwhelmed and distract yourself with busywork.

Habits aren't necessarily negative, but people tend to only think about them when they are aware of one they'd like to change. Because they can either work for you or against you, habits can support you in reaching your dream, or keep you stuck in self-defeating patterns.

PRACTICE PAUSE

Name some of your habits. See if you can
identify at least one habit in each of these
categories: physical (behavioral) and mental
(thinking), those that serve you (help you reach
your dream) and those that do not.

As in every other area of implementing your plan, habits can
bring up a few barriers. Have you ever experienced the following?

+ Noticing a habit you don't like, and either immediately or
   after a few attempts to change it, you think, *I'll never be
   able to break this habit!*

+ You start to create a new habit, mess up and forget, and
   decide it's not worth the effort.

+ You decide to overhaul an area of your life, then can't
   sustain the massive change and give up, feeling like a
   failure.

+ You try to change a habit through willpower or other
   ineffective means, then blame yourself when it doesn't
   seem to work.

+ You judge yourself relentlessly, both for the habits that
   aren't helpful and for your efforts to create or change them.

We've seen how Sally is hampered in her dream of building a
business by using habitual ways of working that are less efficient
and effective than she would like. (Can you identify the habits
that are holding her back?) Let's find out what habits are helping
or hindering Chris, Dawn, and Kevin as they keep working toward their dreams.

CHRIS

"I've been feeling really good lately about the direction I'm going. Most of the time I'm pretty dialed in with my food choices, and I've been moving my body more too. Since those were going so well, I thought I'd take on stress management, since that's an area that I find really impacts my ability to make good choices all around. When I'm stressed, for example, it's so much harder to eat well. So I decided I would take a short walk anytime tension starts to arise at work, take a one-minute pause every hour to breathe and clear my mind, and start leaving work by six p.m. every day. And then yesterday happened. Even though I set an alarm on my phone for the one-minute pause, I ignored it because I was embroiled in a 'crisis' at work. There was so much tension, and I didn't pull myself away to go for a walk. I didn't even remember that it was a possibility. And I ended up staying way later than six o'clock. I'm not sure what happened . . . it's a bit of a mystery."

DAWN

"This process of starting a nonprofit has really challenged me to improve my communication and collaboration skills. Nearly every day I find myself in some situation in which I'm noticing how I would normally act, and also noticing that I'd like to do something different. Sometimes I succeed, sometimes I don't. And sometimes, I'm just not sure, and I feel like I'll never be proficient with these skills. For instance, yesterday I had a phone meeting with the head of the board, and I was really dissatisfied afterwards. This is one of the main people on the board who advocated for a program that goes into the schools instead of a center, which is what I want. We actually had a good conversation as a follow-up from that first board meeting where I felt like I screwed up, yet I still got off the phone feeling heavy and troubled. I don't know what's going on."

KEVIN

"One of the biggest habits I'm working on is my tendency to favor work over anything else. This promotion and job-share situation is giving me lots of opportunity to experience that habit! I had a day off where, again, work called to me. I asked my question about whether it was essential, and I decided that it was. So I worked for about an hour taking care of the one piece I needed to handle, but then I kept going. I knew I was going beyond what was necessary and had the thought that I should stop, but I didn't. I ended up working about half the day before I finally quit, when all I really needed to do was put in an hour. I've mostly been confused about it—I wonder why I kept going, especially when I was aware of what I was doing."

Hopefully, you're beginning to recognize the common patterns of internal barriers that arise on the way to your dream—and you're also beginning to recognize how the processes in previous chapters can contribute when any of these barriers arise.

SCP: As soon as you notice that you are disconnected from yourself, you can reconnect by using the Self-Connection Process, then see if there's another process you'd like to do afterwards.

Self-Empathy: You can empathize with the barrier thought when any of the above occurs, connecting with your needs in that moment.

Internal Mediation: If you can frame what is coming up in terms of two conflicting voices (perhaps "I want to change this, I can't change this"), you can mediate between them.

Chooser Educator: If your internal conflict is between a Chooser (who perhaps chose to do the "bad" habit) and the

Educator (who afterwards tries to educate you about how awful that choice was), you could use CE to mediate between them.

There's one other process we'd like to give you—one that you can use to assess what happened after the fact, making it especially useful for creating and changing habits. It's a process that supports you to debrief, perhaps after what you think of as having failed or succeeded at your new habit behavior. (You'll see later in the chapter why it's just as important to do it after a success as after a failure.) We'll talk through the Mourn Celebrate Learn (MCL) map after a brief primer on habits.

PRACTICE PAUSE

What internal barriers in habit change or
creation are familiar to you?

WHAT IS A HABIT?

A habit is a behavior or thought pattern that you have repeated often enough that it becomes automatic. As a result, the brain takes care of performing the task, and you can be thinking of something else entirely. In other words, you can be unconscious in regard to that behavior.

As we've already said, habitual conduct is not necessarily detrimental; you likely have quite a few habits that support you. When you'd like to create new habits to help you reach your dream, or change habits that are getting in the way, it helps to know a little about habits and how to create and change them.

Many books have been written on this topic (see For Further Reading for our favorites), so we will only give a brief overview here, with suggestions on how you can integrate the Mediate Your Life skills and the MCL map in particular to create and change habits to move toward fulfilling your dream.

According to Charles Duhigg in his excellent book *The Power of Habit*, a habit consists of three parts: cue, routine, and reward. Let's look at these in the context of creating a habit and changing a habit.

HABIT CREATION

Part of your plan may include the creation of habits that are central to your dream or that would support reaching it. For example, if you decide you'd like to learn to play piano, improve your communication skills, or be more productive, creating new habits may be essential to achieving it. In some cases, the entire dream may rest on the creation of new habits. Take Chris, who has the dream of a healthy lifestyle. Since a lifestyle is an entire set of habits, Chris has numerous habits he is working on creating or changing, from how he eats to moving his body to sleep to managing stress.

The habit behavior itself is the *routine*—what you actually think or do that is leading you toward what you desire. Here are some possible routines for the above dreams:

+ Play two scales on the piano every day

+ Practice a Mediate Your Life map every day

+ Check in each morning to set concrete work goals for the day

Next, the *cue* is what prompts you to execute the habit. Since you are creating this habit, you can decide what the cue will be. If the cue is related somehow to the behavior, it usually helps the habit form more quickly or effectively; however, for some habits, like playing scales, you may want to set a time to do it, or simply tie it to some other daily behavior, such as finishing breakfast. For example, the cue for checking in on daily goals would likely follow from sitting down at your desk. If you're striving to master an MYL map, you may choose to practice it before or after your daily meditation. The cue in habit creation is essentially a plan: "After I . . . (cue), then I will . . . (routine)."

The *reward* is what you get from performing the habit. When people think of their dream and creating habits, it may seem like the reward is the dream itself. But long-term rewards don't tend to be very compelling. In fact, rewards that are *directly tied to acting out the behavior* are more likely to succeed in establishing the habit. What does this mean?

For example, if you want to start a habit of walking, enjoying your time outside in nature will help you keep venturing out far more often than the idea that eventually you'll lose weight or be more fit. In other words, being in nature becomes its own reward, and the fitness or weight loss becomes a positive byproduct.

The reward may be something that arises naturally in the course of performing the behavior, or it may be something you create. If you choose to create a reward for yourself, it might be giving a congratulatory pat on the back each time you successfully complete the routine. That may seem small, but even a small reward is significant. You can also look for what is intrinsically rewarding about enacting the behavior itself, as in the example of walking in nature. For the budding pianist, perhaps noticing your improvement each day on scales becomes its own reward. And if you're striving to be more productive, you might notice that you enjoy the few minutes of check-in time before diving into work.

The way we view what is happening with habits is, of course, through the lens of needs. As such, the reward for any habit can be framed in terms of what need you are meeting through the habitual behavior. Therefore, another way to create your reward is to look at what needs you are meeting each time you practice the new habit.

Here's a summary of habit creation:

In creating a habit, plan the behavior (or thinking) you'd like to engage in on a regular basis to help you move toward your dream. This becomes your *routine*. Then plan how you will *cue* yourself to execute this new behavior, or rather, find a way to prompt yourself to perform it. If you can anticipate some way of rewarding yourself early on to help maintain your new habit, while also taking note of intrinsic rewards that come up as you try it, these will both help solidify the habit. Here is a table that shows one possibility for the cue and reward for the examples above.

Cue →	Routine →	Reward
After I finish breakfast, I will →	Play two scales on piano →	Joy of moving my fingers on the piano keys
After I meditate, I will →	Practice one MYL map →	Feeling more connected to myself during the day
After I sit down at my desk in the morning, I will →	Check in about my work goals for the day →	Being in control and proactive in approaching my workday

PRACTICE PAUSE

What new habit would support you to reach your dream? Identify the routine, then decide on at least two possible cues and rewards. Name the needs you anticipate would be met by acting out this behavior.

HABIT CHANGE

If you have patterns or routines of behavior that are unsatisfying, that don't meet some of your needs, or that you regret later, you may have a few habits you'd like to change. Perhaps you notice that you are simply not executing on your plan—if that's the case, you'll want to determine if you have habits that are in the way.

With existing habits, you already have a cue, routine, and reward in existence, and changing the habit requires identifying each of those pieces, and then finding a new routine (new behavior) that will lead to the same reward.

Let's take the example of being distracted from productive activity by going on social media. Here are two possible ways to break down the habit into the cue, routine, and reward.

Cue →	Routine →	Reward
Feeling overwhelmed when seeing your to-do list →	Opening your browser and going to your Facebook feed →	Distracting yourself from the overwhelm
Seeing a difficult task that you have some concern about tackling →	Checking your Instagram feed on your phone →	Avoiding the discomfort of taking on the task

Each of these three parts will be highly individual, and changing a habit depends on identifying each as clearly as you can.

In identifying the reward, again look to the needs you are meeting through the habitual behavior. In the examples above, you might be going on social media to meet a need for ease, comfort, emotional safety, or a number of other possible needs.

It may take some inquiry to identify the reward, and if this is a habit you want to change, you are likely more in touch with how it is not meeting certain needs—in this case, perhaps needs for productivity, accomplishment, integrity, and meaning.

While the cue is the first column in the table, changing the habit requires working backwards, or rather, becoming aware of the reward first. You do this by stating the reward as a need (so that you become aware of the needs you are meeting by performing the habit), then becoming aware of what needs are not being met. Once you determine both sets of needs, you can try different strategies to meet all of them. By substituting in a new routine that you hope will be more successful at meeting all of your needs, you can assess that strategy and repeat until you find one that works. Over time, you'll be able to replace the old routine with the new one.

It's important here to also note that in some cases, you may be able to change a habit by identifying and eliminating the cue—or the trigger. An example of this would be avoiding the trigger altogether, such as if you tend to eat too many sweets, avoid the sweets; if your mother-in-law tends to set you off, avoid your mother-in-law. But this isn't usually possible as a long-term solution, so the other alternative is to change your *relationship* to the trigger, such that it is no longer a cue that prompts the routine.

The clearest example from our work is when someone in your

life pushes your buttons and you react in a habitual way—perhaps your child or spouse says certain words that trigger your anger, or your boss or coworker ignites your frustration with one of their habits. In *From Conflict to Connection*, we talked about the Intensity Exercise, in which you work with the trigger to defuse it, allowing you to completely shift the entire habitual reaction pattern. While a focus on processes for dealing with emotional triggers involving other people is outside the scope of this book, we mention it in case you have some habitual pattern of interacting with others that is hindering your dream—and hence may benefit from changing your relationship to the trigger.

PRACTICE PAUSE

Identify a habit you'd like to change, perhaps one that interferes with your dream. Write down the cue, routine, and reward, and name the needs you are meeting with your behavior.

REPETITION

Creating or changing habits requires repetition, and you'll likely fail, perhaps often, on the way to success. By "fail" we mean that you will create your plan for new behavior or thinking, and then at the time you'd like to do it, you will forget. When changing a habit, even after you know the cue and have identified a routine that you find leads to the reward, it still can take some time to make the change. You must then become aware of *when* the cue is happening in the moment so that you can substitute the new routine. This can require time, and it's likely you'll mess up along the way. Not to worry, though. It's simply part of the process.

How you deal with these "failures" can either stop you from the change you desire, or keep moving you toward your dream. The map below will help you identify the needs (both the needs you are meeting with your current habit and those it is not meeting), as well as assess how your habit change or creation process is progressing. If, instead of blaming yourself for forgetting to perform the habit (which will only serve to demean you), you use the map each time you forget, you will become aware sooner. Before you know it, you'll be aware *in the moment* that you'd like to make a new choice.

MOURN CELEBRATE LEARN (MCL)

In the process of achieving your dream, you may find that you:

+ Do something or fail to do something and feel awful afterwards

+ Notice ways you are avoiding acting on your dream

+ Decide that creating a new habit, or changing an existing one, would support you in moving toward your dream

+ Encounter situations in which you succeed or fail in engaging those habits

In any of these cases, it helps to look at what happened—in the form of a debrief, if you will—so that you can make changes to act more the way you desire in the next situation. The Mourn Celebrate Learn map is the process that will help you do this. In giving you the awareness of habits you have or would like to have, you're better able to create or change them.

Life will always intervene and get in the way of the habits you'd like to create—priorities will change and things will come

up. But using MCL allows you to look at what happened and decide how to shift your priorities, not in a condemning or punitive
manner, but by simply assessing whether what you did met your
needs in the way you desired. If you tend to jump quickly to self-
judgment, MCL will help you convert those thoughts into needs
so that you can move forward. The three steps in this map are
included in the name:

1. Mourn

2. Celebrate

3. Learn

MOURN

The first step puts you in touch with the needs that were not met
in what happened or in what you chose. This often brings up a
sense of sadness, which is why it is called mourning.

To look closely at what occurred, use the components of observation, feelings, and needs. First, if it was something you did,
imagine seeing the scene as if a video recorded it, which will help
you stay away from interpretations and judgments about what you
did. "I ate three cookies and a donut at the office party" is an observation, whereas "I screwed up my commitment to eat healthy"
is a judgment. Your observation can also be what you are *thinking*
about what you did, so you could start with, "I'm thinking that I
screwed up my commitment to eat healthy." This may seem like a
small change, but it makes all the difference between living from
judgment and stepping outside of it to merely observe your thinking.

If what occurred or the habit you're working on is more internal, you can similarly think about stepping outside of what
happened and observing it. For example, perhaps you would like

to change how irritated you get when visiting your parents. But the next time you're there, you find yourself irritated again, then upset with yourself for being irritated. The observation would not be "I'm so stupid for getting irritated again" (though you could say, "I'm thinking I'm so stupid for getting irritated again."), but rather something more akin to "I felt upset and spoke harshly when they commented on how I'm raising my daughter, even after I wanted to remain calm."

After making your observations, check in with how you feel. At this stage your feelings might be anger, frustration, sadness, or disappointment (see the Feelings list in Appendix A for help if needed), which may be difficult to sit with. But in doing so, you will allow your feelings to guide you toward the needs that are not met. You can ask yourself:

+ What needs are not met by having these particular thoughts?

+ More generally, what needs did not get met in the situation?

Using the example of eating at the office party, this step might sound like this:

> I ate three cookies and a donut at the office party, and I'm thinking that I really screwed up. I feel guilty and a bit angry with myself. It didn't meet my needs for well-being, or follow through on my health goals. And my thoughts and feelings afterwards are not meeting my needs for ease and allowance of my choice at that time.

Here is a recap of the step of mourning:

1. Mourn

   a. Identify observations of what happened or the thoughts you have in your mind about what happened.

   b. Notice how you feel when you recall what happened or think those thoughts.

   c. Ask what needs of yours are not met by what happened or what unmet needs you are seeking to express with your thoughts.

CELEBRATE

Mourning is important, as it puts you in touch with the unmet needs in what you did or didn't do, but it is not the entire picture. There were also needs that *did* get met, and celebrating turns your attention to those needs.

Again, use observations, feelings, and needs to empathize with what went well, or what needs you were trying to meet in what you did. Here's how you might celebrate the office party:

> I saw the food there and I wanted it, so I ate it. I can celebrate that I did have a brief thought about whether I wanted the food or not, even if I wouldn't quite say it was a conscious choice. I was enjoying the party and chatting with everyone, and joining in on the food met my needs for enjoyment and belonging. The cookies had also been made by my friend, and it met my needs for contribution to have some of her cookies and compliment her on them.

When working with your habits, think about observations that include any of the following:

+ Observations about what actually happened

+ Thoughts you have about it now

+ What needs you were meeting in what you did

+ What needs you were intending to meet in what you did

+ How you were able to approach the situation differently this time

Notice that you can celebrate what you actually did, and you can also celebrate your *intention*. When it comes to the epic fails that occur on the road to changing habits, celebrating what you did (perhaps the old habit), even if it wasn't what you hoped to do, is key to coming out of judgment and finding new strategies to meet all of your needs.

Here again is the second step of MCL:

2. Celebrate

    a. Identify observations of what happened that you liked.

    b. Notice how you feel when you recall those instances.

    c. Ask what needs of yours are met by what happened.

As you celebrate, you might find that more comes up that didn't meet your needs. It's common to go back and forth between mourning and celebrating, multiple times if necessary, before moving on to the final step. Allow the process to be fluid, following what comes up for you in each moment. You'll know it's time to move on when you feel lighter, when any intrusive thoughts of wrongness have diminished, and when you feel complete and ready to move to learning.

LEARN

After mourning and celebrating, you might find that you see the situation differently. Give yourself a little space to consider what you have learned from identifying your needs, including what you might like to try next. Here are a few questions you can ask:

+ What have I learned in going through this process?

+ How do I feel different now than I did before I began?

+ How can I better meet my needs going forward?

There are three parts to this third step—learn, plan, and practice. Especially as you consider the habit you are trying to create or change, you may have some awareness of what you'd like to try next. So after you consider what you *learned*, you can next *plan* what you'd like to do. Though you may not think of it as a plan, even repeating a habit—such as "I'd like to empty my inbox at the end of the day again tomorrow"—is a plan. A few questions that might help you with planning are:

+ What new patterns or habits of thought and action can I create to better meet all of these needs?

+ What changes in patterns or habits of thought/action would help me better meet these needs?

+ What can I learn from this situation that will help me in general to better meet these needs?

You may not always need to plan something, but consider this a placeholder, reminding you that a plan with regard to this habit may be helpful in meeting your needs moving forward. In habit creation, there are two aspects of planning that studies show are helpful: A) Be small and specific in what you will do, and B) Tie your new habit to something you already do.

For example, if you'd like to add strength training to your day, you might create a plan to do one pushup after brushing your teeth in the morning. The reason this works is that new habits are easier to remember if they follow an already existing habit—one that they are related to in some way. Even better is that small habits will tend to grow. Your one pushup will soon seem silly and you'll do two, then three, and so on. (For a free online course on building these types of habits, see BJ Fogg's Tiny Habits course.) Since this type of plan is in essence making a primary agreement with yourself, you might also think about any supporting and restoring agreements you could make to help you follow through.

Now you'll want to consider whether there is anything you'd like to *practice*. Practice is especially helpful in cases where your plan includes having a difficult conversation with someone else, but practice can also apply to working with your habits. Once you create your plan to do a pushup, for example, you can imagine yourself doing it the next morning after brushing your teeth, mentally rehearsing executing the new habit where you'd like to be doing it. If it's something you can physically practice in that moment, then do so. Practicing either mentally or physically helps you begin to embody that new habit. Each time you perform the habit from then on, you strengthen it.

Learning from the office party might proceed as follows:

It's nice to connect with the needs I did meet in what I did—it got me in touch with how important it is to me to feel connected to folks at work and support my friend. I would also like to find a way to meet those needs that doesn't go quite so far from my health goals, especially since this comes up at most events I go to that involve other people and food. I'd like to plan ahead for future events, and decide beforehand what I'd like to do while I'm there. Maybe limit to one cookie or just a small piece of any food I want. At office parties I'd also like to give input on the food they bring in to make sure there are healthier options to choose from. Maybe I'll also ask my friend for support to see if she'd be willing to make some healthier desserts that I'd feel better about trying. It sounds odd, but one idea I have for practice is to rehearse saying no when someone offers me sweets or other junk. There's another coworker I think would have fun with that, so I'll ask her to help me practice saying no.

Here is the recap of the final step in MCL:

3. Learn

   a. Learn through reflecting on how you feel different now that you've gone through the process.

   b. Plan what you would like to do from here, either in the current situation or in general, to meet your needs.

   c. Practice anything that will help you embody your learning so you will have it available in a similar situation in the future.

PRACTICE PAUSE

Choose a recent incident, perhaps one where you engaged in habitual thinking or behavior, and walk yourself through Mourn Celebrate Learn.

www.mediateyourlife.com/mourn-celebrate-learn-video/

Like Sally at the beginning of the chapter, you might notice that you are frustrated or unhappy about something as you create your dream. If so, you can walk through MCL as she does below to help you identify your met and unmet needs, as well as identify habits that you'd like to create or change.

—*⁓*—

Sally leaves the restaurant feeling grateful for being able to spend a little time with Peg that isn't about taking care of their mom or asking her to help with the kids. She had told Peg about her frustration of the morning, and Peg had asked whether one of the processes she knew might help find a new way forward. The process that came to mind was Mourn Celebrate Learn, and Sally is now excited to try it. She drives to the field where Maggie is still finishing up soccer practice, and sits on a bench nearby to take herself through the process.

She starts with not being able to find the contact information for the woman she'd met. *What are my observations?* she asks herself.

First, I couldn't find the contact info and spent half an hour looking. I had thoughts that I was stupid. I felt frustrated that I couldn't find it and disappointed that I looked for so long. I guess my need there is for ease of pulling up information quickly, and to be able to find it so I can move on. So productivity is important to me. And maybe a need for well-being too, to know I'm organized and can find what I require to get things done.

Sally pauses.

It's so weird . . . I'm so organized at home. I guess I have to be so that everyone has the important numbers handy, like doctors and schools and the kids' friends' parents. But I've never done the same thing with my business. Oops!

Sally shakes her head at this realization, then wonders what she can celebrate about it. She then realizes that it might help to look at what she was doing that led to not having the contact handy.

What's my observation there? she muses. *Well, probably when I got back from the networking event, if it's like other events, I just threw all the business cards I'd collected into the drawer or left them in my bag, instead of doing something with them. That's about ease for sure. And really it's the same with email—when I'm responding to email, I'm doing it quickly because I'm focusing on getting things done that seem more important at that moment. So I'm meeting needs for productivity there, and to keep moving instead of stopping to get organized and add contacts to a list. Wow, it's like I'm meeting these needs in one way, but with consequences of not meeting them in another way! I would like to take some time to set up my contact list, and then develop some system to make sure it stays up to date. I don't know what that would look like yet, so maybe a first step would be to brainstorm some ideas of how I might do that.*

Sally feels confident with those agreements, and begins to think about the rest of the morning.

My observation is that I worked all morning on my website, then still didn't feel good about what I'd accomplished. I felt let down and was thinking I should feel more pleased than I did, so I was unsatisfied. But I guess I can celebrate that I worked on it . . .

What needs was I meeting? Hmm . . . clarity and ease for sure, since I know what to do for that task and other tasks aren't always so clear. And there's something about getting the website done that I'm looking forward to. I think I'm expecting that I'll feel like my business really exists when I have a web presence, that I'll be seen as a businesswoman .

As for the needs that didn't get met spending my time working on it . . .

I'd say sustainability and effectiveness are the biggies. I'd like to spend time doing the things that will most move my business forward, instead of getting caught in that Shiny Object Syndrome. So, what can I learn from this?

Sally thinks for a minute.

I'd like to be more strategic about thinking through what is really important each day, and letting that guide my work, instead of going with what is easy. So in the morning, before I even go to my email, I'm going to choose the important things I can get done that day. Maybe I'll even tackle the first one before I go to email. That would be a nice habit to get into!

Sally jots down her plans to create some new habits, finishing just as Maggie runs up to greet her.

—⁕—

MCL IN PRACTICE AND IN LIFE

We've been talking about using MCL to reflect and debrief when:

+ You feel dissatisfied with how something went, so you identify met and unmet needs and choose what you desire moving forward. Doing this can help you identify places where you might have a habit you'd like to create or change.

+ You are creating a new habit, so you work to stay connected with your needs each time you are successful or unsuccessful with it.

+ You've identified a habit you'd like to change, so you acknowledge what needs you're meeting (reward) with the old one, devise strategies for the new routine, and assess how your effort is producing the desired result each time you engage with the habit.

When using MCL in these ways, you'll want to focus on one particular incident. While habits are general and you may tend to think about them that way, you'll want to take the specific instance that comes to mind when you go through the process. For example, instead of a general statement like, "I go to social media when I'm overwhelmed," be more specific, as in, "I went to Facebook this afternoon to distract me when I looked at how many things were on my to-do list." Or instead of "I always choose unhealthy foods when I go out to eat at a restaurant," start from, "When I went out to lunch with my coworkers today, I chose the hamburger and nachos, then regretted it afterwards."

As you can see, choosing a specific instance of the habit in action allows you to identify the specific needs that were met or not met. These may match the same needs—both met and unmet—with regard to this habit in general, but it's easier to identify them when you start from a concrete example.

Though normally we recommend beginning with mourning, using MCL for habit change lends itself well to starting with mourning *or* with celebrating. For example, if you resumed an old habit you have been trying to change, you might jump immediately to judgments of yourself and start with mourning. However, it might be easier to start with celebrating the needs you were meeting in what you chose. Acknowledging that you were meeting needs—any needs—removes the sense of wrongness about what you did, creating more space to then look at what needs *weren't* met. Sally found this to be the case in looking at her choice to work on her website. Though she initially felt it was wrong because of how she felt, celebrating the needs that she *did* meet opened her to consider more fully the needs that *weren't* met. Through this process, we hope you will begin to see that there is no right or wrong choice; there are only choices you can learn from.

When you are creating a new habit, you can benefit from using MCL even when you are successful at performing the new habit. Let's say you would like to write as part of your dream, and your new habit is writing a specific number of words or for a certain amount of time each day. When you execute this behavior, celebrate that you did it—but also ask what needs might *not* be met, and what you can learn. Inquiring into unmet needs when you actually performed the habit might seem strange, but the fact is that when you create a new habit, you may find it takes some time to adjust to it. Perhaps during the first days of accomplishing the new behavior, you realize that because you are now taking time for writing, you haven't exercised. If you don't acknowledge that and be present with both met and unmet needs, you may find it less likely you will continue the habit.

Why is this? Because if you simply push aside the thought that you didn't exercise, it's more likely to build up, getting stronger each time you push it aside until you sabotage your whole writing project. Without being present to both met and unmet needs, it's easy to fall into thinking that you can do one or the other, instead of looking at how you can do both—in this case, write *and* exercise to meet all of your needs.

People tend to falter in making ongoing change when they are unaware and disconnected from needs, and thus not at choice. Staying connected to all of your needs and being in question about how to meet them on a continuing basis helps you choose *each time*. Even if your choice the next day is to exercise and cut down on your writing time, the fact that you've chosen consciously makes it less likely that you'll give up on the writing (or exercise) completely.

Though it seems odd to talk about conscious choice in a discussion about habits (which by definition are unconscious behaviors), the fact is that at the start, you have to choose, again and again, to engage in the behavior you desire in order for it to become a habit. Once it becomes habit, you no longer have to make the choice, as long as it continues to work for you—or in other words, as long as it meets your needs. When you solidify *choosing* early on, it establishes the kind of pattern that allows you to continue acting in ways that you enjoy, leading you toward fulfilling your dream.

MCL is similar to Chooser Educator in that it is a go-to process for something that happened in the past. In our experience, CE is most helpful when you have a harsh critical voice, whereas MCL is more generalized for situations in which you'd like to assess how something went. However, we encourage you to try out both processes for yourself and find what works best for you to shift into more connection and find a new way forward.

Once you've practiced and internalized the map, you'll find you will be able to do it more quickly and in the moment. Here are a couple of options for integrating MCL into your life and being able to use it in the course of your day.

CONDENSED PATH

For a medium-length version of MCL, you can go through the same process as the full version, but you'll focus only on needs. Once you've practiced the full version and are familiar with naming the observation and feeling, then looking for the need, you can perform a version that jumps right to needs. In other words, when a situation arises, you may be able to simply ask what needs were not met (mourning), what needs were met (celebrating), and what you might learn. Always remember with needs that you are looking for a physiological reaction, not a cognitive analysis, to naming the need, which means you have a strong *sense* of whether the need is met or not. You can do this in a matter of minutes when you notice you are feeling disconnected or displeased after an event or happening.

QUICK PATH

For a short version of MCL, consider combining it with Self-Connection Process. Here's how that might unfold:

1. Notice that you feel bad about something that happened or that you did (or didn't do), then perform SCP and reconnect to your breath, body, and feelings.

2. When you get to the needs segment of SCP, consider both a need that was not met in what happened and a need that was.

3. If it's helpful, ask one of the questions from Step 3 (Learn), such as "What would I like to do to move forward?" and plan what you will do next.

This shorter version flows from one map right into another in a way that doesn't take a lot of effort. As with all shorter versions of maps, try this exercise *after* you've had some experience going through MCL step by step in detail so that you begin to embody the process.

PRACTICE PAUSE

What agreements could you create with yourself to integrate MCL into your life?

Chris, Dawn, and Kevin used the MCL map to work through their respective situations. Let's look at how they described their process.

CHRIS

"When I did MCL, I really got in touch with all my unmet needs in what happened yesterday. I was feeling pretty unhappy about the choices I made to ignore my breaks and stay later than I wanted to. I didn't meet needs for integrity, care, or certainly for well-being. In mourning that, I understood that I let myself get drawn into other people's drama, and it got all blown out of proportion, even though it really wasn't that big a deal. It was hard to celebrate anything initially, especially since I judged myself for getting involved to that extent, but then I saw that I was meeting needs for challenge, to be seen as someone who can handle the issue, and for a kind of fellowship, joining people so we're all in it together. I realize that it's okay to try and meet those needs, but I would like to do that in a different way going forward.

"The other thing that's clear is that I tried to take on too much. I was so excited about how well other aspects of my lifestyle change were going that I got a little ambitious, trying all of these new habits about stress management at the same time. I think it might help if I focus on one at a time, instead of trying them all at once. So for the next few days, I'm going to narrow it down to the one-minute pause and see how I do with that, regardless of what comes up."

DAWN

"I did MCL to try and uncover what was making me feel so blah about the phone conversation with the head of the board. I celebrated that I did listen and reflect back what she said, which met my needs for empathy, care, and respect. That led me to realize, though, that I didn't listen for her needs too. I stayed focused only on my needs, and that didn't meet my need for connection. I noticed that I tend to feel like my needs won't get met when there's any disagreement, which is what leads to that desire for control. What was fun about it was that I could actually celebrate that recognition, instead of feeling like I did something wrong. I like that it gives me a way forward, and in the next few days, I'd like to focus on really listening for people's needs—as well as expressing mine—when I'm talking with them, and see what opens up from that. Maybe there's a new way forward in collaborating that I haven't even been aware of. I may even want to change my agreement with myself about the question I was asking: whether this is a time for collaboration or control. That may not be the right question after all, if I'm thinking of control being about only *my* needs getting met. I'm not sure about that yet . . . it's something I'm going to keep looking at as I do MCL after future conversations."

KEVIN

"I chose MCL to look at what happened on my day off, since I didn't really have a strong judgmental voice about it. I first focused on how I had worked more on my day off than I really wanted to, which didn't meet my needs for balance, enjoying my time off with family and other projects, and integrity. When I looked at what had happened, I realized that I get really engaged in certain aspects of my work, and that's what drew me that morning. I liked what I was doing, so I was meeting needs for enjoyment, accomplishment, and meaning. That led me back into mourning, since I realized that I was aware of not stopping, even when I knew what I was doing was no longer essential. What bothered me about that was that I wasn't really making the choice. I like that I was still meeting needs, but I'd like to do that more consciously. Because continuing to blindly work didn't meet my needs for being at choice *or* being truly connected to my needs in the moment, I'd like to stop and connect with my needs through

Self-Empathy in the future so that I can make a conscious *choice. I'm glad I was at least aware, but it's clear to me that sometimes awareness isn't enough. There's another step to take in order to choose."*

As you take the steps to achieve your dream, notice the opportunities along the way to create behaviors and patterns of thinking that will support you in your efforts. Use the Mourn Celebrate Learn map to stay connected with yourself when you find that dissatisfaction arises after taking action, and see if there are habits you would like to change.

As you're striving for your dream, think of your behavior through the analogy of a sailboat. When sailing, though you are headed for a target, you rarely arrive there directly; it is only through numerous course corrections that you reach your destination. Similarly with habits—through MCL and the other processes in this book that help you reconnect continuously with your needs—you can make frequent course corrections in your habitual thinking and behavior so that you fulfill your dream with greater ease.

NEXT UP

Changing the habits that are in the way of reaching your dream—and creating new ones—are ways of navigating the things you can control: your behavior and mental patterns. As you take action, however, you will also encounter situations that you cannot control. In the next chapter, we'll address how to respond when the unexpected occurs.

RESILIENCE

8

TURNING SETBACKS INTO STEPPING STONES

Life's up and downs provide windows of opportunity to determine your values and goals. Think of using all obstacles as stepping stones to build the life you want.
—SIMON SINEK

———

SALLY ARRIVES AT HER OFFICE AND MAKES A CUP OF TEA. Sitting down with a trade magazine, she leafs through it, barely seeing the pages. *What's going on? Why am I NOT excited to jump into things today?*

She reflects on the busy few weeks prior. Though the lead-up had been a little stressful, she had prepared for the national meeting and presented her session there, receiving a positive response. Sally smiles, remembering feeling on cloud nine that afternoon. Many people told her how much they appreciated her session, and she collected quite a few leads as well—people who said they were interested in following up about her services. She came home feeling satisfied and pleased about the whole experience, as well as looking forward to what she could create with her business through the new connections. The few days following, she'd sent personal notes to everybody she'd talked to about working together. She'd also added all the people she'd met to her contacts list, delighted that she was changing her habits in that area.

Suddenly, Sally feels her mood sink. *I haven't heard back from a single person,* she realizes. *Nothing. Not even a "Nice to meet you," or "I enjoyed our conversation," much less anyone actually following up to discuss work. I guess they were all just being nice at the meeting, saying what I wanted to hear. Maybe none of them really had any intention of hiring me. Maybe they were just being polite. Or maybe I turn people off ... what if there's something about my personality that people don't respond to?*

Sally pauses, remembering her internal conflict about going in the first place. *All that time I spent prepping was a waste, since nothing came of it. Maybe I'm really not cut out for having my own business and won't be able to make it work. I mean, what better opportunity could possibly come along to generate more business? Presenting at a national meeting with all these people in my industry. Where did I go wrong?*

———

It's impossible to plan for everything on the way to your dream. Regardless of how big or small your aspirations, it's likely that the unexpected will happen. You will plan, but your plan will prove to be inadequate, or will proceed differently from what you anticipate. Events out of your control will intervene, threatening to throw you off course. Some examples might be:

+ You plan an event at the community center, and the pipes break and flood the center the night before your event.

+ A key ingredient is unavailable at the store for your carefully planned dinner party, necessitating a last-minute menu change.

+ Your flight gets cancelled while you're on the way to an important meeting for your business.

+ You get sick the night before a final interview for your ideal job.

+ A manufacturing error causes your new product to ship later than anticipated, and publicity has already been sent.

These experiences can bring up more internal barriers—thoughts and feelings that get in the way of clarity and excitement about your dream. If the setback seems significant and the internal barriers proportionately large, it can sometimes be the final straw, causing a person to give up altogether.

> setback *n.*
>
> stalling or reversal of progress

Many of the previous examples in this book could be seen as setbacks: Chris "screwing up" at the wedding and eating more than he intended, Dawn finding that the board wants to take the nonprofit in a different direction than she does, and even Kevin being offered a promotion. From one point of view, these events could be seen as obstacles to the dream they are each working toward. Yet in all of these cases, when approached through connecting with what's going on within, they find a new way forward with increased motivation and commitment to the dream.

In this chapter, we'll talk about the common setbacks that people face, the internal barriers that may arise, and how to use the Mediate Your Life maps to overcome them. We hope that through this chapter you begin to see setbacks as simply another opportunity to connect to yourself, identify your needs, learn from what happens, and make agreements to continue creating your life.

COMMON OBSTACLES AND BARRIERS

We just listed some examples of unanticipated events and issues that can arise in different situations. Though the potential obstacles that can develop are as diverse as the dreams you may have, here are a few common categories of obstacles:

+ Events that are outside your control

+ Someone who impacts your ability to reach your dream, either purposely or inadvertently

+ Pushback from family, friends, or coworkers

+ Your plan doesn't proceed the way you'd hoped, desired, or expected

We've seen already what happens for Sally. She presented at the conference, having worked through her internal conflict in Chapter 4 about it. She believed that the connections she made there would result in more work, yet so far they haven't, creating a setback for her that causes upsetting thoughts and feelings.

Here's how Chris, Dawn, and Kevin experience hindrances as they work toward their respective dreams:

CHRIS

"I'm so angry. I've been doing so well with my dream, making all these changes, and sure, things come up, but I've worked through them every time. And now this . . .

"My family and I have been doing something active

every weekend, sometimes heading out of town for kayaking or some other outdoor activity. I used to skate as a kid and my wife played hockey when she was younger, so it's been really fun to get our kids into rollerblading. But we went last weekend to a park, and I fell and broke my ankle! I was watching out for one of my kids and didn't pay attention to where I put my feet. Now I've got this big brace, and I won't be able to do much for at least six or eight weeks, maybe longer. I guess at least I don't need surgery, but still, this has really thrown a monkey wrench into being able to create healthy habits."

DAWN

"I've been so excited. There's this old factory on the edge of town that's been empty for a long time, and I realized it could be the perfect place for us to create our arts center for the kids. It's not too big, and it has separate rooms that we could make into areas for different arts, with a pretty big area that could be a performance space. Plus we could have offices there too. I contacted the owner and we walked through it, and I could see the possibilities for what it could become. It would definitely take some time and money before it would be at my vision for the space, but we could actually start using it as is. The property owner seemed really nice and said he was interested in what we're doing, and the building was inspected to make sure it was safe. It passed with flying colors, and we were working on a long-term rental contract . . .

"Now it's all turned sour. The owner has come back saying that he wants triple the rent we'd agreed to verbally, and what we'd agreed to was already just at the edge of our budget. I'm so frustrated that he's done this. I don't know what happened. My dream felt so close to becoming a reality in such an amazing way, and now it's slipping away. After seeing this place and my vision for it, if this doesn't work out, I don't know how I can continue working on something that I'm sure will seem like second best."

KEVIN

"I had a tough conversation with Rick, my job-share partner. I think we're through the honeymoon phase where we were both being extra polite, and now that things are starting to be a little more real, we're no longer glossing over the challenges of this arrangement. The tough conversation happened because I went on a four-day trip with my family, and since we were sailing down in the islands, I was completely out of touch those days. I didn't take much time away from work—mostly it was over my normal days off—and I made everything as clear as I could for Rick before I left. But something came up the first day I was away, and because he couldn't reach me, he felt put out. Sometimes it feels like no matter what, someone is going to give me grief. Either I take some time and it's a problem at work, or I take care of work and I hear about it at home."

PRACTICE PAUSE

What setbacks or obstacles have you faced
on the way to your dream?

The barriers that arise when you encounter obstacles in your life are likely to sound familiar, as they're similar to those encountered in other stages of achieving your dream:

+ "I can't do this—it's too hard."

+ "I'm just not cut out for this."

+ "Things never go right for me."

+ "See? The universe is against me."

+ "People are against me."

+ "I'm ahead of my time. No one gets what I'm trying to do."

+ "I'm a failure/I'm not meant to succeed."

+ "What's wrong with me/my plan/my dream?"

+ "I can never get ahead. It's always one step forward, two
  steps back."

As with all internal barriers, sometimes the barrier is less in
words and more in a feeling of hopelessness or powerlessness. If
you notice you are feeling hyper, distracted, depressed, bummed
out, disheartened, or lethargic when you face the unexpected, understand that these feelings may be a sign of an internal barrier.
In that case, you'll want to use the suggestions below to identify
what is going on so you can work through it.

PRACTICE PAUSE

Which internal barriers show up most
commonly for you when setbacks occur?

WHAT TO DO WHEN THINGS DON'T GO AS PLANNED

When facing an obstacle, your thoughts and feelings are likely to
be a habitual reaction and therefore trigger you into a low level of
the fight-flight-freeze response. An obstacle is seen as a threat to
accomplishing the dream, and any intrusive thoughts may trigger
further stress. However, going into the stress response is not likely
to positively contribute to the situation. While initially being am-
ped up may seem helpful for dealing with the issue, it can take
you out of being present with what's going on. Hence, it's more

likely that being clear-headed will assist you, since you are more empowered when you are aware, present, and able to choose.

Returning to presence and choice even in stressful situations is the purpose of the Mediate Your Life maps and tools, including the ones in this book. Whether your setback is big or small, as soon as you notice a barrier thought or feelings consistent with those thoughts, begin with Self-Connection Process as a way to connect to yourself. This short practice is one of the most effective ways to come back to presence—and it helps to practice it regularly, so that when you are in the midst of a crisis situation, you've already embodied the map and can fall back on your practice.

At times, especially in the midst of an emergency, connecting to your needs may be enough to help you take more effective action. It can also lead you to the next map to choose. Any of the maps we've discussed in this book may be appropriate to use when dealing with a setback, and in Chapter 10 we'll have more to say about how to choose a map based on what is going on internally. For this chapter, however, we'll focus on the map that is most likely to be helpful: Mourn Celebrate Learn.

CREATING COMPASSION

Being stopped by forces that seem outside your control can be challenging, and having compassion for yourself will create more ease in moving through the experience. Yet in our experience, simply telling yourself to have self-compassion doesn't work. In contrast, a process like Mourn Celebrate Learn tends to allow compassion to arise naturally. How?

When you get connected to your needs, particularly unmet needs, there's often a sadness that arises between the way things are and the way you wanted them to be, or the way they could be. Many people try to avoid that sadness, but if you stay with it, there's a space created where compassion typically develops, a tenderness and warmth that occurs in being able to hold what happened, what you desire, and the gap between them. Depending on the situation, you might hold what you did or what someone else did that you didn't like, or you might hold how hard the situation is and how you don't like the choices you see available. Either way, when you truly tap into your needs, you can feel compassion for whatever is going on that's difficult.

At the same time, you can also inquire into what you can learn from it to better meet your needs moving forward. That step is built into all of the maps in one way or another, particularly in the Learn step of MCL or in the final step of requests and agreements in the other maps. Not only is learning valuable in seeing how to act differently in the future to better meet your needs, but it's even more effective when you can learn in a compassionate manner.

Kevin used various processes to learn from the difficult conversation with Rick:

"I started with Self-Connection Process, but it pretty quickly morphed into Self-Empathy. I did the Breath and Body parts of SCP, but when I got to Needs I realized I wanted to uncover the observation. It went in a couple different directions from there. First I went with the observation of 'I never get a break.' No matter what, someone is unhappy with my choices. When I think that, I feel exhausted and then go into indifference. With needs, ease came up first, which made me realize that it's pointing me toward this sense of choosing for me. I don't know what the need is exactly, but it's something about including myself in my choices instead of only including other people.

"Another observation was that Rick expressed his upset at my not being available during my trip, so I shifted from Self-Empathy to Mourn Celebrate Learn for that observation. First, I mourned the consequences of not being available, which didn't meet my needs for partnership and to make this job work for us both. I then celebrated that I did unplug for the trip—it was relaxing and nourishing to simply be there with my family, having fun. I also realized I was able to unplug because I trust Rick to handle anything that comes up. Even though we have different responsibilities, I trust his judgment. Perhaps I haven't expressed that well enough to him, or maybe he doubts the decisions he made. Either way, one next step is having a conversation with him, and maybe include our boss, to talk about trust and handling what comes up when the other person is off.

"Another thing I realized is that I might not be able to completely unplug to make this job-share partnership work, though I'd still like to aim for that. While I may not always like my choices either way, it doesn't mean I can't learn from them; at the same time, I can see that being connected to myself and my needs doesn't mean I'll necessarily get to some ideal place where I'll like every choice, or that my choices won't ever have uncomfortable consequences. I'm finally understanding that using these maps is not about some idyllic future, but rather about making choices every moment to the best of my ability."

FINDING MET NEEDS

While learning includes taking into account the needs that you *did* meet, finding met needs can feel challenging when you're upset over a setback.

Taking an example from earlier, let's say you have a workshop scheduled with twenty people signed up, and the night before the workshop the pipes break and the space is flooded, making it unusable. After finding this out in the morning and going into crisis mode, do you try to find a new spot at the last minute to hold the workshop, notifying all attendees about the change? Or do you cancel or postpone the workshop and deal with the consequences of some people wanting their money back?

Hopefully, if you've been practicing the maps and skills in this book, you know to use Self-Connection Process in a situation like this so that you can respond from needs, instead of reacting out of your stress response. But whether you're able to do that or not, there are a few different ways you can look at what needs *were* met when you later consider what happened.

First, you can always appreciate any satisfaction about the lead-up to the workshop, such as all of your preparation, the people who did sign up for it, how ready you felt, and the needs you were meeting in offering that topic. Second, you can look at any needs you met in how you responded in the moment. If you indeed connected with yourself, that's something to celebrate. If there was a period of time where you went crazy and yelled at people, you might mourn that, and then look at what you did to change it. Or, perhaps you met some needs in staying calm and collected, handling everything so the workshop could go ahead, and enjoying how you were able to use the experience as a teaching point in the workshop.

PRACTICE PAUSE

Think of a recent setback you experienced.
What needs were met?

Going through a process such as Internal Mediation helps you connect to the needs you anticipate meeting by taking an action. But in some situations, barrier thoughts may arise from needs you *aren't even aware of,* yet were hoping would be met. In other words, even if you executed one of our processes and connected with your needs, you may have unconscious expectations or hopes about needs being met that you don't fully grasp until barriers come up afterwards.

For example, let's say that Sally feels a vague sense of dissatisfaction immediately after her presentation at the conference. She isn't sure what is going on, so she performs Self-Empathy, looking for the observation—what happened or what she is thinking—behind her current state. She realizes it has to do with judgments about how she spoke: at times she wasn't as articulate as she would have liked, and during a couple of audience questions, she fumbled her answers. She remembers the needs she'd hoped to meet by presenting—sustainability, contribution, growth, fun, and belonging—and realizes that she hadn't named another one, ease in expressing herself, that she'd also hoped would be met. But instead of staying in her judgments about how she spoke, she recognizes that this is an area she would like to improve, and therefore begins looking into how she can enhance those skills. In short, in choosing to execute a process afterwards that connects her with her needs, she discovers how to better meet those needs in the future.

WHEN OTHERS ARE OBSTACLES

If your dream is a departure from the norm, a big dream, or one that impacts those around you, the people in your life may push back against it. Perhaps you'd like to travel around the world, or use a chunk of your savings to start your own business. Your family and friends may not support you the way you'd hoped, or they may express their displeasure in your new direction or disbelief that you can succeed. You may find yourself telling someone, "My family thinks I'm crazy!" or "My friends think I've flipped!"

What's going on with this type of setback?

When you do the internal work of this book, you change; you reach more clarity internally, and make a plan and agreements with yourself that will allow you to create the life you desire. But when you interact with the people in your life—what we call your *reference group*—they know you as you were *before* doing that work, so the new you is a change to them. Since you exist as part of a larger system or network of relationships, when you change, those relationships often have to change as well. As a result, your reference group may resist this change and offer pushback, making you feel like you have to justify your new direction.

Other people besides your reference group may also seem to impact your ability to reach your dream, either through being actively against it or unintentionally standing in your way. Whether you see someone in your reference group or outside of it as an obstacle, you may feel like you are in conflict with that person. But when you work with the internal barriers that arise in these situations, you can change how you feel about the person and how you approach them (we will cover another way to work with these situations in the next chapter). Conversely, you may want to work through the conflict directly with the other person (in *From Conflict to Connection*, we outline the maps and tools to use in working with interpersonal conflicts).

Here's how Dawn responded when she became aware of her internal barriers arising from the setback of the factory owner asking for more money:

Realizing how upset she was over the building, Dawn chose Self-Connection Process and after focusing on her breathing, she named her feelings as irate, despairing, and anxious. Tapping into her needs in that moment, she came up with predictability, openness, and support. "From there, I realized that my judgments of the building owner were really strong, so I worked with those first.* In doing that, I connected more deeply to my needs for support and honoring my word. When I empathized with him, I guessed that he had been really hopeless about this building, which I know he'd tried to sell many times, and therefore might be trying to meet needs for financial security.

"When I uncovered his potential need, it helped me to at least not be so angry, and it also opened up the next piece, which was an internal conflict I had about what to do next. Part of me still wanted to stick it to him: by refusing communication with him and letting him sit with knowing he could have made some money from the building, I would silently convey that he ruined it by going back on his word. Yet part of me still loves my vision for the space and what it could become, so I don't know that I want to sever ties with him. I also saw how the other board members really got on the bandwagon with the idea of having a center when I shared my vision with them. They could see the possibilities, and I'm afraid this setback will send them back to their original idea of merely putting the program into the schools.

"So I did IM, and it was so interesting. The part of me that wanted to make this guy suffer had a need for empowerment, which is familiar to me. When anyone stands in my way, I tend to go into this mode of 'Well, I'll create it despite what you say.' But this time, I found I opened up to what other options might be available, and I decided to present it this way to the board, asking what the possibilities are that we haven't even considered, instead of focusing on it as a problem. I feel much more energized again, and I trust that no matter what—whether we end up being able to use this space or not—we will create something fabulous."

*See *From Conflict to Connection* for transforming judgments of others

SETBACK AS DREAM RENEWAL

An obstacle can cause you to wonder whether you will reach your dream or even whether this dream is right for you. Thus, it's an ideal time to reconnect to the needs for your dream itself. When you revisit the earlier stages of creating your dream, you may find that there's some shift in the dream or in the plan. Since needs can be met in any number of ways, when you reconnect to the needs motivating your dream in a time when reaching it feels in question, it may open you to other possibilities. In fact, one of the most important outcomes from a setback can be reconnecting with your dream.

Chris finds this true as he faces the setback of breaking his ankle:

"I was really feeling down about breaking my ankle, so I did Self-Empathy. My observations focused on my thinking that I won't be able to stay on track with my commitment, which means I'll fail and gain back the weight I've lost and more—again. My feelings were upset, angry, and sad. My needs were about being consistent with my goals and in integrity with what I've said.

"Then I was prompted to look at my dream again. This is enough of a setback that I had to look at whether my dream is still important, whether it's still meeting the same needs, or if it has changed. I was afraid to look at that for awhile, but when I finally did, I was so glad. I reflected on the strides I've made and how much more I've been enjoying my life lately. I expanded the number of needs that my dream is meeting in doing that reflection, so I ended up recommitting to it.

"I also realize that the plan is going to have to change, at least for the period of time that my ankle is healing. I made some new requests and agreements with myself and my family. I'm focusing on food, stress, and sleep for now, and I'll also see a physical therapist to get some exercises I can do in the meantime, since my normal activity won't work.

I'm back to being excited about the lifestyle I'm creating,
and I see this as a chance to focus more on certain areas,
and maybe even learn a few things that will contribute to my
dream well beyond this obstacle."

People tend to think of a dream, or any commitment, as a
one-time deal: you commit and that's it. But we find that it's more
about continual renewal of your commitment and consistent reconnection with the needs you hope to be met. Why?

If you see your dream as a one-time commitment that you are
beholden to forever, then you are in essence making a demand on
yourself in the future. But the part of you that plans for the future
is different from the part of you that acts in the moment that future arrives. If you don't reconnect to the needs your dream is
meeting, you will act from the *demand* of the part of you that
planned.

In other words, people may start out in connection with the
needs they hope will be met, but if they begin to *make* themselves
take the actions expressly because they committed to them in the
past, they will resist. This is why people so often fail to sustain
exactly the type of health-related lifestyle changes that Chris is
working on. More willpower is not the answer here; rather, continuing to connect with the needs in each moment they take those
actions allows forward movement without the resistance.

If you've faced a setback, ask yourself, "Do I want to renew
my commitment to the dream? Is it still going to meet my needs?"
Think about the needs you were connected with when you first
created the dream and plan, then check in with yourself to see if
those are still relevant to you now. Because you have changed
since you created the dream, gaining new information and learning along the way, your needs and even your larger dream may
have changed. Allowing the space for that to occur will keep your

dream alive for you, even if it's not the same one you started with. In short, forcing yourself to follow an old dream simply because you committed to it some time ago generates a lot of effort to merely bring a dead dream into existence.

LIVING INTO "WHAT IS"

One of the common responses when facing a setback is to reframe it from a negative into a positive. This can sound something like:

- "This is actually a good thing."
- "It's showing me there's a different, maybe even better, pathway to take to reach my goal."
- "It's the universe pushing me in a different direction."
- "It will make me stronger in the long run."
- "It's about finding the new way around the obstacle."

When people try to reframe something as a positive that in the moment they see as a negative, they're using an intellectual framework to understand and cope with life events. That framework might be summarized as: "Just because you see it one way right now doesn't mean that future events won't shed a new light on it."

This is the teaching of the Taoist story of the farmer who faces a series of situations that the neighbors think of as either a misfortune or a blessing (his horse runs away, then returns bringing wild horses; his son rides one of them and falls off, breaking his leg; the soldiers come and take all able-bodied men, leaving the son). To each the farmer simply says, "That's the way it is."

Intellectual frameworks can be helpful, but where they fall

short is *they don't give you the way to bring them into your behavior.*
The fact is, if you're facing a setback, in the moment it happens
it's dissatisfying, unpleasant, and perhaps even painful or scary,
and you might feel hopeless or terrified or irate.

You can try to take this intellectual frame of mind and impose it on yourself by saying, "No, really, this is a good thing.
Even though I feel really crappy about it right now, it will all work
out for the best," and try to bypass or ignore how you currently
feel. You could also go into the trauma and drama of it ("Oh this
is terrible, woe is me . . .") and pull the ash heap over yourself,
but that's not likely to produce something you'll enjoy in the future. Neither of these options provides you any guidance about
what to choose in the next moment.

So what do you do?

All that you can truly know is that something is the way it is.
And this doesn't apply only to what happens in the outer world, it
also applies to the inner world—to where you are *in relation to*
what happens. If you can work from where you are, connecting to
your observations, feelings, needs, and requests, mourning and
celebrating what happened and learning from it, you increase the
likelihood that you can make choices that create *more* instead of
less. When you use these tools, you are staying with "what is" in
each moment, both in the outer world (what happened) and the
inner world (your response to it). You then don't have to impose a
belief on yourself about this event being a good thing; instead, you
make choices moment by moment that help you experience the
knowing of it.

A key learning that can come out of facing the unexpected is how
to develop awareness as soon as you become triggered or stressed
so you can respond effectively in the moment. In the early stages

of working with these maps and skills, particularly when habits and the stress response are involved, you may find that it takes many iterations of going into your habitual stress pattern, then realizing it sometime later and working through one of the maps. As you repeat this again and again, you will develop ways to be aware earlier that you are not connected with yourself and are acting out of alignment with your values. As you become aware in the moment instead of some time later, you can intervene quickly to connect with your needs, thereby acting in a more favorable way. Similar to developing any other skill, it takes practice and repetition to be able to respond in the face of urgency, distress, challenge, or aggravation. To be present in the moments when life throws a setback your way, make a choice, accept what that choice creates, and then choose again, over and over. Isn't that a skill worth developing?

—⁓—

Sally catches herself at the end of the long train of thought that concludes with, *What did I do wrong?* Then she thinks, *Wait a minute, that's not where I want to go!* Sally sits back in her chair and takes a deep breath, noticing the tension in her torso and face. *At least I can celebrate catching myself quickly and not letting myself go into a slump based on those thoughts.* Sally remembers times she would have spent days or even weeks feeling down on herself, and she is pleased that this time she catches it right away.

Okay, she reflects, *so I'm bummed that people haven't responded to me. I didn't think everybody would, but I had a lot of hope that some would. I'm disappointed, sad, and I guess a bit hurt too. I thought there was a connection with some of these people. What needs aren't met in this?*

She considers this for a few moments.

Connection, and of course respect . . . being seen and valued, knowing I matter enough for someone to want to respond to a message. I really went outside my comfort zone on this one, both with the conference and with the way I talked with people afterwards, which met a need for challenge and growth . . . and still I'd love to have some feedback that there was some meaning in doing that. I tried, and now I'm in this gap between the response I'd hoped for and what I've actually gotten. I'm sad about that. I guess I'm also a bit afraid. If none of this potential business comes through, what then? Can I really sustain this business?

The phone rings and Sally answers it, interrupting her process to chat for a few minutes with a client. After completing the call, she refocuses.

Okay, so I mourned, and those needs are about sustainability in my business, connection, respect, and being seen and valued. So what can I celebrate? Well, that I did go, stretching outside my comfort zone . . . so meeting needs for growth and challenge. And that I did make all of those connections . . . I really enjoyed talking with a few people and that's important too, not just what might come of it in the future. I can also celebrate the follow-up I did, writing the notes to people. I made an effort to put myself into those, not just send some generic email to everyone. I like that I did that . . . I acted congruent with how I want to act in my business.

Even in the midst of celebrating this, Sally feels the disappointment flood in again. *I'd still like some response, though. I guess I'd like to be seen for the effort I've made. Maybe I could at least acknowledge myself for that . . . and I could also consider that there's something more I could do. Perhaps I could call some of these people, just to say hi and connect again, not necessarily with some agenda.*

Sally stops suddenly, awareness dawning. Just then her phone rings again. Seeing Alicia's name on her phone, she picks up.

"Alicia, perfect timing! You won't believe what I just real-ized!"

Alicia laughs. "Well, you sound excited. I can't wait to hear it. Tell me!"

Sally says, "I've been mourning and celebrating from the conference, because this morning I felt so down about not hear-ing back from any of the people I connected with. But what I just understood was how much interpretation and meaning I was putting on their silence. I went to how wrong they were for not responding, and how wrong I am for any number of things, from my personality to how I followed up, and then it went right to failure in business. I just leapt from one right into the next. But I just realized that I don't actually know why no one has responded. Maybe it just means they're busy and haven't gotten around to it yet. It's weird, though . . . I mean, it's so clear now, but a few minutes ago, I didn't see anything but my own failure."

Alicia chuckles. "But look how quickly you realized you were interpreting their silence as a bad thing when it might not be. You didn't stay for days believing all your judgments were true and then feel awful about it. You recognized it and did something to change it."

Sally agrees. "That's true. I started out saying, 'What did I do wrong?' But then I caught myself and celebrated that I caught it . . . it would have taken me so much longer a year ago."

"So, what are you going to do from here?" Alicia asks.

"That's what I was just getting to. I may take a look back at the list and give the people I felt most connected to a call. I'd like to check in, just to say how much I enjoyed meeting them and see what the conference did for them. Sometimes I think I put too much pressure on needing to find clients, even when I know that building relationships with people is usually the most effective way of building a business like this. I'd like to learn how to have a better balance between those."

Alicia asks, "Would practicing one of those conversations be helpful?"

"Yes! Would you be willing?"

"Sure!"

"It would be great to see what might come up and work with it instead of waiting until the real thing."

"Well, I was calling to plan an evening out with the four of us, but let's plan the role-play chat too. I know Shawn mentioned us getting together to James, but of course they leave the planning to us."

Sally laughs. "Just as well—if we left it to them, we might not get together until the next decade."

After planning the dates, Sally hangs up the phone, relieved and ready to see what she can create in her business today.

—ᴠᴠᴠ—

NEXT UP

One of the setbacks we mentioned you might face is when other people either push back against your dream or stand in the way of your reaching it. In the next chapter, you'll learn how to apply the Internal Mediation map when you are in conflict with other people, addressing your role in the conflict to shift the situation.

9 | WORKING WITH OTHERS

INTERNAL MEDIATION FOR EXTERNAL CONFLICTS

The most dangerous psychological mistake is the projection of the shadow onto others: this is the root of almost all conflicts.
—CARL JUNG

———

JAMES GLANCES AT THE CLOCK. *FIVE MINUTES UNTIL MY meeting with Scott.* He shuffles through the papers on his desk looking for the acceptance letter for the conference and the printout of the white paper he's written that they've published on their website. *I can't wait to tell Scott about this!* James thinks. *How great this will look for the company. He should be pleased.*

Just then, a momentary doubt flits across James's mind. *Maybe I should have talked to him earlier about it.* But James brushes the thought aside as he walks to Scott's office.

He knocks on the open door. "This still a good time, Scott?"

"Sure, sure, come on in," Scott says from his desk, indicating the chair opposite.

James sits down. "I wanted to let you know some exciting news, a little project I've been working on 'offline,' so to speak."

Handing over the papers to Scott, knowing that he will recognize the name of the national organization prominently displayed on the top of the first page, he continues. "I've written this white paper, which is on the website, and they've asked me to present next month at their annual meeting. Just a session on best practices in training, so it's specific to folks in similar positions as me. It'll be a small session, but I'm really excited about it."

Scott glances through the white paper and the letter, his face impassive. James becomes increasingly nervous the longer it takes for Scott to respond. Finally Scott sighs and looks up.

"I wish you'd talked to me about this before. It takes a lot of time and energy to do this kind of thing . . ." Scott waves the papers in the air, ". . . and it's no walk in the park to be good at all of it, both the writing and presenting. Maybe you're thinking it's good for the company for you to be out doing this, but if you don't do it well, it will reflect badly on us. You'd really need training and mentoring, and that's a big commitment. I think you've got enough on your plate already without taking something like this on."

James sits stunned for a moment. His next impulse is to get out of Scott's office, so not knowing exactly how to respond, he mumbles, "Okay, then" and leaves.

Walking back to his office, James moves through feeling numb to furious. *How dare he try to sabotage me and what I'm trying to do? What right does he have to tell me that doing this won't be a contribution? He can't just write me off that way.* Fuming, James finds it difficult to focus on his next tasks.

Other people will inevitably be involved as you take action to reach your dream. You may require other people's help, or you may find that your vision enrolls others and they wish to support you. When involving other people in pursuit of your dream, you may also encounter conflict, as people close to you may have unfavorable thoughts and reactions to your new path.

When conflicts are with other people, you might think they are not internal at all. If, for example, you have a conflict with your boss over the caliber of a project you did or you disagree with your landlord over who is responsible for paying for repairs, these can seem like entirely external arguments. As in James's conversation with Scott, James sees Scott as standing in the way of his dream and is therefore in conflict with him.

Generally speaking, if you're in conflict with another person, you may see it as an interpersonal conflict and turn to our book *From Conflict to Connection* for the maps and tools to use. Another place you might look, however, is to what is driving *your* side of the conflict.

Conflict does not exist in some external realm; it is always an internal experience for the people who are involved. Conflict is based on people's perception, and perception is always internal. Even if one person can get lots of people to agree that their perspective is most favorable—such as the one likely to be upheld by the courts—the conflict still resides in the minds of the conflictants.

Now, if the person you are in conflict with is aggressive, judgmental, or demanding, we are not suggesting that you are responsible for their behavior. What we *are* suggesting, however, is that you look within, because what's driving the energy from your side of the conflict likely has to do with your perceptions. As such, when you work with the conflict internally first, you may experience a shift in your perspective regarding how you'd like to respond to the other person. In this chapter, we'll address the internal aspect of external conflict and how to use the Internal Mediation map to address conflicts with other people.

Chris, Dawn, and Kevin each have other people they interact with as part of their dream. Let's see how they encounter conflict with others as they pursue the changes they're making.

CHRIS

Chris's family plays an integral role in his quest to transition to a healthier lifestyle, and extended family, friends, and coworkers can be supporters or detractors:

> "I had kind of a surprising and nasty interaction recently with my wife's brother and sister-in-law at a large family gathering. We hadn't seen them for some time—probably since before I began living a healthier lifestyle. They commented on how little I was eating, and then when dessert came and I turned down the cake, they got downright snarky. They made little jokey comments about how I should 'live a little' and how 'surely one little piece of cake wouldn't hurt,' and 'what, are you trying to be Mr. America?' I finally got so tired of it I snapped back at them, then avoided them the rest of the afternoon. It really irritated me, and I complained to my wife about it all the way home. She thought they were just trying to be funny and that I was taking it too seriously and should let it go, but I didn't find anything amusing about it."

DAWN

Dawn requires other people to create her vision of a nonprofit, from the board of directors to staff to people in the community who will be impacted. In addition, as we've already seen, her is-

sue of finding a suitable place for the arts center has her reacting
to the owner of a building she'd like to rent:

"I'm so angry with the owner of the old factory we'd like to
convert into the arts space. Although we had a board meeting and we're exploring some different options, we're still
continuing to negotiate with him. He agreed to a meeting
with me and the head of the board, but he was a jerk during
the entire exchange, claiming that he never agreed to the
price we'd discussed when I walked through the building
with him. I was trying to understand his viewpoint, and reminded him that he said how much he liked the idea of the
space being used for this purpose. But he totally did a one-
egihty, saying he hadn't really thought I was serious about
the whole thing, that he saw me as just a bored housewife
and thought he'd 'humor me' a little. I started seeing red
about then."

KEVIN

Kevin would like more balance between his work and home life,
and to reach that dream he finds he has to balance relationships
on each side—his wife and kids at home, and Rick—his job-
sharing partner—his boss, and his direct reports at work:

"I don't know what's going on. I thought I was doing okay
with creating work/life balance, but in the last day I've had
an argument with my wife, followed by another tough conversation with Rick. My wife and I were talking about how
great the trip was, and suddenly it turned into all this pressure to be around more, and she was implying that I was still
missing out on all this stuff at home and working too much.
Then I go to work and Rick is basically saying I shouldn't take
time off or be away at all, that I'm senior management and
that we need to be on 24/7 because that's the job. I said

earlier that I feel like I get it from both sides, and then I really did get it from both sides."

Each of them would say at this point that they are in conflict. The way people typically think about conflict is that all the responsibility lies with the other person. It's not unusual to think, *If they would just agree with me, we wouldn't be in conflict!* From our perspective, however, if you are in conflict, then your conduct is in some way contributing to it. As such, the most effective way to shift a conflict is to uncover how *you* are contributing and then work to change it. When you change yourself, you will shift the dynamic between you and the other person.

> ## PRACTICE PAUSE
>
> Have you encountered conflict with other people in pursuit of your dream? Bring to mind the situation, who is involved, and what the conflict is about.

THE INTERNAL COMPONENT TO EXTERNAL CONFLICT

When you react to someone else, have a problem with them, or are triggered by what they are saying or doing, consider that the reason you react is because there is a dynamic within you that is activated. You may be surprised to learn that the conflict with the other person may not be about them at all, but rather a result of something that pre-exists within you.

How might this show up?

1. Whatever the other person is doing or saying, there may be
    some part of you that does or says the same thing, and that
    is why you react.

    For example, if someone is judging you and you are react-
    ing to it, it is an opportunity to look within and see if you
    may also be judging yourself—perhaps some part of you
    is in agreement with their judgment, or you are judging
    yourself for judging. Anytime you're upset, angry, or hurt
    from someone else's words or actions, one way to shift
    what's going on is to look to the internal dynamic within
    you that represents the same pattern activated by their
    conduct.

2. When you have a barrier thought—like any of the ones
    we've listed in the previous chapters—you may project that
    thought onto something or someone outside of you. This is
    especially likely if it's a thought that brings up difficult or
    painful feelings you'd rather avoid. After all, it's not easy to
    face the part of you saying "I'll never succeed" when you
    believe it. So instead of seeing it within, it's interpreted in
    what other people say. Projecting onto other people is a
    way of hiding what you actually think about yourself, and
    further, hiding that it's *your core thinking* that is the source
    of the external conflict you perceive yourself to be in.

    For example, James recalls times when he reacted to co-
    workers or his boss giving him feedback about an idea.
    When he looked back on it, he recognized that although
    the person was only giving an opinion, James was triggered
    by it. His interpretation was that the other person was
    saying he didn't have good ideas, and that what he wanted
    to do wouldn't work. When James looked within, he real-

ized that he had an internal voice saying that he can't be trusted, his ideas aren't any good, and he should give them up because they won't work anyway. Since James has this barrier thought arise when he has an idea (and it may not even be a thought, but rather more a general sense or feeling), the same barrier is triggered in a similar situation, such as telling another person an idea and hearing their feedback. If James didn't have that internal voice, he would be less likely to interpret other people's feedback as saying the same thing, causing a negative reaction.

When you find yourself in conflict with another person, look at your interpretation of what they are doing and then ask yourself, "Where do I do that to myself?" Is there some part of you that does the same thing or treats yourself in the same way that the other person is treating you? If you find that the other person's conduct does reflect some way you treat yourself, it's likely you have an internal conflict in place. Part of you treats yourself badly, and another part reacts to it, much like you are reacting to the other person. In fact, you are reacting to the other person precisely because you are reacting to the part of you that treats yourself that way.

It's a good practice to think of times when you have an external conflict as an opportunity to uncover beliefs about yourself you may not even be aware of. Because core beliefs about oneself are sometimes so enmeshed that they remain hidden, noticing when you get triggered with situations or people can illuminate those beliefs. You can therefore think of your relationships with other people as a mirror of deeper internal conflicts that are difficult to unmask. In short, what you react to outside is a way to find out what's going on inside.

So how does this show up with regard to your dream?

If you feel triggered by what someone else says about your dream, perhaps being flooded with doubt or feeling paralyzed, then what that person is saying may be stimulating and reinforcing your internal barriers that you haven't yet overcome.

Let's say your dream is to have a child, but you have an internal conflict that says that because you work full-time, you'd have to put the child in daycare, which you deem bad and harmful. Then, in talking to a family member one day about having a child, that person says, "Oh, honey, you'd have to quit your job. You don't want to have your baby taken care of by others, do you? That's not good for the child." You may feel upset and in conflict with that person, but it's driven by the fact that you have an internal conflict mirroring the outside one. If you didn't have that internal conflict, you'd be more likely to brush off the other person's comment, recognizing that you simply have a different point of view.

Since this can be a challenging idea to grasp, let's take another example to see how an "external" conflict can be driven by each party's perceptions and internal conflicts.

A few years ago, when Corey and Maggie were a bit younger, Sally and James had a conflict one evening. Both of them were exhausted from having young children and trying to handle the necessities of life, and Sally said, with some insistence, that she would like some help with the children, and would James please read to Maggie and put her to bed. But James was trying to get all the bills paid before bedtime, and he was already wishing he could climb into bed and crash. From past experience, he knew that Maggie would want him to read a book over and over, dragging out the process of going to sleep. Not only would he be irritated and frustrated by it, he would still have the looming task of paying the bills. So he said to Sally, "I would really like to finish the bills and get to bed, I'm beat."

Sally retorted with, "You're so selfish . . . you always just think about yourself. What about me? I'm exhausted too. And they're not just *my* children. The least you could do is help get them to bed. You're gone all day as it is."

The thoughts running through James's mind went something like this:

She's so demanding and unreasonable. I never get a break, never get any understanding for what it's like to be in my shoes. She doesn't see or appreciate all the things I do for this family, or how I need to be able to focus on doing the work so that we can survive. I can't be drained of energy doing all this other stuff. If she really cared about me, she would see how exhausted I am and not be doing this.

Sally, on the other hand, was thinking:

He says he's exhausted, but what about me? I'm tired too. He never does anything around the house to help with the kids . . . I have to deal with them all day. He has no idea how much work it is to take care of little kids all day. Sometimes I would just like to take a week and go away and leave him to deal with all of it. And not leave with a full refrigerator, either! Let him find out what it takes to get everyone up and keep them fed and get them where they need to go and take care of the house. He always puts other things ahead of the family and he doesn't spend enough time with the kids. He should know spending time with them is the most important thing.

Both Sally and James were generating a whole series of thoughts that boiled down to "he/she doesn't care about me; if he/she cared he/she would see the pain I'm in and would help."

Thus, each had interpretations of what was going on that caused the conflict within them.

In this case, each had an additional internal conflict that was feeding the conflict with the other. For James, it came when he heard Sally say that he's selfish—a part of him also judged himself, thinking, *I really don't do enough to be present with the family, and I should be better about that.* Having these thoughts then caused James to be angry and defensive, because while there's a part of him that said he should be doing more, another part of him responded by saying he's doing as much as he can.

The internal conflict in Sally had to do with thinking she maybe shouldn't ask James for more help with the kids. *He does work all day and provide for us, so maybe I should give him a break.* Yet another part of her was still angry that he was missing out on an important part of the kids' lives and that he didn't seem to understand what she was going through. The conflict between them was driven and maintained by their interpretation of the other person's behavior as well as their own internal conflict.

> ## PRACTICE PAUSE
>
> Think of the situation that came to mind in the previous Practice Pause: In what way might you be contributing to your conflict with others?

Regardless of how entrenched an external conflict is (and the type of conflict Sally and James were in can easily become entrenched), it is possible to shift your internal state such that the conflict no longer lives within you. You may still have a disagreement with the other person, but you can work with the conflict in a way that you have no charge around it and can be in connection with yourself and with them. Before going into how to do this internal work, let's examine what happens when you disagree *without* conflict.

WHAT IT MEANS TO BE IN CONFLICT

What is your experience of being in conflict with someone? How do you know that you are in conflict?

Imagine yourself in a scenario in which you have a meeting with a coworker to discuss a joint project. You know your co-worker would like to use strategy A while you prefer strategy B. Here are two ways this scenario might proceed:

SCENARIO 1

Before even going into the meeting, you prepare all of your arguments for using strategy B, anticipating all the arguments your colleague will supply for strategy A and how to effectively refute them. You feel tight and wound up, expecting at best a difficult conversation, and at worst a fight to get your way. During the discussion, it feels like the two of you are at loggerheads, each of you rigidly advocating for your point of view, and the exchange gets more heated as time goes on. You finally both agree to a compromise, but leave the meeting feeling angry and frustrated, thinking of your coworker as an intractable jerk, and dreading the work going forward.

SCENARIO 2

Before going into the meeting, you use any process from this book to be connected to yourself and the needs you antici-pate would be met with Strategy B. During the meeting, you listen for the needs your colleague is seeking to meet and reflect those, and continue to connect with your own needs, expressing those to your coworker. At times you notice frustration coming up but always link it back to your needs. Eventually, after much discussion, you reach an agreement about a strategy to move forward on the project. You leave the meeting feeling connected to yourself and your coworker, and on board with the strategy that you mutually agreed to.

We would suggest that in the first case, you are in *conflict* with your coworker, and in the second, you have a *difference of opinion* regarding strategies, but you disagree and work toward solutions without having the experience of being in conflict. You're instead solving a problem together, which may entail feeling frustrated, hopeless, disheartened, or having a lack of clarity, but when you stay present with your feelings and needs, you can be in the disagreement without being in conflict with the other person.

As we've noted, in conflict there is often some way you are *reacting* to the other person. When you remove that reaction, the difference of opinion may remain, but the actual conflict dissolves.

So how do you step out of the reaction?

INTERNAL MEDIATION FOR EXTERNAL CONFLICT

When you are part of a conflict with someone else, it's crucial to check where the conflict is living within you. It may be in the thoughts about what's going on and the reactions to the thoughts; it could be in the interpretations, analyses, diagnoses, and judgments of yourself or other people. Often it can feel like you are possessed, where the thoughts take over and have a life of their own. In short, you do not feel at choice.

If you can uncover how you are contributing to the conflict, it gives you a starting place to do your internal work. To do this, you find the first voice (likely the one reacting to the other person) and the voice in conflict with it—perhaps the voice inside you that treats you in a way you don't appreciate, or the part of you judging that you're reacting. Using the Internal Mediation process, you give both parts of yourself empathy, allowing them to be heard by each other. The result is that by resolving your internal conflict, the outer situation transforms and thereby seems less daunting and more resolvable.

Here is a reminder of the Internal Mediation process from Chapter 4:

	CONNECTION		RESOLUTION
Mediating Between Two Parts of Yourself	**A's Needs**	**B's Needs**	**Synthesis/ Strategy to Meet All Needs**
Process	Empathize with A: surface A's needs	Empathize with B: surface B's needs	Consider what strategy might meet the needs of both A and B
IM Steps	1. Empathize with A 2. Empathize with B 3. Ask B to empathize with A 4. Ask A to empathize with B		5. Make Solution Requests and Agreements

The process is exactly the same as in Chapter 4, except you are identifying your *internal* conflict through an *external* conflict, instead of through internal voices coming up due to barrier thoughts about your dream.

How do you find the internal conflict that is being played out with the other person?

To begin the IM process, you can either jump in with whichever voice is most clear and see how the process unfolds, or you can identify the two parts in conflict first, and then follow the IM process.

When you're reacting to what someone has said or done, that can be a starting place. To do this, you'll set up your two chairs, then empathize with that voice as Part A. Let it speak, telling you its judgments or analyses of the other person and how awful they are, and listen for the observations, feelings, needs, and requests. When that part of you feels heard, switch to Mediator Mind and simply ask yourself, *What other part of me would like to respond?* Another part of you may have already tried to speak up as you were empathizing with Part A, or another voice may have something to say. That part of you is Part B, and you can empathize with it in the same way, identifying what part of you it is and what needs it would like to meet. Continue from there with the other steps of the IM map.

Another option is to identify the two parts of you for each chair before starting the process. You may have a voice that is judgmental about the other person, and you may also be aware of a voice that is judging you for judging, and these two can be enough to start your internal mediation. Or, your reaction to the other person may actually be a reaction to the part of you that does something similar. Since this second case is more confusing, let's take a closer look at identifying these parts of you.

As we said before, you sometimes react to what the other person is saying because there's a part of you that regularly says something similar—so you are actually reacting to that part of yourself. When you decipher what it is you are saying or doing, then you can mediate between those two parts of yourself. For example, let's say you react to your coworker telling you that your idea won't work. You recognize you are triggered because there's an inner voice telling you that you don't have good ideas. Therefore, your reaction to the other person is the same as your reaction to that voice inside you. Your internal conflict, then, is between the part of you saying you don't have any good ideas, and the part of you reacting to it.

Because this internal conflict comes up through your reaction to the other person, you might start there. In other words, Part A is the part of you in reaction, and Part B is the part of you doing or saying something (i.e., telling you that you have no good ideas) that Part A is reacting to. Again, you might request the name of these parts of you when you begin so that you can keep straight which part of you is speaking as you go through the process. Follow the Internal Mediation process exactly as laid out in Chapter 4, the only difference is how you arrive at the two parts of yourself that are in conflict.

When you get to Step 5, Solution Requests and Agreements, your request will be of yourself, as you're working on an internal conflict. At this point, you'll ask, "How do I want to take action to meet my needs?"

After you make the requests and agreements with yourself, you may also wish to address the outer situation to "close the loop," meaning that once you become aware of the internal conflict through a conflict or reaction to someone else and have resolved the internal conflict, you can now address the outer conflict. Hopefully, you now see the other person and situation in an entirely new light, perhaps even seeing that you are no longer in conflict with them at all, even if you hold a different perspective than they do.

PRACTICE PAUSE

Use the Internal Mediation map with a situation in which you are in conflict with another person.

———*∿∿*———

James continues ruminating on his anger at Scott, then notices a small voice of doubt. *Maybe Scott's right. Maybe I won't be any good at this, and if I'm not it won't look good for me or the company. Maybe I don't have much to offer and my point of view isn't valuable. Perhaps I should stick to managing the team . . . at least I know I'm good at that.*

The anger at Scott arises again, and James vacillates between the two until he suddenly stops. *Wait a minute! This doubt is actually really similar to what Scott was saying. I'm upset with him because he's saying what some part of me already thinks and is telling me. So this conflict is as much within me as it is between Scott and me. Let me mediate it and see what happens.*

James sets up two chairs, one for the part of him that is angry and the other for the part doubting himself. James starts in the chair of the part of him that is angry. Tapping into that voice, he listens to its point of view:

Voice A: *I do have something to say, and I have every right to go for this dream.*

MM (empathizing): *So, you'd like to believe in yourself and trust in your dreams and ability to reach them?*

Voice A: *Yeah, and trust that it will be a contribution, not just to whoever is at the session but to the field and at work too.*

MM: *You're meeting needs for contribution and trust . . . and is believing in yourself also about self-esteem or self-actualization?*

Voice A: *Absolutely, both of those.*

Upon hearing this, James asks and receives confirmation that this part would like to be called Trust. Feeling clear about where Trust is coming from, he switches to the other chair, the part of him that has doubts.

MM: *What do you want to say?*

James feels fear close to the surface.

Doubt: *Maybe we aren't really capable of doing this and should just stick with what we know we can do well. This might be too hard and too much to take on.*

MM: *Are you trying to stay safe, and not take risks that might be damaging in some way?*

Doubt: *We'll feel bad if we fail or get negative feedback, and it will reflect badly on us and on the company, so yeah, I'd like to avoid that.*

MM (again, empathizing): *Okay, you're protecting me from loss, like loss of respect from those I value at work and in my field, and loss of community and sense of belonging. Is that right?*

James feels himself relax as he asks this and receives an affirmative response.

Feeling complete with Doubt, James asks Doubt to reflect back Trust's needs, and then switches back to have Trust reflect Doubt's needs. After this step, James feels confident that both parts have heard each other, and suspects that since Doubt has been heard, it might be willing to go ahead with the current plans. Pondering this, from mediator mind he comes up with some language he can use to talk to himself and allay Doubt's fears: *"Even in the worst-case scenario, whatever is likely to happen in this situation is not so bad . . . I'm safe and secure in the sense that the world will not end and that I trust my boss and colleagues will appreciate my having tried."*

James then checks to see if this will work for Doubt, at least for a period of time. Doubt agrees to try it. James then checks with Trust, who is similarly willing to use this strategy. James ends by reassuring both Trust and Doubt that if this strategy doesn't work, they will together come up with another strategy to experiment with, and in so doing change the agreement.

Feeling good with this agreement for now, James's thoughts return to what happened with Scott. He notices that his anger at Scott has diminished, and he begins to wonder what really motivated Scott to say what he said. James spends a few minutes thinking through what he guesses might have been going on. After coming up with a few ideas that help him understand what might be motivating Scott, James decides to talk to him again tomorrow to see if any of his notions are on track.

—◦∿∿◦—

THE VALUE OF WORKING WITHIN

Have you ever told a friend about being upset by a comment from someone else, and they told you not to take it personally, to let it be like "water off a duck's back"? It likely didn't help much, did it? Sure, not taking anything personally is a nice idea, but the truth is that you are probably already taking it personally, so *what* exactly do you do to change that?

In this chapter, we're giving you the tools to create that "water off a duck's back" sense—or in other words, what to do once you have already reacted, and also over time to become less reactive.

When you notice what you react to, you become more self-aware about the limiting beliefs you hold. In empathizing with the voices that come up when you react, you reduce the hold those core beliefs have on you. As a result, you become much less reactive in general, because you no longer have as many sticky core beliefs that become triggered by what people around you say or do. When you react less, it's then much easier to be present and empathize with other people, and therefore be more effective in coming up with strategies that will address the issue at hand. In short, you're removing the static of your own reaction from the interaction with people around you.

Before covering the other benefits of doing internal work when in external conflict, let's hear what Chris, Dawn, and Kevin discover when they focus internally.

CHRIS

"I didn't stay angry very long, but I did keep running through the events of the day in my mind. I realized that what my wife's brother and sister-in-law were saying triggered a voice in me that judges me for not eating foods I know I really enjoy. It tells me I'm living for some future instead of enjoying today, and that part of the dream is to enjoy today too, so how is avoiding all these things I like in alignment with that?

"I was angry with my relatives because I react to that part of myself. So I mediated that conflict within because I know it can come up anytime I'm at an event, or even at home where there's food I like but doesn't fit my plan right now. I discovered that the part of me in reaction would like to meet needs for integrity and commitment as well as for health. Then I found that the other part is trying to meet needs for joy and pleasure, but also well-being, and since part of the dream is about enjoying the now, it's actually looking out for the dream too. The mediation turned into constructively thinking about what really brings enjoyment and pleasure, and where the choices I make are bringing up my need for autonomy—to be able to do what I want, when I want to do it. As I thought about these ideas, I again got in touch with how much more I'm already enjoying my life.

"Now, it's like a weight has lifted and I no longer feel a charge around any of it. Thinking back on the day, I can see my wife's perspective that they may have been joking, but I also see more clearly the possibility that my choices might have triggered them into internal conflict about their choices. In a similar situation, I get now that if I'm in touch with my needs, I can just be with whatever they say and it doesn't have to affect me."

DAWN

"I was so ticked off about what the factory owner said in our meeting that I had to jump right in with empathy. It was clear that part of me wanted to be taken seriously and that respect was a key need. I also saw how important it is to matter, and to be seen for what I'm creating. This center will make a difference, and it felt like by discounting *me* entirely, he was discounting *it* entirely. The funny thing was, as I was empathizing with that part, it occurred to me that I don't take myself seriously. I have that "imposter syndrome" people talk about, where I don't really see myself as a nonprofit founder, or a powerhouse woman in my community. I'm just a housewife and who am I kidding? People will see right through me. No wonder I got so angry with him!

"In empathizing with that part of me, I right away saw the need to trust that I can take care of myself emotionally. Because there's familiarity and comfort in the role I'm used to, stepping out of my comfort zone in such a big way is challenging, and there's a need for trust that I can handle whatever might come up. I sat with both of these parts of myself and when they connected with each other, something really opened up. It's hard to put into words, but it was like the level of respect I have for myself went up a notch and I stepped into seeing myself in a new light. In recognizing the ways I'm already powerful and capable, I know I'm growing my capacity to be present in ever more challenging situations, which is helping me be able to think more clearly under pressure.

"When I thought about the factory owner again and our interaction, he now seems almost like a caricature. He's this old-school kind of guy who expects women to be in the kitchen . . . it's almost laughable. So now that I know that's just the way he is, I began to think of a few men his age who I might ask to join the board and negotiate with him. Before I did this internal mediation, that idea would have absolutely infuriated me, but now I'm thinking, 'Why not? If that's what it takes to create what I'd like in the world, so be it.' I have a new understanding about being free to deal effectively with 'what is' and continue creating my life with my particular vision."

KEVIN

"I felt so confused that at first I wasn't even sure what process I could use, so I just did Self-Connection Process for awhile, connecting to my needs for clarity and ease in all of this. As I settled down a bit, I recognized that my wife and Rick were saying the exact things I say to myself, so they were each representing one side of my own internal conflict about my dream. It seems so obvious now but when I comprehended that, it was a revelation. I also felt a little frustrated, thinking, 'Haven't I done this internal mediation already?' Sometimes it seems like I'm going in circles. But I empathized with that part of me (that wants movement and clarity and consensus within), and then recognized that if this is coming up, it's because these parts of me are not feeling heard.

"The needs for each part of me came readily. Those related to working less are about integrity of my dream, enjoyment, and family, and the part that advocates for being available at work is motivated by a desire to be seen as responsible, and as embodying integrity, excellence, and dependability. There's also some fear there that if I don't go

above and beyond, I'll be fired. So I realized there's a pro-
tective nature in that voice as well.

"As I sat with each side, I really tapped into what it
would be like for the needs to be met, which was very satisfying. I also made some agreements with the fearful part
about checking in and what would help meet its needs while
also meeting others. These two parts of me seem much more
connected now, and I have more peace internally, even though
I know more conversations will be happening, both within
me and with my wife and Rick. I'm less concerned about
those, though, because I trust that we'll find a way through."

If you find an internal dynamic driving your external conflicts, you have more power to work with them and shift them,
which will change the dynamic of your relationship with the
other person. As the saying goes, "It takes two to tango," so think
of a conflict with one or more people as a system: anytime you
stop adding energy into a system, it begins to wind down; if one
person stops dancing, it's much more difficult for the other to
continue in the same way.

By using the IM map to reconnect with yourself, you can alter
the dynamic in the system, using the reconnection to then re-
engage with the other person. In being present with and hearing
the other person from a place of connection with yourself, the
whole dynamic of the conflict can begin to shift. Because changing the internal allows you to respond to the other person in a
different way, you show up with a fresh perspective, no longer in
reaction to the other person. And when *you* respond in a new way,
they will typically react differently in kind.

Though working with internal conflicts *is* extremely powerful,
it is not a magic bullet for solving external conflicts. In other
words, doing your internal work doesn't necessarily mean the
other person will be immediately placated and the stormy conflict

waters calmed. In fact, you may find that if you show up differently, the other person will react in a negative way and be *more* difficult. Even if you do your inner work—shifting out of judgments and back to reconnection with yourself, such that the conflict no longer lives within you—there still may be conflict living in the other person. They might still be hurt or angry, and you have no control over that, but in being reconnected with yourself, you are no longer *adding* anything to the conflict. At the very least, you will have stopped adding fuel to the fire, and at best, by being more present in your interactions with the other person, you will be more effective at finding ways to connect with that person as a bridge to building trust with them. Once you have trust, collaboration becomes possible.

Perhaps the most important takeaway is that when you show up differently and the situation changes, *you will then see that you have power*. In other words, however that person may react to you, you can simply do your internal work and show up yet again in a new way. Within this learning process, the more you can stay connected to yourself in the moment, the more you have choice about how to respond to the other person's reaction to your showing up in a new way.

In the best case scenario, when you do your internal work, the conflict can actually disappear and you won't need to use the maps for interpersonal conflict; you deal with it internally and it's not an issue anymore. In other cases, the interpersonal maps in *From Conflict to Connection* will still benefit you and your relationship with that person. But either way, uncovering internal conflicts that are contributing to arguments with other people and applying the Internal Mediation map gives you another means to exercise your power to choose. As with all of the Mediate Your Life maps, it also helps you return to connection with yourself in the midst of whatever difficult conversations you may be in. You can then engage more with people you find yourself disagreeing with from a place of connection.

———∿∿———

James knocks on Scott's door. "Hey, do you have a couple of minutes?"

"Yeah," Scott says, "come in."

James takes a deep breath and connects with himself as he launches into what he wants to say to Scott. "I wanted to follow up about what you said yesterday about the conference. I was a little upset when I left, but I've thought more about what you said, and I wondered if you're worried that I'll get distracted with this interest and might not be as reliable to pull the weight you'd like me to . . . that I won't be as plugged into my work and that might affect you and the team."

Scott nods. "Yeah, exactly. I'm concerned it might be too much . . . and I'm worried we'll lose some of the energy you put into your work here to this other activity."

James empathizes. "So you're focused on making sure that everyone in our division is doing what we need to do and not distracted by other things?"

Scott agrees and adds, "It's not personal . . . it's great that you'd like to be involved this way, and I don't want to take that interest away . . . I really value you and the work you do. It's just that you really take on a lot around here, and I'm concerned about you being able to do as good a job as you already do while also writing and presenting at events."

James feels himself relax inside, hearing Scott's affirmation of his value. "I really appreciate hearing that from you, Scott. And I *would* want to make sure I didn't lose any energy for my work here. In fact, what I've found so far is that it's energized me even more."

"Really?" Scott says.

"Yes. So since I do want to stay aware of overextending myself and making sure I'm not taking it to the point where it would affect my work, would you be willing to set up some ways to check in on that?"

"I guess so. Do you have something in mind?"

"Well, for example, if you perceive that I'm losing momentum, I would want that feedback. And since this presentation is coming up in a month, perhaps we could check in after that, before I commit to anything else. I would really love your support on this because it means a lot to me to take it on and to see how I can contribute in this way. I've realized it's kind of a dream for me, and that's why I've been really excited."

"Okay," Scott says. "How about we see this as a trial period?"

"Great."

"And hey . . . I read your paper after you left yesterday and it's quite good. I think others will really benefit from it."

"Wow. Thanks."

"What are you doing to prepare for your session?"

James smiles. "I have an outline in place and a time set up with Steve—I think you know him . . . he's on the board there and I worked with him before coming here—to run it by him beforehand. And in terms of presenting, I'm seeing it as very similar to what I do with trainings, so I feel confident about that. I'm just taking it all slowly and planning way ahead since I'm doing it on my own time. I'm really looking forward to it!"

James and Scott chat for a few more minutes, then James returns to his office, noting that he feels much lighter.

—~~—

NEXT UP

Whether you're dreaming, planning, or immersed in implementing
your plan, myriad barrier thoughts can appear to stop you. We've
discussed a set of maps and tools to use in various situations, but
how do you put it all together? In the final chapter, you'll see how
to move through all stages of creating and actualizing your dream,
choosing the map that will most support you to address any self-
sabotaging thought that threatens to halt your progress.

10 | COUNTERING SELF-SABOTAGE

BECOMING A COMPASSIONATE NINJA

You can't change what's going on around you until you start changing what's going on within you.

—UNKNOWN

———◈———

"I T'S SUCH A BEAUTIFUL AFTERNOON, LET'S EAT OUTSIDE!" Sally says to James as she finishes mixing her special salad dressing.

James glances out the window. "I was just thinking the same thing. Peg and Mom should be here soon, right?"

"Yeah, Peg texted that they were on their way."

Just then, the door opens and Peg walks in with Doris. "Hey, sis, we're here! What smells so good?"

She and Sally hug as James welcomes Doris, then settles her at the head of the table on the back patio with a glass of iced tea. Corey and Maggie follow, happy to see their grandma.

As plates are filled, Peg asks, "Hey James, didn't you just present at that conference? How'd it go?"

"It went well, thanks for asking. I really enjoyed the talk—it was actually kind of a high. The group was small, only about forty people, but that turned out perfectly because we got into a fruitful conversation."

Sally asks, "And what about Scott? Has he said anything?" Turning to Peg and Doris, she adds, "James's boss wasn't very on board with this idea initially."

James shrugs. "Well, he hasn't expressed any more concern about it, but I did set up a time to check in with him next week from our earlier agreement, so we'll see what he says then."

Sally nods.

"I'm just not sure what's next," James continues. "I mean, it was great, and part of me is saying, 'What, that's it?' So I'm not sure what's behind that. How about you, Peg? How are the caregiver kits going?"

Peg sighs. "Well, it's so interesting that you say that . . . it makes me realize what I've been thinking. Starting the kits has been such a learning experience, and it's going well. I have a good workflow . . . small but steady orders are coming in, and having Maggie over to help has been a blessing."

Maggie looks up from her plate and grins.

"As I hear feedback from people, though, they're sharing their struggles and I feel like these kits aren't enough. There's a much bigger need here, and while I still like the kits, they aren't having the effect I'd like to have. I'm just not sure what would have the bigger impact I'm going for. And I haven't really allowed myself to think much about it because I'm not sure I have anything more to offer."

Peg reaches for a roll and says to Corey, "Speaking of impact, how's your video game going? I loved your idea of a game that would address bullying. Where are you with that?"

Corey shakes his head, looking glum. "Nowhere. We just got turned down by a gaming company yesterday."

"Wait, you mean you already put in a proposal to a company?" Peg exclaims in surprise. "Where've I been? Last I heard it was just an idea!"

Sally jumps in proudly. "Oh, it's moved way beyond idea stage. Corey has had a lot to celebrate about it lately, haven't you, hon?"

Corey brightens a little. "I guess so. I talked to Mr. Loewen at school and he was really into the idea. He helped me map out the story and some simple graphics, enough to take to a friend of his. That guy thought it could be big and we worked up a full storyboard to present to the game company."

"Corey!" Doris says. "That's wonderful! I don't know anything about video games, but it sounds like a lot of people think your idea is really good!"

Peg nods in agreement. "And that they're willing to help you make it a reality. What are you going to do next?"

Corey shrugs half-heartedly. "I don't know. We just found out yesterday about the proposal. It bummed me out."

Doris says, "It sounds like your friend will be able to help figure out where to go from here."

"We think so," James says. "And what about you, Mom? We're all talking about our dreams . . . what about you? What dream do you have?"

Doris's infectious laugh makes everyone at the table grin. "Oh, honey, I have most of what I need right here . . . my family all well and happy, just missing your brother overseas. I guess the one thing I'd say is that I'd like to be able to enjoy whatever time I have left with you all and not be a burden on you."

The adults at the table all protest at once and Doris laughs again. "I know you all say that, and I appreciate it, but I know you're all busy, and I don't want to put more on you with my health. Peg's already changed her life to help out."

"Oh, Mom, you know I enjoy spending time with you. And I needed the change too," Peg affirms.

"We still haven't heard from Maggie or Sally," Doris says, shifting the focus off herself. "Maggie, what do you have going on?"

Maggie squirms in her chair. "I dunno. Just school and stuff."

Sally gives her a playful push. "There's quite a lot included in 'stuff'—chess club, animal shelter volunteering, soccer, and the science program."

Maggie rolls her eyes. "Oh yeah, all of that. But science, yeah, they just announced the science fair. I guess I'd like to have a cool project to enter in it. Some of the other kids have come up with cool things, but I don't have any good ideas."

Reflecting on the conversation, Sally says, "It's interesting . . . most of us are kind of stuck somewhere—Maggie with her science project, James unsure what's next with his dream, Corey in a setback with the company turning down his proposal, and Peg liking the kits but wanting a bigger impact."

James nods. "Yeah, and I also noticed we all had some thought that was in the way, keeping us stuck." He looks at Sally. "It seems this is the way it goes. I've seen you stuck or in conflict at all different points in wanting some balance between your company and family and taking care of yourself. It seems like you've been in a good place, though. How do you feel about it?"

"Well, I'm starting to feel like I have all of that better dialed in. I have a new client, things have been smooth at home, and I've been taking better care of myself. What hearing all of you brings up is how much I see my family as part of my well-being. I'm thinking how great it would be to have some sort of shared dream, like what we'd all like to create together as a family. I'm not entirely sure what I mean by that, but I love the idea."

"What a sweet thought," Doris says.

James squeezes Sally's hand. "Now we just need to figure out what that shared dream might be."

———⁓———

You've dreamed, planned, and implemented your plan, coming up against the internal barriers that can arise at each step, and having the conversations that help you continue. You've also seen how to address the common situations that surface in pursuit of your dream, from creating or changing habits to dealing with setbacks and conflicts with others.

By now, through using this book, we hope you have experienced the value of mediating your internal conflicts so you are no longer divided in taking action on creating the life you desire. We also hope you have experienced that connecting with the parts of you who show up with concerns actually enriches the process of achieving your dream. But at this point, you have likewise discovered that mediating once between conflicting parts isn't the end of the story. Internal barriers tend to show up again and again, as many of the examples in this book have illustrated. The truth is, if you've spent years not listening to some part of you, it may not believe you're truly listening now. And, as you encounter new situations, it may bring up other parts of you that suspect needs won't be met when you step outside your comfort zone. Hence, learning the maps and tools in this book is only the beginning, though it's an excellent foundation that will serve you for a lifetime.

With practice, you will become adept at integrating what's in this book. As you do, instead of a part of you stopping you for days, weeks, or even months or years, it will take only minutes to recognize that you are in conflict and connect with the different parts of yourself. In short, you'll become a ninja, aware the moment self-sabotaging thoughts arise and whipping out a process to address them. Instead of a sword, however, your tools are maps that connect you with yourself, help you mediate between voices, and increase your internal harmony and alignment.

THE BIG PICTURE: FROM DREAM TO ACCOMPLISHMENT

The three stages to actualizing what you desire in your life are dream, plan, and implement. At each stage, you may have barrier thoughts—self-sabotaging thoughts that threaten to stop your progress—and if and when that happens, you can use the maps and tools in this book as soon as you become aware of them. As we've discussed, internal barriers can occur each step of the way of creating your dream, and now you know how to work with those barriers so they no longer have the ability to stop you.

While the process of creating and actualizing your dream is laid out in a linear fashion in a book, you probably realize that it's far from linear in real life. As such, while you reconnect with your needs through listening to your internal voices, you may find that you choose to modify your dream, plan, or approach to implementation. For example, you may begin with a dream and plan, then as you implement it, you find that you have to revisit that plan, perhaps again and again. You may also discover that the dream itself changes, or that *your* needs change, and you therefore shift the dream accordingly. This back and forth is a fluid process, and staying aware of the conversations you are having with yourself allows you to navigate the process with more ease.

For example, Peg started in Chapter 5 with a dream of creating carekits for caregivers. James helped her come to agreements about moving forward on her dream, and she's taken all the actions and had the conversations to bring her dream into existence. But while she now has a small business selling the kits, she sees other needs that aren't being met through her products alone. She is therefore considering that her dream may change, perhaps expanding to include something else entirely.

Regardless of what comes up for you in dreaming, planning, and taking action to reach your dream, all the processes in this book are a moment-by-moment toolbox to choose from so you can stay connected with yourself—and so you can navigate the entire process of creating and actualizing a dream using all of them. We presented certain tools and processes at particular points for ease of learning them; however, the maps later in the book might be appropriate at earlier stages too. Let's take another look at each stage of the journey and how different processes might be appropriate.

DREAM

During the dream stage, self-sabotaging thoughts can indicate an internal conflict. If you think of a dream you'd like to achieve and then go into judgments about how you can't achieve it, you may want to use the Internal Mediation process to resolve the conflict between the part that desires your dream and the part with judgment. Similarly, if you have more than one dream and don't see a way to do both now, you could also use the IM map to connect with the needs you're hoping to meet, allowing you to make an informed choice about how to proceed.

As it's possible to judge how you are pursuing any choice you make, the Chooser Educator process may even be appropriate at this stage. For example, you may notice that you are judging yourself simply for the way you *approach* the dream stage, as in "I tried to come up with a dream and couldn't even do that" or "I came up with a dream, but it's not the right/good/perfect dream." Chooser Educator can help you uncover what the Educator would truly like for you.

PLAN

During the planning stage, any thoughts that keep you from planning (and therefore from moving toward your dream) are indicative of a dispute between (at least) two parts of you. If you think you need to know how you're going to achieve it, aren't sure what steps to take first, resist planning at all, or feel overwhelmed by the process, the IM map can help you have the conversation between the parts of you showing up. If you create a plan and then judge yourself for not planning correctly, or if you mess up somehow on making a plan, then Chooser Educator might benefit you, since you're beating yourself up for your supposed lack of planning prowess.

IMPLEMENTATION

Implementation encompasses everything beyond the plan, including how you take action, deal with obstacles, handle your habits, and work with others. While these can bring up several issues within you that a map could assist with, we recommend always starting with Self-Connection Process, as it's a quick way to reconnect to yourself through breath, body, and needs. From there, you are more present to choose what other process might be helpful. Below, we'll give you some guidelines on how to make that choice, whatever stage of reaching your dream you are in.

ACCOMPLISHMENT

Some dreams have a definite point of accomplishment, while others—particularly larger visions—may have many stages. Once you've reached your dream or completed some stage of it, please take time out to celebrate! Even if it's a tiny dream (like organizing that junk drawer in the kitchen), plan to do a Celebrate Mourn Learn upon accomplishing it. Celebrate your process, including any awareness you had and the choices you made to empathize with yourself. Then, mourn anything that didn't work as well as you'd hoped or times you forgot to pay attention to parts of yourself that were speaking up. Finally, consider what you might learn from all the conversations you had to reach this point that you might apply to reaching the next one.

PRACTICE PAUSE

Think about where you are with a particular dream. Based on what's coming up for you, what is your next step? Which map would be helpful for taking it?

HELP! WHICH MAP DO I USE?

In learning these processes, people are sometimes confused about the differences between them. Here are some clarifications about the common confusions, as well as additional guidelines about when to choose each process.

SELF-CONNECTION PROCESS (SCP) VERSUS SELF-EMPATHY

Anytime you become aware that you are disconnected, Self-Connection Process is the go-to process, as it's a quick way to reconnect with yourself and step into mediator mind. From that state of presence, you can then choose what you would like to do next by focusing your mind and deciding what action to take, which may entail choosing another process.

Different from Self-Connection Process, Self-Empathy is a tool to use anytime you would like to connect with a *specific voice* you hear. Listening for the observations, feelings, needs, and requests of that voice allows it to be heard as it desires. This tool is also particularly helpful when you're aware you don't feel good, yet aren't quite sure why, by guiding you toward the observation creating your current state. For example, if you feel glum and don't know the cause, you might use Self-Empathy to find the observation—when the feeling started, what happened, or what you were saying to yourself that led to feeling that way. This can lead you to the internal voice and a deeper connection to what is going on. In sum, while SCP helps you connect to *the fact that* you feel the way you do and what your needs are, Self-Empathy can help you uncover *why* you are feeling that way.

CHOOSER EDUCATOR (CE) VERSUS
MOURN CELEBRATE LEARN (MCL)

Chooser Educator and Mourn Celebrate Learn can seem like similar maps because they are both used after you have taken an action or something has happened to you. So how do you differentiate between them?

Chooser Educator is a type of internal mediation, following the same basic steps as the IM map. When you have a strong judgment about yourself following an action or event, it's likely you have a Chooser Educator conflict: your Educator is judging you for what you did, while your Chooser had good reasons for choosing it.

If you don't have a strong judgmental voice, but would still like to debrief a situation to learn from it, Mourn Celebrate Learn is the map to choose. It will not only help you find both met and unmet needs, but it will also allow you to think through what might help you better meet your needs now and in the future.

For example, let's say Sally is working on creating the habit of entering names into her contact list. She goes to a networking event and forgets afterward to enter the cards she collected into her contact manager.

If she . . .	Then she might choose . . .
Realizes it the next day and judges herself, thinking *Wow, that habit didn't last long ... I already forgot! How stupid is that? I collected all of these cards and didn't even think about adding them to my contacts. I'll never get this right . . .*	Chooser Educator, where her Educator is speaking, and she's likely to also have another voice, either saying why she didn't enter them (*"I was too busy!"*), or simply saying, *"I forgot! Stop judging me!"*
Realizes the next day that she forgot to enter the names, and she wants to examine what happened and how she might remember better next time . . .	Mourn Celebrate Learn, connecting to the needs she was meeting, the needs that weren't met, and what she can learn from it, in particular what agreement she might put in place to remember next time she goes to an event.

INTERNAL MEDIATION (IM) VERSUS CHOOSER EDUCATOR (CE)

Internal Mediation and Chooser Educator are the two internal mediation processes, so when you experience two or more voices that each advocate for a different strategy, one of these processes will be your best choice. The clearest way to think about when to use which one is based on time. If you have a situation that is present or future-based, then use Internal Mediation; if it's regarding something in the past for which one of your internal voices is in strong judgment about what you did or didn't do, then it's more likely Chooser Educator.

Keep in mind too that Chooser Educator can arise not only about aspects of creating and actualizing your dream, but also as you attempt to use the maps and tools in this book. You'll know your Educator has stepped in if at any point you hear yourself saying something like:

+ "You should have used a map there."

+ "Wow, you really messed up on choosing (map)—a different one would have been better."

+ "You can't even recognize when you have a self-sabotaging thought. How screwed up is that?"

+ "You don't even know how to get the benefit out of doing these processes."

In these cases your Educator is attempting to educate you about how you're not doing the process correctly. This is a perfect time to practice the CE map—connecting with the part educating you and with the part of you that made the choice.

Here's a quick guide to help you recognize when to choose a particular map or tool:

If you …	Try this map or exercise
Become aware of feeling out of sorts without being sure what it's about	Self-Connection Process (SCP) OR Self-Empathy
Notice a barrier thought that is keeping you from taking action	Internal Mediation (IM)
Are beating yourself up for not keeping an agreement or habit	Chooser Educator (CE)
Feel distracted and not present	Self-Connection Process (SCP)
Don't like how you feel about a past situation	Mourn Celebrate Learn (MCL)
Have multiple options and feel undecided about which to choose	Internal Mediation (IM)
Would like to learn from something that happened	Mourn Celebrate Learn (MCL)
Experience conflict with someone else and would like to address your contribution to that conflict	Internal Mediation (IM) for external conflict
Judge yourself for how you acted when faced with a setback	Chooser Educator (CE)
Feel stuck and weighted down, or sense resistance, reluctance, or heaviness	Self-Empathy
Cringe from an internal voice commenting harshly about what you did	Chooser Educator (CE)

As you take action toward living the life you desire, consider that every moment of your life you are facilitating yourself. As such, we've introduced the idea of mediator mind, which is the part of you that facilitates, focusing your attention in certain ways and making requests of yourself and other people. The maps and skills in this book give mediator mind a lens, or framework, to know what question will be helpful in any given situation, presenting a limited set of options to choose from that are likely to lead to connecting with yourself and taking action to meet your needs.

There isn't one right way (or wrong way) to go about having these conversations; in each situation it's your choice what tool to use. But if you feel stuck, start with SCP, and once you are present, choose a map and see where it leads you. If you don't find a deeper level of connection and understanding, pick another map. And remember that all of the maps are strategies to meet your need for empathy, so regardless of which map you choose, you will be empathizing with yourself—listening to your internal voices and their observations, feelings, needs, and requests. Repeated over time, you will create the habit of turning toward yourself in times of disconnection. If, however, you are in more troubling or difficult situations and find it a challenge to unwind what is going on within, you may want to seek help from someone else, so let's turn to how you might work with others.

PRACTICING WITH OTHERS

Unless you are already practiced in noticing your inner dialogue, you—like many people—may find it challenging to navigate an internal mediation process on your own when you're first learning. Distinguishing the two different voices can be confusing, and you may not have the clarity to mediate between them. In addition, the process can seem complex, difficult, and even arduous to undertake. This is when enlisting another person's help, either as a support person or to role-play the mediation, can achieve the same ends.

SUPPORT

If you know someone who is familiar with the maps in this book, they can facilitate you through all aspects of an internal mediation. If they're not familiar with the maps, they can still be of help with a bit of direction by reading through Chapter 4.

First, it's sometimes easier for another person to help you distinguish your internal voices if you have trouble identifying them on your own; talking out what you're hearing will likely help the other person categorize each voice. This person can then either support you to move through the process, or act as the mediator, taking you through the steps and empathizing with the voices that show up.

Having a friend support you can also help you with each component of empathy—observations, feelings, needs, and requests. Since being clear about the observation/judgment distinction is critical in internal conflict, a support person can make sure you identify observations, not judgments. In guessing or reflecting your feelings and needs, a support person can also help you be clear about the deeper motivation each voice is expressing. In making those guesses, each part of you is receiving empathy as well as gaining understanding of the other side. During the final step of making requests and agreements, an outside person can be instrumental in assisting you in finding a strategy that meets all of your needs. Finally, you may be clearer when you work with a support person—when someone else reflects what they've heard, it stimulates internal clarity.

ROLE-PLAYING INTERNAL MEDIATION

While a support person can help you with clarity and empathy, many people find that externalizing the voices through having others role-play with them brings an even deeper level of understanding and resolution. The idea of role-playing internal conflict may sound strange; after all, you may wonder, "How can someone else play *my* internal voice?" But while some people are initially concerned that another person can't represent one of their parts adequately, we rarely find this to be a problem. As much as internal voices feel like they are yours alone, it turns out they are surprisingly universal.

You can set up a role-play with one or two other people (or more, if you have more than two internal voices!). Each person plays the part of one of your internal voices. Here's how to set up this practice if you have two friends to work with.

If you're in the same location, set up two chairs across from one another, and the third at ninety degrees for the mediator. You will play one voice, someone else will play the other voice, and the third person will mediate (you'll each switch chairs to play each role). You can also set up a triad practice over the phone, in which case each person can set up three chairs to move between.

To begin, tell your partner playing the other part of you a little bit about that part's perspective; often all that is necessary as a starting point is the language that the voice uses, perhaps the main phrase and emotion. If you already sense what needs that part of you is trying to meet, you might share that too, but that may not be clear until you get further into the mediation.

Since it's your issue, once the other person has the starting phrase for their role, you begin talking from the point of view of the voice you're playing. Remember, you're not talking *about* the issue, you *are* that part of you. The mediator then empathizes, guesses what needs that voice is trying to meet, and guides the conversation.

The key to internal mediation as a triad practice is to switch roles so that eventually you will sit in each of the chairs. Set a timer at the beginning for some period of time, perhaps fifteen to twenty minutes. Following the same basic IM process, you speak first and the mediator empathizes with you, then your partner speaks and the mediator empathizes with them. When the timer rings, wherever in the process you are, everyone rotates one chair. You now play the role of the other voice, the previous mediator plays the role you were just in, and the other partner becomes the mediator. Reset the timer, and then simply continue the conversation from where you left off. Go a few more rounds of both voices being able to speak and get some empathy, and then when the timer rings, again rotate chairs, so you are now in the mediator chair, mediating between these two parts of you, played by your practice partners. Continue the conversation again from where you left off.

People often have striking insights into their internal conflicts by externalizing the voices and taking on the perspective of each part of themselves, ending in the mediator role.

If you are working with a single partner, you can do a role-play in which you take on the role of one voice, and your partner takes the role of the other voice, empathizing with you *from that perspective*. In this scenario, instead of a mediation, this role-play is an empathy session.

For example, if you have a Chooser Educator conflict regarding treating your daughter harshly, you would first inhabit the role of the Educator, and your partner would be in the role of the Chooser. You would simply speak as the Educator, saying the words to your role-playing partner as if that person is your

Chooser, in the voice you hear speaking in your mind. Your Educator might say:

> "I can't believe you did that! You're such an idiot. I thought you were supposed to be compassionate. You're hurting her emotionally. What were you thinking?"

The "Chooser's" role, then, is to empathize with you; they reflect back what they hear you saying, turning it into feelings and needs.

When the Educator has spoken their piece, switch roles. Now you speak as the Chooser, and your role-playing partner takes on the role of the Educator to empathize. As the Chooser, you say what comes up in hearing the Educator's judgments. From the above example, it might sound like:

> "Hey, give me a break, I was angry! I don't want her to grow up and be disrespectful of others. What do you want me to do, just sit there and do nothing?"

Your partner as the Educator empathizes, helping you as the Chooser connect with your feelings and needs.

After the Chooser and Educator both receive empathy, you can stay in the role of the Chooser with your partner as the Educator, and consider other actions you could have chosen. Keeping all the needs in mind, you might dialogue with the Educator about what you could do that would also meet the Educator's needs. In the example, it might sound like:

> "So, if I had chosen to take a breath and remind myself of my needs for love and connection, while still expressing my need for respect, would that work for you? Would that address your needs?"

Once you come up with a strategy that both parts of you like, you might want to practice it. That practice can take place internally, but if the situation involves communicating with someone else in a different way, you can ask your partner to role-play the other person. By role-playing the situation and acting in a new way, you practice being able to do what you desire in the moment.

Though similar to simply having a support person empathize with you, we find that in role-playing this way, people reach a much deeper level of empathy. It's somewhat mysterious, but when the other person is playing a part of you giving another part of you empathy, it begins to feel like each part is actually giving empathy to the other. It is even more powerful than simply receiving empathy from a support person.

PRACTICE PAUSE

Who can you ask to practice with you and what request can you make? If you need a practice partner, check out our book page online at:

www.mediateyourlife.com/
when-your-mind-sabotages-your-dreams/

INNER CACOPHONY: WHEN MORE THAN TWO VOICES SHOW UP

We've focused on internal conflicts in which you only have two parts of you in conflict, but you may find times when three, four, or even five parts of you are all vying for attention. What do you do then?

It can be confusing enough when you have two voices to contend with, much less a horde of them. The most effective way we've found to mediate in this case is to keep the conversation between two of the voices. If you are aware of more than two voices from the start, you can ask, *Which two parts most need to have the conversation right now?* Identify the two voices that 1) have the most energy or discord between them, and 2) that would be most valuable to resolve their differences. If it isn't clear which two have the most charge between them, you can also simply choose two to put in the chairs first.

Sometimes, you have two voices at the beginning, but then a third shows up somewhere in the process. At whatever point another voice arises, empathize with it first. Then ask the question above, seeing if it makes sense to shift the two parts having the conversation, or continue as you are, assuring the new voice that you will come back to it later.

Once you have completed the Internal Mediation process with the two parts, check in again and see if there is another conversation required. Often, going through the IM process with the two voices that have the most charge between them is enough to create a sense of connection within about the issue, and the other voices integrate easily into the resolution. If not, ask who would still like to voice concerns and who that part would like to be heard by, and have that conversation.

Always keeping the conversation as a one-to-one between two parts of you maintains a sense of order in what can be a complex process of multiple voices clamoring to be heard. Ultimately, remember that the underlying goal is to uncover the needs of any voice that speaks up and to encourage connection within.

LIVING AS A NINJA

As we've discussed, using the Mediate Your Life maps and tools helps you become aware in the moment that you have a self-sabotaging thought. Once aware, you can be present with what's going on for you, connect with your needs, and then choose what's next from that connection. Each time you create a dream and begin the process of actualizing it, the journey will be different. Yet we've seen common themes emerge as people become more ninja-like in applying the MYL maps. To elucidate these themes, let's check in with Chris, Dawn, and Kevin, and hear their reflections on the process of actualizing their dreams.

CHRIS

We've followed Chris as he developed his dream of a healthy lifestyle that would allow him to enjoy today and live many tomorrows. Any dream that involves so many daily choices is likely to bring numerous opportunities to practice the MYL maps. Here's how Chris reflects on where he currently is with his dream:

"I've gone through so much in the time I've been using the MYL maps: choosing my dream of a healthy lifestyle, entering into the program at work, and all the small and large changes along the way. It's so easy at the beginning to think that it will all be straightforward and easy—just eat a bit better, get more movement, sleep a bit more—but it hasn't been, not even close. Working through each situation that has come up, like the trip to Vegas with the guys, the broken ankle (which is still mending), and the conflict with my wife's family, all have helped me find new ways to act consistent with what I'd like my life to look like. Each time something comes up, even when it initially feels like a setback, I see how much it has contributed—once I get through it—to being more fully in this journey. It's like each time I get in touch with what a voice really desires, it puts me in touch with a part of myself I may have ignored before. The result is that I get more of me all the time!

"The changes I'm noticing in my health have almost become a side benefit, even though they started as my main dream. But I've seen changes for sure—I'm more than half-way to my target weight, I'm sleeping better and don't wake up exhausted anymore, I feel more energy throughout the day, and I'm happier than I've been in a long time. I have a ways to go and I'm sure challenges will still come up, but I have the skills and the confidence to keep going. I think it will keep getting easier, since the more I'm in touch with my-self, the easier it is to make healthy choices. It's like the more I honor myself through connecting with all parts of me, the more I naturally want to make other choices that honor me as well."

DAWN

Dawn's journey from not knowing her dream to starting a nonprofit organization has had her looking at her relationship with herself and other people in a new way. Similar to Chris, she found that it was a process that unfolded in ways she couldn't have imagined:

"I'm so amazed when I think about the journey I've been on—I remember when I started, I didn't think I had any right to even have a dream! And look at how far I've come. It's all a work in progress, of course. But still, I'm celebrating all that I've put into my dream and all the personal work to do it in a way I feel good about. Starting this nonprofit is such a collaborative effort, and I've had to look at a lot of my own challenges with desiring control and my relationship with power, not to mention how I see and treat myself. I'm learn-ing so much in using the MYL maps about meeting my own needs, and in working with others in a way that creates more in the world for everyone. Even when it's challenging, I'm be-ginning to trust that if I just keep going—choose some process to use, go through it, and get help if I need to—I'll find a way forward, often one that's better than I could imagine before.

"This situation with the owner of the building I've been dealing with over the last few weeks is a perfect example. I went through all of the angst about his actions and my reaction to what he said, but I kept connecting to myself and to what I thought might be going on for him. The board and I stayed in communication about our options and reached out to our respective communities, and we may have hit the jackpot. We have a funder willing to purchase the building for us! They are negotiating right now, and there's still a lot of uncertainty, but we're hopeful that this will work out. We already have kids from the high school interested in helping with the changes we'd like on the building, so it looks like we may be able to give kids more than just an arts experience. Because shop classes have been cut too, one of the teachers who used to teach shop is talking to the school about creating a class where the kids will work on projects for us and get credit. I'm thrilled seeing how people are getting behind my dream and creating more than I ever imagined."

KEVIN

In his process to bring more balance to his life so he can enjoy his family and lifestyle, Kevin has also discovered that the path turned out to have as much to do with how he related to himself and the world:

"When I think back on where I started with my dream, I remember how resistant I was to having a dream at all, and how unwilling I was initially to use the MYL maps. I've always relied on my intellect to figure things out, and when I couldn't see a way to do that, I tended to avoid the maps. That's why I resisted my dream. It's taken some time and experience, but I now recognize how much I didn't trust that this would give me a way through that would work—and I still have to frequently remind myself that I now have another option. My experience is that connecting with myself in the ways I've learned actually does give me new ways forward that my rational mind wouldn't have come up with. I knew I would need a personality adjustment to create more balance in my life, but it turned into a much bigger one having to do with how I relate to myself—and to everything else!

"In terms of my challenges with this job-share situation and having more time with my family, it often still feels difficult. I keep reminding myself that it's not about some perfect solution that will take care of everything, it's about being able to be present and consciously choose from needs. The more I stay in touch with the different parts of myself, especially the ones that have been in conflict about my dream, the easier it is to have conversations with others. Rick and I are continuing to discuss how to work effectively together, and I have more compassion for where he's coming from. My wife has been supportive, especially as I make more effort to unplug and do more things with the family. I'm still at the beginning of this journey, but I notice the ways I'm already living more in alignment with my dream than I was earlier. I'm able to appreciate and enjoy more time with my family away from work, while still enjoying my professional career. I no longer feel like I'm avoiding a difficult situation that I can't find a way through. I'm consciously creating the life I want to live."

As Chris, Dawn, and Kevin all discovered, the process is not about cognitively figuring out what is holding you back or what to do next. While you do include thinking in the process, using these tools allows a deeper wisdom to play a substantial role in actualizing the life you desire. Even when the path is difficult and you're up against your biggest self-sabotaging tendencies, keep going! You will discover more of yourself and be more fully in your journey each time you become aware of holding yourself back and then choose from presence. You and your life are worth it.

—◠◠◠—

Pushing her empty plate aside, Peg says, "Well, if we're all stuck and have some thought getting in the way, let's work through them. We have two experts here, after all!" She grins at Sally and James.

"I'm game," James says. "Let's see if we can first each identify the barrier thoughts getting in our way."

"Okay," the group says in unison.

"For me," James says, "it's that sense of disappointment. A part of me is saying something like, 'You put in all that work and where's the big result?'" He turns to Maggie. "I heard you say you don't have good ideas . . . is that your barrier?"

Maggie twists her hair around her finger. "Yeah, I guess. I want a great project like the other kids have and I can't come up with anything."

Corey speaks up next, as Maggie's barrier thought triggers his own. "I thought I had a great project, but since it was turned down, now I'm wondering if it's really any good. Maybe I've been wrong about it."

James nods, recollecting their earlier conversation. "It sounds similar to the doubt that stopped you from going from the dream to the plan." He turns to Peg. "What about you?"

"I think doubt is there for me too," she says, crunching her face. "I'm seeing this bigger need and thinking I may not be the person who can address it, for a number of reasons." She pauses. "Mom? Sally? What are yours?"

Doris shakes her head. "I don't have any thoughts that are getting in the way."

Sally looks thoughtful. "Mom, I wonder if the belief that you're a burden on us is a barrier thought. I could see it taking away from being able to enjoy being with us when you interpret that you might be a burden."

"I hadn't thought of that!" Doris says. "I do feel sad think-ing that, so perhaps you're right."

Sally shrugs. "Maybe. And for me . . . there's confusion about what a shared dream might be. But in terms of something in my way, maybe I shouldn't even bring it up. We're all work-ing on so many things and here I want to add something else . . . and maybe you don't all have the same desire, so I should just be quiet." Sally's eyes widen. "Wow, that sounds like a barrier thought right there, doesn't it?"

"Yeah," James says, "one that would keep you from even bringing it up!"

Everyone laughs.

"So we've all identified what's holding us back," James de-clares, "so let's work through one."

Everyone looks around the table. "Peg," Sally ventures, "would you be willing? I think there's something else holding you back and would love to help figure out what it is."

"Sure," Peg says, giving it some thought. "Well . . . the first thing that comes up is time. I can't take anything else on right now. But that's also the easy excuse, if you know what I mean. If I'm really being honest with myself, what's there is this sense of 'who am I to think I could really help people that way?'"

Sally nods. "Is that part trying to protect you from judg-ment?"

"I think so. In part, it's about credentials, but there's also this deeper belief about what would I really be able to do for people that would make a difference?"

James guesses the need in what he hears Peg say. "Is it that you would like to matter?"

Peg nods slowly. "Yes . . . I'd really like to help people be in a position of caregiving in a different way, a healthier way than people tend to be."

"Sounds like it's also meeting a need for care," Sally says. "Maybe the care *you'd* like for yourself being in this position?"

"Probably so, yes," Peg affirms. "And to share what I've learned from doing this."

"So contribution as well," Sally reflects. "Since you've been there, you know the territory and what to do or not do."

Peg laughs. "So I guess I do have something to offer. But there's still this voice saying I can't have a big enough impact."

James wonders out loud, "Is that again reflecting the need to matter, or is it something else?"

"Maybe meaning?" Sally adds.

Peg ponders their suggestions. "Maybe some of both. I guess the word coming up is more like value, something about what I or this experience have that's valuable."

"Would you like to trust that you and your experiences have value?" James asks.

Peg's shoulders relax slightly and her face softens. "Yeah, I'd really like that."

Sally mirrors what she's heard. "Okay, so you'd like to help people in a bigger way than the kits are doing . . . meet needs for care, contribution, and to matter . . . and you'd like to trust that you have value. Is there anything else?"

Peg chuckles. "Hearing you say that, I realize I'm defining value as something much bigger than what I'm doing—taking care of Mom." She turns to Doris. "It reminds me of you, Mom, and how you always said that your role as our mom was the most important thing you could do with your time. I do understand that, even though I seem to easily forget it sometimes." Peg rolls her eyes. "It's like this is the most valuable thing I could be doing, and maybe at some point I can do something more than the kits, or maybe I can find a small way to start bringing in this other piece to the kits . . . I don't know, but just having this conversation reminds me of that perspective."

Sally says, "It's interesting how much clearer all of us are on the value of what you're doing than you are! I know I'm so grateful every day, knowing you're with Mom. It's not just contributing to her, it's contributing to all of us. And I know Gerry would agree too . . . remember he said so before he went back overseas."

Doris and James both agree.

James asks Peg if she feels complete for now, and when she affirms that she does, he says, "Listening to you work through that helped me see that I'm also stuck on a similar point about value, wondering what value I can bring beyond my actual job. I guess that's behind my barrier thought. Are you guys up for working on this with me?"

Jumping into the discussion, the family all take turns empathizing with the sabotaging thoughts stopping James from taking the next step, using whatever MYL map seems appropriate. James realizes that he was expecting a grand result from his presentation, reflecting a part of him that also would like to make a bigger impact. He decides to revisit his dream over the next couple of weeks and see whether there's a shift in the dream itself, or merely in the plan, that would help him feel more satisfied.

When the conversation shifts to other members of the family, Corey revisits the doubt about himself and his project, recognizing that it is protecting him from disappointment if it doesn't work out, and identifies it as a pattern that he'd like to change. He makes an agreement to pay attention to what people are actually saying about his idea, and when his doubting voice arises, to empathize with it first, and then ask what he can learn from it.

Maggie's a little vague about hers, so Sally and James help

her get in touch with her desire to be seen as smart and creative through her science project, while also enjoying the process, and the whole family helps her begin to brainstorm some ideas. She agrees to continue that process and choose a project that would be fun for her, asking for help if she would like it.

The theme of asking for help brings up Doris's thought about being a burden. With James and Sally empathizing, Doris taps into her needs to feel capable and independent, as well as her desire for the time she spends with the family to feel like quality time, not merely time spent on medical issues. This prompts a discussion about what she means by quality time, and strategies to make all time, regardless of what they are do-ing, into quality time—which Sally realizes is exactly the kind of family dream she had in mind.

Conclusion

Achieving Your Dream One Conversation at a Time

Until you make the unconscious conscious,
it will direct your life and you will call it fate.
—C.G. Jung

What is the tenor of your internal conversations? Do they tend toward a kind meeting of voices all collaborating to achieve your dream life? Or are they more like a dysfunctional family, where bickering and judgment hinder your momentum to create and your enjoyment of life?

If you're like most people, it's likely the latter. But we are hopeful that through reading this book, you've become more aware of the numerous internal conversations you have each day, and how those conversations unfold in either helpful or unhelpful ways. Once cognizant of them, we hope that you can better recognize barriers that may arise as you create a dream, plan how to achieve it, and implement that plan. Further, through the illustrations that followed Sally, James, Corey, and Maggie—as well as Chris establishing a healthier lifestyle, Dawn launching a nonprofit, and Kevin seeking balance and enjoyment between work and home—we hope you've become more familiar with when and how to apply the maps and tools we've taught you to use at all the stages you're likely to go through in achieving a dream:

- ✦ Creating a dream while thinking you have no right to, don't know what a dream is, or are unaware of what your dream is

- ✦ Resisting the planning process, perhaps through feeling overwhelmed or facing self-doubt

- ✦ Making choices about taking action and finding arguments within about what choice to make, what you should do, or avoiding what you said you would do

- ✦ Judging yourself after taking an action for not taking the "right" one, for how you took action, or for the outcome

- ✦ Creating and changing habits to help you reach your dream

- ✦ Experiencing setbacks, whether they come through unexpected events or other people, or your plan simply doesn't proceed as expected

- ✦ Being in conflict with other people, and working with those conflicts internally, which can then shift your interactions with the other person

We also hope the examples have highlighted another perspective:

Every moment is a chance to create your dream life.

You may have noticed by this point that the multiple aspects of achieving a specific dream apply in a larger way to your life as a whole. In other words, you likely formulate some sort of plan for your day, whether written out or as a vague sense of what you'll do when. You take multiple actions during the day, some of which may have various options to choose between, and some of which you may judge yourself for afterwards. You also engage in creating and changing habits to increase your effectiveness, even if you are not aware of doing so. Setbacks and obstacles arise that you have to deal with, and you interact with others in personal and professional relationships.

In short, your dreams—whether big world-changing ones or simple daily ones—are not separate from your life. At every moment, you are creating your life with the choices you make, in particular the choices about how you focus your attention and what action you take. "I'm going to get up, go to the gym, take a shower, eat breakfast, and drive to work" may not be a world-changing plan, but it's part of the bigger plan for living the life you desire.

If you think about it, the conversations you have with yourself as you implement your morning plan impact how you feel and the subsequent actions you take. For example, how your morning will go doesn't seem like much of a dream, but how often has your morning plan been disrupted, and then negatively impacted the rest of your day? As the saying goes, "Life is what happens to us while we are making other plans." Whether it's a big, hairy, audacious plan to change the world, or simply the plan to get from your bed to work, being derailed happens, and it can set off an internal conversation that, unless you notice and change it, can lead you away from your dream life instead of toward it.

Where the aspiration for your life can similarly falter is in those behaviors where you don't feel like you have much control—perhaps the habits that stand in your way, or the ways you do or don't take action. These behaviors arise because a part of you intrudes and takes over consciousness for a small burst of time, producing conduct that you feel like you don't have control over. Whether it's eating the chocolate cake straight from the refrigerator in the middle of the night, yelling at your child—again— when he doesn't do what you asked, or spending time on social media instead of marketing your business, you act in ways that are not congruent with the way you've said you wanted to act.

What are those behaviors for you that you've uncovered while reading the book?

As you now know, whether a part of you impacts your behavior, or voices are directly in conflict, different parts of yourself will show up—which is not crazy, but rather an accepted understanding of the mind. Because behaviors like these arise from not communicating well in the mental ecosystem, the internal parts of you become the worst kind of dysfunctional group, in which ignoring, belittling, and lambasting take place with immunity. In fact, until you pay attention to it, you may not even realize the extent to which your internal voices are behaving toward one another in ways you would never treat someone you cared about. Yet, most people were not given an operating manual for how to live with this mind, so they try to actualize their dreams through inner conflict, often with minimal success. The good news is, you now have a functional operating manual for the mind; this book—and the entire Mediate Your Life series—focuses on bringing you into connection with yourself and all the parts of you, enabling you to understand and reconcile those negative voices with clarity and confidence.

As you've read in this book, and hopefully experienced in practicing the maps, our approach to changing this internal landscape into a friendlier, more compassionate space involves using the tools of Nonviolent Communication (NVC) to listen to, empathize with, and mediate between the parts of yourself. Since you may not have been aware that multiple parts of you existed, these tools are designed to surface what has not been overtly conscious for you. As Jung said, if you don't make the unconscious conscious, it will tend to run your life.

What you likely realize by now is that when different parts of you are in conflict, you're not connected with yourself, and if you're not connected with yourself, it's difficult, if not impossible, to truly connect with other people, or to take the most effective action to create the life you desire. In bringing these parts of you to conscious awareness and mediating between your internal voices, you are no longer run by them. You can be integrated within, and the way you then present to the world and interact with others has more ease and effectiveness.

What's more, when you bring your internal voices to conscious awareness, you can experience serenity more often. Why? Because the comments and actions that normally "hook" you can fly right past; you may notice them, but you won't be provoked by them in the same way.

As we've discussed, people get triggered because something happens that some internal voice takes issue with and reacts, hence going off course from their main purpose to attack, defend, or make their point, even when they know that doing so will not get them what they truly want.

For example, your main purpose with your child may be to love and support them, but when they have a certain tone of voice, it triggers a part of you that interprets that your need for respect is not being met. In another situation, your main purpose may be to move your business forward, yet a part of you sees danger and stops you. Surfacing these parts of you and mediating your internal conversation allows you to stay focused on creating the life you desire, instead of being diverted.

But diversions aren't all bad; in fact, they are pointing you to the parts of yourself that seek to become part of your conscious awareness. Once you recognize this and subsequently work with an internal conflict, you diminish the likelihood that these parts of you will be able to sabotage your efforts in the future. In short, the more they become conscious, the less they will have to undermine you in order to be heard.

An analogy we like to use is meditation practice. People often start meditating and find that they feel a sense of peace and calm. They notice the thoughts in their mind, and use whatever technique their practice dictates to handle those thoughts, resulting in the sense of being able to watch the stream of thoughts without getting caught up in it. However, as soon as they return to their lives, that equanimity dissipates, and they are unclear on how to incorporate that state of meditation into their day-to-day life—or rather, they have difficulty finding the bridge between the two.

We've discovered, in our own lives and the lives of our many workshop participants, that the tools in this book provide that bridge. By giving you concrete ways to notice your internal voices, step into mediator mind (where you are not caught up in the thoughts of either voice), and then connect with what is going on inside of you, the tools assist you in forming a continuation of heightened mindfulness beyond your meditation practice.

THE MEASURE OF SUCCESS

When it comes to creating your dream or your dream life, the obvious measure of success would be achieving it. Nonetheless, that is not the measure of success we recommend—nor is it to complete every plan you create, or have every implementation task proceed as you initially intend.

Instead, success lies in being able to be present with whatever happens—whether your plan succeeds beyond your wishes or has to be scrapped completely. When you've been diverted, whether from a plan for your morning or your life, you are in a moment of asking yourself: "What can I do?" "Where do I focus my attention now?" and "What conduct should I engage in?"

Being present in that moment, you now know how to connect with your current needs, assess what your dream and plan were, create them anew or make modifications if necessary, and consciously choose a next step from that connection with yourself. Further, by consistently practicing the tools and maps in this book, you notice the different voices that come up at each step of the journey. Empathize with those voices, and if they're in conflict—creating a barrier that produces disconnection and threatens your forward movement—mediate between them.

In short, success is:

+ cultivating awareness of what is going on for you moment by moment

+ increasing your skill to return to presence, regardless of what is happening

+ nurturing your ability to choose what to do instead of react

+ learning from whatever happens so that your skills, experience, and effectiveness expand over time

The benefit to seeing success in this way is that it is directly under your control. The bigger your dream, the more factors will be outside of your control, and the more likely that your plans will progress in unanticipated, and perhaps sudden, changes of direction.

But remember that you always have this present moment to make a choice, to focus your attention and take action to reach your dreams. Noticing your thoughts, realizing the power and impact of them, and being able to affect them so that they don't run your behavior in unconscious or habitual ways, allows you to be present and make choices about the life you are creating now.

INNER WORK, OUTER WORLD

While this book is about creating the life you desire, it's also about how you treat yourself, and how all the parts within you have an impact outside of you in ways that are sometimes mysterious.

For example, developing the ability to inquire about your internal experience gives you the capacity to reach out to other people. Hence, from your internal connection, you can connect with others and build trust with them. Once you have trust established, you can collaborate, focusing on meeting needs. Doing so effectively—without the conclusions, judgments, and analyses that tend to dominate interactions—is the foundation for a healthy relationship, whether it is among family members, coworkers, or opponents on any social or political issue. In this way, even across the divides of religion, politics, nationalities, and belief systems, collaboration is possible.

This isn't always an easy path, particularly when hurt on either side is long-standing and hope is hard to find. Yet the path of increasing divisiveness, hatred, and separation is guaranteed to not only not be an easy path, but also one in which fewer and fewer people's needs will truly be met. If the skills to be integrated within each one of us—whether it's through MYL, NVC, Internal Family Systems, or any of numerous other modalities—were more widespread, it's likely there would be a different public discourse, not to mention less friction in families and workplaces.

Peace and harmony start within. It's easy to look outside and berate the state of the world—its conflict-torn areas, the discord endemic in the political system, and hatred and prejudice seeming to gain ground—and feel hopeless and helpless about making a difference. Yet, when you get a grasp on the warring voices within, you can contribute to creating the world within which you would like your dream to exist. As the Dalai Lama says, "Peace starts within each one of us. When we have inner peace, we can be at peace with those around us."

In doing the work of this book, you are not only working toward the life you most desire to live, but also contributing to a world where people can cross the gulfs that divide them, connect, and collaborate to create a global community that supports the dreams of everyone.

APPENDICES

Feelings List

Feelings are bodily felt experiences and tell us about our needs being met or not met, and about what we are observing, thinking, and wanting.

PEACEFUL	LOVING
tranquil	warm
calm	affectionate
content	tender
engrossed	appreciative
absorbed	friendly
expansive	sensitive
serene	compassionate
loving	grateful
blissful	nurtured
satisfied	amorous
relaxed	trusting
relieved	open
quiet	thankful
carefree	radiant
composed	adoring
fulfilled	passionate

GLAD	PLAYFUL	INTERESTED
happy	energetic	involved
excited	effervescent	inquisitive
hopeful	invigorated	intense
joyful	zestful	enriched
satisfied	refreshed	absorbed
delighted	impish	alert
encouraged	alive	aroused
grateful	lively	astonished
confident	exuberant	concerned
inspired	giddy	curious
touched	adventurous	eager
proud	mischievous	enthusiastic
exhilarated	jubilant	fascinated
ecstatic	goofy	intrigued
optimistic	buoyant	surprised
glorious	electrified	helpful

MAD	SAD
impatient	lonely
pessimistic	heavy
disgruntled	troubled
frustrated	helpless
irritable	gloomy
edgy	overwhelmed
grouchy	distant
agitated	despondent
exasperated	discouraged
disgusted	distressed
irked	dismayed
cantankerous	disheartened
animosity	despairing
bitter	sorrowful
rancorous	unhappy
irate, furious	depressed
angry	blue
hostile	miserable
enraged	dejected
violent	melancholy

SCARED	TIRED	CONFUSED
afraid	exhausted	frustrated
fearful	fatigued	perplexed
terrified	inert	hesitant
startled	lethargic	troubled
nervous	indifferent	uncomfortable
jittery	weary	withdrawn
horrified	overwhelmed	apathetic
anxious	fidgety	embarrassed
worried	helpless	hurt
anguished	heavy	uneasy
lonely	sleepy	irritated
insecure	disinterested	suspicious
sensitive	reluctant	unsteady
shocked	passive	puzzled
apprehensive	dull	restless
dread	bored	boggled
jealous	listless	chagrined
desperate	blah	unglued
suspicious	mopey	detached
frightened	comatose	skeptical

For a printable version, visit:

www.mediateyourlife.com/

when-your-mind-sabotages-your-dreams/

B | UNIVERSAL HUMAN NEEDS / VALUES LIST

The needs below are grouped into categories of core needs, three meta-categories, and nine subcategories.

WELL-BEING

SUSTENANCE/ HEALTH	SAFETY/ SECURITY	BEAUTY/ PEACE/PLAY
abundance/thriving	comfort	acceptance
exercise	confidence	appreciation
food/nutrition	emotional safety	gratitude
nourishment	familiarity	awareness
rest/sleep	order	balance
relaxation	structure	ease
shelter	predictability	equanimity
sustainability	protection from harm	humor
support/help	stability	presence
wellness	trust	rejuvenation
vitality	faith	simplicity
energy		space
		tranquility
		wholeness
		wonder

CONNECTION

LOVE/ CARING	EMPATHY/ UNDER- STANDING	COMMUNITY/ BELONGING
affection/warmth		cooperation
beauty	awareness/clarity	fellowship
closeness/touch	acceptance	generosity
companionship	acknowledgment	inclusion
compassion	communication	interdependence
kindness	consideration	harmony/peace
intimacy	hearing	hospitality/welcoming
mattering	(hear/be heard)	mutuality
importance	knowing	reciprocity
nurturing	(know/be known)	partnership
sexual connection	presence/listening	relationship
respect	respect/equality	support/solidarity
honoring	receptivity/openness	trust
valuing/prizing	recognition	dependability
	seeing (see/be seen)	transparency
	self-esteem	openness
	sensitivity	

SELF-EXPRESSION

AUTONOMY/ FREEDOM	AUTHEN- TICITY	MEANING/ CONTRIBUTION
choice	adventure	appreciation/gratitude
clarity	aliveness	achievement
congruence	discovery	productivity
consistency	honesty	celebration/mourning
continuity	initiative	challenge
dignity	innovation	efficacy
freedom	inspiration	effectiveness
independence	joy	excellence
integrity	mystery	growth
power	passion	learning/clarity
empowerment	spontaneity	mystery
self-responsibility		participation
		purpose/value
		self-actualization
		self-esteem
		skill/mastery

For a printable version, visit:
www.mediateyourlife.com/
when-your-mind-sabotages-your-dreams/

C | SELF-EMPATHY

Self-Empathy utilizes the four components of communication—observations, feelings, needs, and requests—to empathize with yourself or one of your internal voices.

Here are the steps of Self-Empathy:

1. Identify Observations

    a. What happened?

    b. What do you notice about your internal state? (thoughts, beliefs, attitudes, assumptions, feelings, sensations)

2. Feel and Name your Feelings

    a. Be present with your experience without describing: feel the sensations arising.

    b. Describe the sensations in your body.

    c. Name your feelings.

3. Find the Needs

    a. Ask, "If I'm feeling this way, what need of mine is not met?"

    b. Check in with your body, allowing your physiological reaction to confirm to you when you've correctly identified the need.

    c. Imagine your needs being fully met.

4. Make Requests

    a. What strategies might meet your needs?

    b. Requests are positive, present-tense, action language, and not a demand.

For a printable version, visit:
www.mediateyourlife.com/
when-your-mind-sabotages-your-dreams/

D | SELF-CONNECTION PROCESS (SCP)

BREATH *(Awareness: being in the present moment)*

1. Focus on your breathing. Deepen the inhale as you breathe in, and extend the exhale longer than the inhale.

2. Repeat this several times while staying aware of your breathing.

3. Continue to deepen your inhale and extend your exhale as you do the next steps.

BODY *(Presence: being with feelings and accepting what is)*

1. Focus on what you are feeling. Feel the sensations and emotions, the aliveness and energy, by being in your body and experiencing it fully. At this stage you are solely being present with and experiencing sensations, scanning your body and noticing your sensations and where they are located. As much as possible, sense what you are experiencing without talking to yourself about it.

2. Describe what you're experiencing, using whatever language you are comfortable with to describe your

sensations. This is when you talk to yourself about what you are experiencing, using whatever words come to you to describe it.

3.   Name the feelings you are experiencing.

NEEDS *(Choice: choosing thoughts, beliefs, and actions to meet needs)*

1.   Now that you're aware of your feelings from Step 2, look into what is prompting you to feel as you are. Connect with the needs that are met or not met in your current situation. A way to do this is to ask yourself, *If I am feeling this way, what need is the unconscious part of me interpreting as met or not met?* The idea here is that your unconscious is communicating to your conscious mind that needs are being met or not met by prompting feelings to arise in you. You use these feelings to work backwards to find your needs. (Refer to Appendix B for a list of needs.)

2.   Check in with your body as you consider the needs. It's not a cognitive process of "figuring out" what they are. When you name the need that most closely fits, your body will respond. It may take some time and practice to learn your particular physiological response that signals you are naming the need that is met or not met—it may be a feeling of warmth, relaxation, a sense of something falling into place, or just a knowing and certainty.

3.   Deepen into the needs you've identified by imagining what it would feel like for those needs to be

fully met. Savor what that would be like, and how your life would be if those needs were fully met.

We encourage you to set aside at least five minutes a day to practice SCP, and also to practice throughout the day, in as many moments as you can, when you're not in a fight-flight-freeze reaction. In doing so, you will prepare your neural pathways to more likely be accessible when you are experiencing fight-flight-freeze reaction.

SELF-CONNECTION PROCESS: EXPANDED VERSION

BREATH

1. Slow and deepen your breathing.

2. Notice the number of counts you are inhaling and the number you are exhaling. Breathe in, hold your breath, breathe out—all three to the same count.

3. Practice relating to thoughts with kindness, humor, and friendliness.

BODY

1. Feel your feelings without naming, analyzing, or thinking about them.

2. Focus attention on three body centers—belly, heart, head (called the "triune brain": reptilian/ instinctual, mammalian/emotional, neocortex/ intellectual/intuitive).

3. Relax your muscles; allow openness, softness, and flexibility in your posture.

4. Mind-body practices

- Relax your muscles (e.g., eyes, tongue, jaw, shoulders, arms, belly).
- Open your posture (e.g., open chest and arms, say "Ahhhhh").
- Align and balance around your spinal core.

NEEDS

1. Breathe into three body centers (the spinal "chakras"—belly, heart, head).

2. Connect core needs to the body centers.

- Well-being (peace)—sustenance, safety, order
- Connection (love)—care, understanding, community
- Self-expression (joy)—freedom, honesty, meaning

3. Focus on a "chemistry-changing" positive image for each body center.

4. Imagine the needs fully and completely met.

5. Gratitude practice: Celebrate how needs are met in your life; mourn any ways needs are not currently met.

6. Tonglen—breathe in suffering of self, others, the world; breathe out peace, love, joy, happiness, well-being, connection, self-expression.

SCP AS A MEDIATOR MIND MINDFULNESS PRACTICE

BREATH

1. Focus attention on your breathing, following the in-flow, extending the out-flow.

2. Observe your sense perceptions (sight, sound, scent, touch, taste).

3. Shift attention from thoughts and "stories" back to breath and sense perception.

BODY

1. Feel what is happening in your body, including internal sensations and feelings

NEEDS

1. In focusing on need, find the inner place of felt well-being that is not tied to what is happening externally, where you already know that you are safe, loved, cared for, accepted, and connected.

2. Use the phrase "I am ..." to tap into this knowing, repeating to yourself, *I am safe, I am valued, I am connected ...*

3. Focus on finding the place within that experiences the felt sense and inner knowing of what you are saying.

For a printable version, visit:
www.mediateyourlife.com/
when-your-mind-sabotages-your-dreams/

E | INTERNAL MEDIATION (IM) MAP

The Internal Mediation (IM) process is one of the inner mediation maps for navigating a conflict between different voices within ourselves in the present about a choice to make in the future. The IM process can also be used for "shadow work," finding and working with unconscious inner conflicts (i.e., in the "shadows" outside the light of awareness) that are being triggered by external conflicts with others.

INTERNAL MEDIATION STEPS

1. Empathize with the first voice that wants to be heard (Voice A)

Ask what voice wants to be heard first, and empathize with that voice (Voice A). Reflect back your understanding and get to the feelings and needs. It can help to ask this voice what its name is, and the role or function it is playing. You can think of this as akin to being in a dark room, and needing to ask questions to find out who's there. In shadow work, Voice A speaks about reactions to the external other.

2. Empathize with the second voice that wants to be heard (Voice B)

Ask what other voice wants to speak and be heard in relation to what Voice A has said. Empathize with that voice (Voice B). Reflect back your understanding as well as uncovering the feelings and needs. You can ask this voice, too, about its name, role, function, etc.

+ Sometimes other parts or aspects of the self emerge to be heard. If this happens, empathize with each.

+ When using IM for shadow work, have the external person with whom there is conflict become an inner part or aspect of the self (Voice B), and empathize with this voice. Another option is to look for some other part or parts of the self that are somehow related to the person, pattern, or dynamic in the external conflict.

3. Ask Voice B to empathize with Voice A

Ask Voice B if it would say to Voice A what it heard A say, focusing on needs.

4. Ask Voice A to empathize with Voice B

Ask Voice A if it would say to Voice B what it heard B say, focusing on needs.

[Cycle through steps 1–4 as needed to create inner understanding and connection.]

5. Solution Requests and Agreements

Ask Voices A and B if they have solution requests of each other to meet the needs of both. You can also shift into the perspective of the mediator chair for this phase. Make agreements with yourself or others to meet your needs.

    a. Agreements

        i. Primary—what both parts of you agree to do to meet your needs

        ii. Supporting—what to do to support the primary agreements

        iii. Restoring—what to do if the primary agreements are not kept

If additional voices speak up, empathize with them as they arise, but keep the conversation focused between the two voices that are in the most conflict with each other. If you complete the process between those two and find another pair in conflict, repeat the process with those two voices.

For a printable version, visit:
www.mediateyourlife.com/
when-your-mind-sabotages-your-dreams/

F | CHOOSER EDUCATOR (CE) MAP

The Chooser Educator (CE) process is one of the inner mediation maps for navigating conflicts between different parts or aspects of ourselves, when we are evaluating ourselves negatively after we have taken an action in the past (i.e., through a conscious or unconscious choice).

CHOOSER EDUCATOR STEPS

1. Empathy with the inner Educator (the voice of self-evaluation/judgment)

Listen to what the voice of the Educator is saying, and empathize with it. Reflect back your understanding and get to the feelings and needs of the Educator. The Educator is expressing, or communicating about, needs not met by the action or actions of the Chooser. The Educator may express its needs through the language of moralistic self-judgments, "stories," or demands—language stating or implying wrongness, badness, "should have," criticism, blame, or punishment. The emotion that tends to come from the Educator is anger, with fear underneath. By transforming the language of the Educator into a language of needs, there is a shift from self-blame to "mourning"—natural feelings of sadness and regret.

2. Empathy with the inner Chooser (the part of ourselves that did or chose what the Educator is evaluating)

Ask the inner Chooser to say what it wants to be heard about, and empathize with it. You could ask how the Chooser feels about how the Educator is talking to it. Often the emotions that come from the Chooser are guilt, shame, and anxiety, but also sometimes anger toward the Educator. You can then ask what needs the Chooser was trying to meet when it did what it did. The Chooser used a particular strategy to meet a need or needs. Through empathy for the Chooser, you begin to understand how that strategy was the best the Chooser knew to do at the time to meet the needs it was trying to meet. This understanding brings self-compassion. Even if the strategy was not successful, there can be an appreciation, or even celebration, for how the Chooser was trying to meet needs.

3. Ask the Chooser to empathize with the Educator

Ask the Chooser if it would say to the Educator what it heard the Educator say, focusing on needs.

4. Ask the Educator to empathize with the Chooser

Ask the Educator if it would say to the Chooser what it heard the Chooser say, focusing on needs.

[Cycle through steps 1–4 as needed to create inner understanding and connection.]

5. Solution Requests and Agreements

Ask Educator and Chooser if they have requests of each other for how to meet the needs of both. You can also do this from the perspective of the mediator chair for this phase. A way to gain clarity on requests is to look back and imagine other ways of responding. See if you can reach an inner agreement.

a. Agreements

i.   Primary—what both parts of you agree to do to meet your needs

ii. Supporting—what to do to support the primary agreements

iii. Restoring—what to do if the primary agreements are not kept

For a printable version, visit:
www.mediateyourlife.com/
when-your-mind-sabotages-your-dreams/

G | MOURN CELEBRATE LEARN (MCL)

PART I: MOURN

Empathy with needs *not met* for you by what happened.

1. Observations

   a. What happened that did not meet your needs?

   b. Do you have any negative thoughts, judgments, or "stories" about this?

2. Feelings: Sensations and emotions in your body

3. Needs: Connect your observations, thoughts, and feelings to your needs

CYCLING: Move through the three steps in whatever order works for you. Continue to cycle through the steps until you feel an inner calm and are connected to your needs.

PART II: CELEBRATE

Empathy with needs *met* for you by what happened.

1. Observations

    a. What happened that met your needs, including
        good things that might happen in the future
        from what occurred?

2. Feelings: Sensations and emotions in your body

3. Needs: Connect your observations, thoughts, and
    feelings to your needs

CYCLING: As with Part I, you may cycle through the
steps multiple times. Also, as you are in Part II, you may
also notice more thoughts and feelings relating to unmet
needs coming up. At any point, you can cycle back to Part
I, and back and forth between Parts I and II.

PART III: LEARN

1. Learn from doing Parts I and II. Any new ideas,
    insights, or possibilities you now see?

2. Plan a specific action for how you want to meet
    your needs, now that you have connected with met
    and unmet needs. See if you can form a specific,
    action-language, "doable" (what you *do* want)
    request of yourself. One way to achieve this is to
    do a "post-hearsal"—imagine redoing the situation
    and what you might have said or done differently.

3. Practice: After forming an action request and a
    plan, you may want to practice whatever you came

up with in order to make it into a new habit. One way to do this is to role-play with a practice partner or coach, or to do this in journaling.

CYCLING: After reaching step three, you may notice you have more learning and insights. If so, you can cycle back through the steps. You might also notice more needs (met or not met) coming up to empathize with. If so, you can go back to Parts I and II.

For a printable version, visit:
www.mediateyourlife.com/
when-your-mind-sabotages-your-dreams/

ACKNOWLEDGMENTS

It takes many people to make a book like this. There is the writing that went into it, for which John and Ike tip their hats to Julie Stiles with our deepest appreciation and thanks for all that she has done to bring this and our prior books to fruition. Without her, we doubt whether we would have a Mediate Your Life book series. We are also grateful to Stacey Aaronson, who once again shepherded this book through the final stages of editing and design.

In addition to the writing, there is all that we have experienced that inspires what we write. These experiences are rooted in our interactions with participants in our trainings and mediations, and in our interactions with family, friends, and colleagues.

We have attempted to live what we write, and in so doing have made collaborators of all we meet.

FOR FURTHER READING

Allen, David. *Getting Things Done: The Art of Stress-Free Productivity.* New York: Penguin Books, 2001.

Baumeister, Roy F., and John Tierney. *Willpower: Rediscovering the Greatest Human Strength.* New York: The Penguin Press, 2011.

Duhigg, Charles. *The Power of Habit: Why We Do What We Do in Life and Business.* New York: Random House, 2012.

Gazzaniga, Michael. *Who's in Charge? Free Will and the Science of the Brain.* New York: HarperCollins, 2011.

Goldsmith, Marshall, and Mark Reiter. *Triggers: Creating Behavior That Lasts—Becoming the Person You Want to Be.* New York: Crown Business, 2015.

Haidt, Jonathan. *The Happiness Hypothesis: Finding Modern Truth in Ancient Wisdom.* New York: Basic Books, 2006.

———— *The Righteous Mind: Why Good People Are Divided by Politics and Religion.* New York: Pantheon Books, 2012.

Heath, Chip, and Dan Heath. *Switch: How to Change When Change Is Hard.* New York: Broadway Books, 2010.

Kahneman, Daniel. *Thinking, Fast and Slow.* New York: Farrar, Straus, and Giroux, 2011.

Kenrick, Douglas T., and Vladas Griskevicius. *The Rational Animal: How Evolution Made Us Smarter Than We Think.* New York: Basic Books, 2013.

McGonigal, Kelly. *The Willpower Instinct: How Self-Control Works, Why It Matters, and What You Can Do to Get More of It.* New York: The Penguin Group, 2012.

Neff, Kristin. *Self-Compassion: The Proven Power of Being Kind to Yourself.* New York: William Morrow, 2011.

Patterson, Kerry, and Joseph Greeny, David Maxfield, Ron McMillan, and Al Switzler. *Change Anything: The New Science of Personal Success.* New York: Business Plus, 2011.

Rosenberg, Marshall B. *Nonviolent Communication: A Language of Compassion.* Encinitas, CA: PuddleDancer Press, 1999.

Rubin, Gretchen. *Better Than Before: Mastering the Habits of Our Everyday Lives.* New York: Crown Publishers, 2015.

Schwartz, Richard C. *Internal Family Systems Therapy.* New York: The Guilford Press, 1995.

——— *Introduction to the Internal Family Systems Model.* Oak Park, IL: Trailhead Publications, 2001.

Stone, Hal, and Sidra L. Stone. *Embracing Our Selves: The Voice Dialogue Manual.* Novato, CA: Nataraj Publishing, 1989.

Williams, Mark, and Danny Penman. *Mindfulness: An Eight-Week Plan for Finding Peace in a Frantic World.* New York: Rodale, Inc., 2011.

ABOUT MEDIATE YOUR LIFE

Email: ikelasater@mediateyourlife.com
johnkinyon@mediateyourlife.com
Website: mediateyourlife.com

Facebook: Mediate Your Life
facebook.com/pages/Mediate-Your-Life/277226242307687
Twitter: @MediateYourLife
twitter.com/MediateYourLife

ABOUT THE TRAININGS

Mediate Your Life integrates compassion, mindfulness, and clear communication to help you learn to create and choose peace with yourself, with others, and with society at large. We offer step-by-step, highly effective processes and exercises that rewire your brain to return to presence and create connection between yourself and others.

At its core the Mediate Your Life program is about listening to—and really hearing—ourselves and others. It is about increasing our capacity for empathy so that when triggered we can overcome the body's natural "fight-flight-freeze" reaction. The process teaches how to replace conflict with true collaboration, new possibilities, and compassionate support.

We offer a variety of trainings to suit your needs. The year-long immersion program consists of three four-day in-person intensives, with practice suggestions in between. You can take any of these workshops as a standalone course or sign up for the full year. We also have shorter in-person classes, and offer the intensives as a telecourse for those who prefer.

Ike Lasater, JD, MCP

As a mediator and trainer, Ike coaches individuals and organizations to foster successful collaboration through learning skills to effectively handle difficult conversations, improve productivity, give and receive meaningful and productive feedback, and reduce interpersonal conflict and stress. These skills help teams to thrive in an environment that encourages individual risk taking, where members listen to each other's ideas, no matter the cultural differences within the team or perceived differences in power.

A former civil trial attorney, Ike founded a twenty-person law firm, litigating complex, multi-party commercial and environmental cases for twenty years in the state and federal courts of California. As he trained extensively with psychologist Marshall B. Rosenberg, PhD, founder of Nonviolent Communication (NVC), for over a decade, he grew to see that conflict can be an opportunity for connection, and shifted his focus from law to training. NVC's approach was congruent with his values, developed through long-term practices of Zen meditation, yoga (he cofounded *The Yoga Journal* in 1975), and aikido.

Ike has served on the boards of the Center for Non-violent Communication and the Association for Dispute Resolution of Northern California, and on the mediation panel for the United States District Court for the Northern District of California. He has facilitated workshops in twenty countries in North and South America, Europe, Africa, Australia, and Asia.

You can find Ike online at www.ikelasater.com

JOHN KINYON

John Kinyon provides training, coaching, and facilitation/mediation to the public and to organizations. John is a speaker and author, and is co-creator of the Mediate Your Life training program that is offered in different parts of the US and internationally in Asia, Europe, and Australia. For over two decades, John has mediated conflicts in a wide range of contexts, including families, businesses, and organizations. He worked closely with Nonviolent Communication (NVC) founder Marshall Rosenberg for over a decade before he retired. John has been a certified trainer of the Center for Nonviolent Communication (CNVC) since 2000, and a leader in the worldwide NVC community.

John received his undergraduate degree from the University of San Francisco, where he studied psychology and philosophy, and played for USF's nationally ranked soccer team. He went on to graduate training in clinical psychology at Penn State University. After graduate school, John helped launch and develop a small commercial business before embracing full-time communication and conflict-resolution work, which began with cofounding the Bay Area NVC organization (BayNVC) in 2002. John lives with his wife and children in the San Francisco Bay Area.

You can find John online at www.johnkinyon.com

JULIE STILES

Besides working with Ike and John for over the past ten years, Julie is a Health and Transformation Coach, ThetaHealing® Practitioner, Access Consciousness Bars® Facilitator, writer, and speaker who empowers people to fully live their healing journey, as well as radically alter their relationship to healing and wholeness through reclaiming their power over their well-being. She is a graduate of the Institute for Integrative Nutrition and has an MA in Consciousness Studies from John F. Kennedy University.

Julie's work focuses on lifestyle changes, including nutrition and fitness, that promote better health, as well as on the deeper process of transformation that is often required when people step onto the path of improving their overall well-being. She has supported people to eat healthier, lose weight, honor and accept their bodies, increase balance in their lives, create reasonable goals and reach them, move through their blocks to making change, and resolve internal conflicts. Creator and host of the podcasts Autoimmune Adventures and Being Well, Julie has also appeared on Voice America and radio shows nationwide, inspiring people to live their challenges as an adventure and create the change they'd like to see in their lives.

Julie offers private and group coaching, energy healing, workshops, and webinars, and she works with people in person and worldwide via phone and the Internet.

You can find Julie online at www.juliestiles.com

CPSIA information can be obtained
at www.ICGtesting.com
Printed in the USA
BVHW081326301218
536481BV00041B/184/P